CHRISTIANS AND EVOLUTION

CHRISTIANS

AND

EVOLUTION

Christian Scholars Change Their Mind

Edited by **Professor R. J. Berry**

MONARCH
BOOKS
Oxford, UK & Grand Rapids, Michigan, USA

Published by Monarch Books
an imprint of
Lion Hudson plc
Wilkinson House, Jordan Hill Road,
Oxford OX2 8DR, England
Email: monarch@lionhudson.com
www.lionhudson.com/monarch

ISBN 978 0 85721 524 6
e-ISBN 978 0 85721 525 3

First edition 2014

Acknowledgments
Extracts from The Authorized (King
James) Version. Rights in the Authorized
Version are vested in the Crown.
Reproduced by permission of the
Crown's patentee, Cambridge University
Press.
Scripture quotations [marked ESV] are
from The Holy Bible, English Standard
Version® (ESV®) copyright © 2001 by
Crossway, a publishing ministry of Good
News Publishers. All rights reserved.
Scripture [marked NASB] taken from
the New American Standard Bible®,
Copyright © 1960, 1962, 1963, 1968,
1971, 1972, 1973, 1975, 1977, 1995
by The Lockman Foundation. Used by
permission.
Scripture quotations taken from
the Holy Bible, New International
Version, copyright © 1973, 1978, 1984
International Bible Society. Used by
permission of Hodder & Stoughton, a
member of the Hodder Headline Group.
All rights reserved. 'NIV' is a trademark
of International Bible Society. UK
trademark number 1448790.
Scripture quotations [marked NLT] are
taken from the Holy Bible, New Living
Translation, copyright © 1996, 2004,
2007 by Tyndale House Foundation.
Used by permission of Tyndale House
Publishers, Inc., Carol Stream, Illinois
60188. All rights reserved.
Scripture quotations [marked NRSV]
are from The New Revised Standard
Version of the Bible copyright © 1989
by the Division of Christian Education
of the National Council of Churches in
the USA. Used by permission. All Rights
Reserved.
p. 29: Extract from The Limits of Science
by Peter Medawar copyright © 1984,
Peter Medawar. Printed by permission of
Oxford University Press.
p. 35: "He's Still Working on Me" by Joel
Hemphill copyright © Joel Hemphill.
Printed by permission of Song Solutions.
pp. 201, 203, 205–206, 208–209, 213:
Extracts from Stages of Faith by James
W. Fowler copyright © 1981, James
W. Fowler. Printed by permission of
HarperCollins.
pp. 326–37: Extract from "Approaching
the Conflict Between Religion and
Evolution" by L. Meadows in Teaching
About Scientific Origins edited by Leslie S.
Jones and Michael J. Reiss copyright ©
2007, Peter Lang Publishing. Printed by
permission of Peter Lang Publishing.

A catalogue record for this book is
available from the British Library

Printed and bound in the UK, October
2014, LH26

Contents

Foreword

Bible-believing Christians are possibly more divided about evolution than over any other subject. How ought we to interpret Genesis 1–3? Were there men and women before Adam? Did virtually all life perish in a global flood? How should we regard scientific understanding – the age of the earth, the fossil record, the implications of molecular genetics? Did Charles Darwin make reasoned faith impossible? Many have written on these things, making the case for one or another answer. This book is not concerned to argue any particular point of view. It simply sets out the testimonies of a group of assorted Christians and how they have reconciled their faith with scientific understanding. For some it involved a long and painful struggle; for others the pieces of the jigsaw fell more easily into place. Some issues occur again and again, but underlying every contribution is a recognition that accepting the authority of the Bible requires also an interpretation of its meaning; and the confidence that, with the Spirit's help, a determined search for an informed faith in the twenty-first century need not be in vain; biblical authority and current evolutionary science are not – and should not be – inevitably opposed. There will be some who will be uncomfortable with the testimonies herein, but it would be reckless and pastorally dangerous to ignore them. Hopefully there will be those who will be helped in their own spiritual journey and growth into maturity.

However, we have to recognize that questions about evolution have wider pastoral and evangelistic implications. One of the main reasons that teenagers feel disconnected from their church is a tension they feel between Christianity and science, and an impression (rightly or wrongly) that churches do not understand scientific issues. Probably the most acute of these issues is that of origins and the evolution-creation debate. It is no help to a questioner merely to point to Bible texts and insist on their truth.[1] We must be able to interpret and expound the Bible in ways which are consistent not only with itself but also with God's "other book", his Book of Works – which is creation, the study-book of science.

R. J. Berry

---

[1] Petteri Nieminem, Anne-Mari Mustonen and Esko Ryökäs (2014). Theological implications of Young Earth Creationism and Intelligent Design: emerging tendencies of scientism and agnosticism. *Theology and Science*, 13: 260–84.

In the Beginning God

R. J. (Sam) Berry was Professor of Genetics at University College London 1978–2000. He is a former president of the Linnean Society, the society to which Darwin's announcement of evolution by natural selection was made in 1858 and where the then president announced that "the year that has passed has not been marked by any of those discoveries which at once revolutionize the science on which they bear". He has also served as president of Christians in Science, an organization whose aim is "to develop and promote biblical Christian views on the nature, scope and limitations of science, and on the changing interactions between science and faith". He is the author of *God and Evolution* (Regent, 2001) and *God and the Biologist* (Apollos, 1996), and editor of *The Lion Handbook of Science and Christianity* (2012).

This book is the stories of eighteen people – all of them Christians and all but two of them scientists – who have wrestled to resolve their personal conflicts over evolutionary science and Christian faith. The contributors have been intentionally chosen to reflect a variety of backgrounds and Christian experience. The issue of how God works in the world which He created is not something peculiar to any one group. It is something that every Christian who takes the Bible seriously has to face. The testimonies here are presented in the hope that the difficulties – and often misunderstandings – described will help those facing their own tensions and having to make their own decisions over evolution. The book concludes with a review of academic studies of people who have faced problems about faith and evolution from a professional educationalist, and an epilogue from a distinguished theologian.

As far as I am concerned, I only met the evolution-creation debate two or three years after I became a Christian in my teens. Following my conversion, I was happy to accept that God had made the world and its contents, and I never bothered to think how this related to the actual creation in which we live. I was brought up short at university by a friend announcing he could never become a Christian, because "it would mean not believing in evolution". I was flabbergasted. What did a set of scientific ideas have to do with eternal life? I can't remember our subsequent discussion, but I know it prompted me to find out what the Bible said on the subject and to see how this debate had arisen.

It is said that the only doctrine upon which all Christians agree is that God is the creator of everything. I don't know whether this is true, but there is no doubt whatsoever that Christians are very divided about *how* God created. These divisions are the subject of this book: Christians from a range of backgrounds and experiences describe how they have faced up to understanding God's creating work, and for some of them, the pain they went through in arriving at their final conclusion. It is not irrelevant that most of them are scientists, trained in evaluating evidence and exploring different explanations of phenomena.

How cause and effect (or creator and creation) relate to each other is an old problem, but advances in science have made us increasingly aware and interested in mechanisms of all sorts. Four centuries before Christ, Aristotle identified the possibility of four different causes for an event. Notwithstanding, the biblical writers say very little about causes. They thought of the world as being as it always has been, "established immovably" (Psalm 96:10), with the sun moving daily from east to west under a solid sky (Psalm 19:6). God was in heaven "up there". The idea that the earth was a sphere rather than a flat disc was understood by Greek astronomers from at least the third century BC and was accepted by most scholars in the Christian era, but the notion that the earth goes round the sun and that the sun is only a minor star in an immense universe came much later. Copernicus proposed the idea of a moving earth in 1543, but it took another century before Galileo's telescope gave experimental backing to the concept.

The Bible does not even tell us when creation began. The traditional date is that it was relatively recent, perhaps 6–10,000 years ago. The date most people remember is 4004 BC, proposed by Archbishop Ussher in 1650 on the basis of the genealogies in Genesis and Luke, but there are many other calculations giving similar answers. However, questions about such dates became more acute towards the end of the eighteenth century. The fossils of marine organisms high in mountains indicated that the earth must have gone through major changes in its past. The recognition of different rock strata stretching over large distances with their own characteristic fossil faunas implied a long time span. The identification of geological discontinuities built on this, indicating that there had been changes in rock formations. Before the development of radioactive decay techniques, there was no way of knowing the actual dates when these events took place, but by the beginning of the nineteenth century there was general agreement about a long period of "deep time" – and acceptance of this by Bible scholars.[1] In 1890, Princeton professor William Green

> conclude[d] that the Scriptures furnish no data for a
> chronological computation prior to the life of Abraham;
> and that the Mosaic records do not fix and were not
> intended to fix the precise date either of the Flood or of the
> creation of the world.

Francis Schaeffer has written similarly, "Prior to the time of Abraham, there is no possible way to date the history of what we find in Scripture."[2]

Assuming that we take the Bible seriously and in some way as God's revelation to us, how are we to interpret the creation stories in the light of this "deep time"? There are some (Young Earth Creationists) who insist that "deep time" does not exist. They maintain we must read the accounts of creation in the first two chapters of Genesis as literal history and that creation did in fact take place a few thousand years ago. Any geological changes must therefore be recent, mainly as a result of Noah's flood. Probably most people disagree with this interpretation and accept that the earth has indeed had a long history. Many Christians consent to this, but believe that God directly intervened on occasions during this time to produce our present world and its organisms (Old Earth Creationists). Then there are those who accept that evolutionary change has happened in both the geological and biological past as described by science, but insist that it has been overseen and ultimately under the sovereignty of God (Theistic Evolutionists, or

---

[1] Cherry Lewis and Simon Knell (eds), *The Age of the Earth: From 4004 BC to AD 2002*, London: Geological Society of London, 2001.

[2] Francis Schaeffer, *Genesis in Space and Time*, Leicester: IVP, 1972, p. 124.

Evolutionary Creationists). Finally, there are some who deny that the beautiful and detailed adaptations that we find in the natural world can arise from known scientific mechanisms and require a "designer" to intervene occasionally as required (Intelligent Design theorists). This four-fold grouping is not exact. Each group contains individuals with different nuances or emphases and there are no fixed boundaries between the groups; indeed Intelligent Design adherents have largely replaced Old Earth Creationists over the last few decades. However, the four positions need to be examined from two very different challenges: biblical interpretation and understanding God's workings in His world.

How should we interpret Genesis 1–11? Is it legitimate to take these chapters as conveying truth but not literal history like the Battle of Hastings or the emancipation of slaves? In the *Word Biblical Commentary* on Genesis, Gordon Wenham calls Genesis 1–11 "paradigmatic and protohistorical".[3] What about the "days" in Genesis 1? Are they literal 24-hour periods or can they have some other significance? Many have treated them as indicators of the passage of time – perhaps even geological eras. Another interpretation has been that the "waste" or "chaos" mentioned in Genesis 1:2 describes the beginning of the present dispensation following the demolition of previous creations (such as almost happened prior to Noah's flood: Genesis 6:7). This means that the Genesis "days" need not be understood as primary creation events. This "day-gap" (or "ruin-restoration") theory used to be widely accepted by evangelicals because they learned it from the notes in Schofield's Reference Bible. A very different proposal is that the "days" indicate days of "revelation" to whoever

---

[3] Gordon J. Wenham, *Word Biblical Commentary*, Nashville, TN: Thomas Nelson, 1987.

received them from God (traditionally Moses).[4] Arguably most compelling is to recognize that the creation account has a literary shape – the six days represent two triads – days one to three are days of separation (or shapelessness) and are followed by three days of adorning (or filling): the light of day one is matched by the luminaries of day four; the creation of the expanse of the sky and the separation of the waters (day two) corresponds to their occupation by winged animals and fish in day five; and the appearance of the dry land and vegetation (day three) corresponds to the appearance of the land animals, including humankind (day six).

However, by concentrating on days one to six, we tend to neglect day seven – the day of rest, a concept of high significance in the culture and practice of the ancient Israelites (Exodus 16:23–29; 20:8–10; 23:10–12; 31:12–17; Leviticus 23:3; 25:1–22; Nehemiah 9:14; 10:31; Isaiah 58:13; Mark 2:27; Hebrews 4:9 etc.). Calvin comments on the seventh day, "After the world was created, man was placed in it as in a theatre, that he, beholding the wonderful works of God, might reverently adore their Author." Old Testament scholar John Walton suggests that the whole creation narrative would imply God and His dwelling-place to its first readers – and that the whole of creation would have no sense if God was not in His Temple, which is why day seven is crucial to the whole.[5]

This interpretation from Walton should recall us to one of the first principles of biblical interpretation: to ask what the text would have meant to its original readers. We need to be very

---

[4] Peter Wiseman, *Creation Revealed in Seven Days*, London: Marshall, Morgan & Scott, 1948.

[5] John Walton, *The Lost World of Genesis One: Ancient Cosmology and the Origins Debate*, Downers Grove, IL: IVP Academic, 2009.

clear: the Bible cannot be read as if it is a twenty-first century textbook. It must be in language that can be understood by people of all generations; this recognition is crucial wherever there is a potential overlap or conflict with science. It is often said that the Bible uses "phenomenological" language. We do the same. We speak of the sun rising or setting, whereas the physical reality is that the visibility of the sun is the result of the rotation of the earth and nothing to do with the movement of the sun itself. In the IVF *New Bible Commentary*, Ernest Kevan wrote:

> *The biblical record of creation is to be regarded as a picturesque narrative, affording a graphic representation of those things which could not be understood with the formal precision of science. It is in this pictorial style that the divine wisdom in the inspiration of the writing is so signally exhibited. Only a record presented in this way could have met the needs of all time.*

In the second edition of the same commentary, Meredith Kline argued similarly: "The prologue's (Genesis 1:1–2:3) literary character limits its use for constructing scientific models, for its language is that of simple observation and a poetic quality, reflected in the strophic structure, permeates the style." To quote Francis Schaeffer again:

> *We must remember the purpose of the Bible: it is God's message to fallen men ... The Bible is not a scientific textbook if by that one means that its purpose is to give us exhaustive truth or that scientific fact is its central theme and purpose. Therefore, we must be careful when we say we know the flow of history: we must not claim, on the one*

> *hand, that science is unnecessary or meaningless, nor, on the other hand, that the extensions we make from Scripture are absolutely accurate or that these extensions have the same validity as the statements of Scripture itself.*[6]

John Bimson summarizes the meaning of Genesis 2 and 3:

> *The narrative refers to a real event within history. But it does so with great literary freedom in language that is culturally encoded, symbolic and metaphorical. Put simply, it speaks of a real disruption at the start of the human story, but does not require us to believe this involved two people, a piece of fruit and a talking snake.*[7]

In the light of these caveats about interpretation and particularly the need to avoid treating the creation stories as if they were science in the modern sense, why do debates about creation and evolution raise so many problems? Is it completely out of the question that God used scientifically investigable evolutionary mechanisms to work out His purposes? The Bible repeatedly records God's use of natural processes. He provides food and habitats for the animals (Job 39:6–8, 27, 28; Psalm 104:10–14, 17–18; 147:9; Matthew 6:26) – even for carnivores, such as lions (Psalm 104:21); He controls the weather (Psalm 147:16–18; Matthew 8:26–27; Acts 14:17). We are rarely told anything about the methods God uses, but even in His miracle-working He is sometimes recorded as using natural forces, as when He "drove the sea back with a strong east wind", so allowing the

---

[6] *Op. cit.*, pp. 35–36.

[7] "Doctrines of the Fall and Sin after Darwin", in Michael Northcott and R. J. Berry (eds), *Theology After Darwin*, Milton Keynes: Paternoster, 2009, pp. 106–122, p. 109.

fleeing Israelites to escape their pursuers (Exodus 14:21, NIV). It is sometimes objected that evolution by natural selection is wasteful and cruel and therefore inappropriate for a loving God, but this is not a compelling argument; it is not for us to judge the methods that God uses for His purposes.

1859 and all that

What about Charles Darwin himself? Was he a devil incarnate? What did his actual contributions amount to? It is important to distinguish between the *fact* that evolutionary change has occurred and the *mechanism(s)* by which it comes about. The *fact* of evolution was freely discussed before the *Origin of Species* appeared in 1859. Darwin lists in the *Origin* thirty-four authors who had proposed evolution in one way or another before him. One of his achievements was to present an enormous amount of evidence that it had in fact happened. There was little dissension at the time about this *fact*. Darwin's originality was to propose (together with Alfred Russel Wallace) natural selection as the mechanism by which adaptation to the environment could take place and hence evolutionary change occur.

Like any new idea, this suggestion had a mixed reception, but most readers of the *Origin* seem to have reacted positively. Charles Kingsley, Regius Professor of Modern History at Cambridge, wrote "God's greatness, goodness and perpetual care I never understood as I have since I became a convert to Mr Darwin's views". The Bishop of Carlisle, preaching at Darwin's funeral in Westminster Abbey, proclaimed:

> *It would have been unfortunate if anything had occurred to give weight and currency to the foolish notion which some*

have diligently propagated, but for which Mr Darwin is not
responsible, that there is an necessary conflict between a
knowledge of Nature and a belief in God.

Darwin wrote to his friend, the Harvard botanist Asa Gray:

I cannot be contented to view this wonderful universe
and especially the nature of man, and to conclude that
everything is the result of brute force. Not that this notion
at all satisfies me. I feel most deeply that the whole subject
is too profound for the human intellect … I can see no
reason, why a man, or other animal, may not have been
aboriginally produced by other laws; and that all these laws
may have been expressly designed by an omniscient Creator,
who foresaw every future event and consequence. But the
more I think the more bewildered I become.

Near the end of his life, he commented: "It seems to me absurd
to doubt that a man may be an ardent Theist and an evolutionist.
In my most extreme fluctuations I have never been an atheist
in the sense of denying the existence of a God." One of his last
letters was to William Graham, Professor of Political Economy in
Belfast, in which he declared "my inward conviction [is] that the
Universe is not the result of chance".

The infamous debate between the Bishop of Oxford and
Thomas Huxley at the 1860 meeting of the British Association
for the Advancement of Science was not really about evolution
versus creation or even science *versus* religion. On the bishop's
side it was about the danger of legitimizing change in an age
when he believed it was having deleterious social and theological
effects; Huxley's agenda was the secularization of society, trying

to establish the legitimacy of science against what he regarded as the improper influence of church leaders. The two were really talking across each other rather than against the other. Certainly the debate is routinely misrepresented; as far as the audience on the day was concerned, many scored it as an entertaining draw. It was reported that the bishop (Samuel Wilberforce) went away happy that he had given Huxley a bloody nose, while Joseph Hooker (who spoke after Huxley) told Darwin that Huxley had been largely inaudible.[8] Despite this, the common understanding – and lasting tragedy – has been a legacy of inevitable conflict between science and faith, encouraged by Huxley himself, fuelled by two much-read (and much criticized) manifestos by John William Draper (*History of the Conflict between Religion and Science*, 1875) and Andrew Dickson White (*A History of the Warfare of Science with Theology in Christendom*, 1886), and regularly regurgitated by the media.

Darwin's ideas were apparently accepted more readily by conservative theologians than by liberals, probably because of their stronger doctrine of providence.[9] Ironically, in view of later history, many of the authors of the "Fundamentals", a series of booklets produced between 1910 and 1915 to expound the "fundamental beliefs" of Protestant theology as defined by the General Assembly of the American Presbyterian Church, were sympathetic to evolution. One of the contributors (G. F. Wright) wrote: "If only the evolutionists would incorporate into their system the sweetness of the Calvinistic doctrine of

---

[8] John Hedley Brooke, "The Wilberforce-Huxley Debate. Why Did It Happen?", *Science & Christian Belief*, 13 (2001), pp. 127–141.

[9] David Livingstone, *Darwin's Forgotten Defenders: The Encounter Between Evangelical Theology and Evolutionary Thought* , Grand Rapids, MI: Eerdmans, 1987.

Divine Sovereignty, the church would make no objection to their speculations." Princeton theologian B. B. Warfield, a passionate advocate of the inerrancy of the Bible, argued that evolution could provide a tenable "theory of the method of divine providence in the creation of mankind".

Historian Owen Chadwick judged that "the compatibility of evolution and Christian doctrine was increasingly acknowledged 'among more educated Christians' between 1860 and 1885; after 1876, acceptance of evolution was both permissible and respectable." A generation after the *Origin* appeared, it was said there were only two "working naturalists of repute" in North America who were not evolutionists. In 1889 Oxford theologian Aubrey Moore made the somewhat startling claim that Darwin did the work of a friend under the guise of a foe by making it impossible to accept the image of an occasionally interfering absentee landlord. For Moore, Darwinism

> *is infinitely more Christian than the theory of "special*
> *creation" for it implies the immanence of God in nature,*
> *and the omnipresence of His creative power … Deism, even*
> *when it struggled to be orthodox, constantly spoke of God as*
> *we might speak of an absentee landlord, who cares nothing*
> *for his property so long as he gets his rent. Yet nothing more*
> *opposed to the language of the Bible and the Fathers can*
> *hardly be imagined.*

Reasons for dissension

In the light of this history, it seems odd at first sight that evolution remains so contentious for Christians. Why is this so? There are at least six reasons.

1. A technical problem that troubled Darwin himself was that natural selection depends on the availability of variation between individuals, and variation seems to be lost in every generation, because offspring tend to be intermediate between their parents. This was a misunderstanding and was resolved by the discovery of particulate inheritance – that inherited elements (genes) are transmitted unchanged between generations. The appearance of blending arises because the expression of every gene is modified by other genes. This was the essence of Gregor Mendel's work, published in 1865 but only realized as significant when it was "rediscovered" in 1900. But in solving one problem, it raised another for the Darwinians: the genes studied by the early geneticists (or Mendelians, as they were called) were almost all deleterious to their carriers, had large effects, and were inherited as recessives – all properties which seemed counter to the progressive gradualism expected under Darwinism. A rift appeared between the biometricians studying the evidence of evolution in living or fossil populations and the geneticists who were unquestionably exploring the physical basis of heredity.

This impasse persisted and widened through the first decades of the twentieth century. There were no real doubts that large-scale evolution had occurred, but it did not seem to have been driven by natural selection. Vernon Kellogg spoke of "the death-bed of Darwinism" in his introduction to a book written for the Jubilee of the *Origin*. Into this apparent void, an extravagance of other evolutionary theories poured: Berg's nomogenesis, Willis's age and area, Smut's holism, Driesch's entelechy, Osborn's aristogenesis and orthogenesis. Their common feature was some form of inner progressionist urge or *élan vital*. Three standard and still-read histories of biology (by Nordenskiöld in 1928,

Rádl in 1930, and Singer in 1931) were written during this time, perpetuating the idea that evolutionary theory is an illogical mess and that Darwinism is completely eclipsed.

The irrelevance of this frenzy of evolutionary speculating was exposed in the 1920s by a series of theoretical analyses by R. A. Fisher and J. B. S. Haldane in Britain and Sewall Wright in the United States, supported by studies of inherited variation in natural populations by E. B. Ford in Britain and Theodosius Dobzhansky in the USA. Their conclusions, together with results from many other sources, were brought together by Julian Huxley in a summarizing volume, *Evolution: The Modern Synthesis*[10] which showed how Mendelian genetics and the insights of Darwin were completely reconcilable. As is proper for any scientific consensus, this neo-Darwinian synthesis has been challenged on various occasions (particularly by discoveries in molecular genetics in the 1960s and 1970s), but remains scientifically robust.

Unfortunately – but perhaps not unreasonably – the scientific doubts of the early 1900s were taken as permanent defects by Christians who saw Darwinism as removing the creator God from His world, an assumption which enabled Richard Dawkins to write that "although atheism might have been tenable before Darwin, Darwin made it possible to be an intellectually fulfilled atheist". This is probably the reason for the recent popularity (particularly among evangelicals) of "Intelligent Design" as a way of smuggling God back into His world.

2. Theologians had a different problem. It concerned the fact rather than the mechanism of evolution. The problem

---

[10] Julian Huxley, *Evolution: The Modern Synthesis*, London: George Allen & Unwin, 1942.

was the Fall. Ironically it was highlighted by an atheist, Robert Blatchford, writing in 1903:

> *Accepting evolution, how can one believe in a Fall? When did man fall? Was it before he ceased to be a monkey, or after? Was it when he was a tree man, or later? Was it in the Stone Age, or the Bronze Age, or the Age of Iron? And if there never was a Fall, why should there be any atonement?*

Taking his cue from Blatchford, the energetic and self-publicizing Adventist George McCready Price proclaimed, "No Adam, no Fall; no Fall, no Atonement; no Atonement, no Savior", using this clarion call to build on the version of extreme literalism espoused by the first generation of Seventh-day Adventists.

Price's legacy fuelled (and continues to fuel) anti-evolutionism among conservatives. By the end of the 1920s, three American states (Tennessee, Mississippi, and Arkansas) had passed laws banning the teaching of evolution in government-funded schools. In Dayton, Tennessee, John Scopes was convicted in 1925 in the notorious "Monkey Trial". The negative publicity from this proved a disaster for anti-evolutionists,[11] and organized "creationism" in the US lapsed into relative quiescence for several decades. This uneasy peace was shattered in 1961 with the publication of *The Genesis Flood*, a highly influential book written by John Whitcomb, a Bible teacher, and Henry Morris, a hydraulic engineer.[12] It rapidly became a key text for Young Earth Creationism. The authors rejected the established findings

---

[11] Edward Larson, *Summer for the Gods,* Cambridge, MA: Harvard University Press, 1998.

[12] John C. Whitcomb and Henry M. Morris, *The Genesis Flood*, Grand Rapids, MI: Baker, 1961.

of geology, palaeontology, and archaeology on the grounds that the world has been so ravaged by a worldwide flood that (they claimed) orthodox stratigraphy cannot be applied. They argued that Genesis tells of a canopy of water which surrounded the early earth and protected its surface from cosmic rays, accounting for the long lives of the patriarchs, and then provided the waters for Noah's flood. Such Young Earth Creationism continues to attract a large number of adherents; Bibles are still produced with the date "4004 BC" heading the references at the beginning of Genesis.

3. Another problem was the seeming randomness of evolution. The idea that evolution might be driven by some sort of purpose was influentially espoused by several distinguished scientists – the zoologist Ray Lankester and the physiologist J. S. Haldane, the psychologists Lloyd Morgan, William McDougall, and E. S. Russell, physicists such as Oliver Lodge, and the cosmologists A. S. Eddington and James Jeans; as well as by popularizers such as Arthur Thomson and politicians such as Arthur Balfour. Not surprisingly with such apparently informed authorities, these ideas were seized upon by churchmen, prominent among them being Charles Gore, and somewhat later W. R. Inge, Hensley Henson, R. J. Campbell, Frederick Tennant, Charles Raven and E. W. Barnes in Britain, and Shailer Mathews and Harry Fosdick in the US. This optimistic progressionism flourished for a time but then died through the perceived ineffectiveness of the theology rather than conscious rejection:

> *The Modernists saw themselves marginalized not by the new science, of which many remained unaware, but by*

changing values within the churches, which brought back
a sense of human sinfulness and alienation from God
incompatible with the idea of progress.[13]

One can have some sympathy with the theologians. It took the scientists a long time to reach an evolutionary synthesis and deal with the apparent purposelessness of evolution,[14] but this does not excuse uncritical use of inadequate science.

4. There is no doubt that evolutionary processes can be described without invoking any metaphysical agent. This is the message trumpeted by Richard Dawkins and other so-called "new atheists". It certainly makes many Christians uncomfortable and leads to them trying to find room for God somewhere in the evolutionary mechanism, most commonly in somehow directing the nature of mutational events. But behind this is a bigger worry: is God necessary? Is evolution wholly naturalistic? Has the demise of Paley's watchmaker meant that God is irrelevant in and therefore excluded from the evolutionary process? This problem is compounded by some Christian apologists defining "naturalism" (the assumption that the laws of nature determine natural events) in an unnecessarily limited way – as implying the non-existence of any supernatural agent. This is a wholly arbitrary restriction. It has been answered powerfully on philosophical grounds by Elliott Sober.[15]

The concern about naturalism seems to be the reason for the popularity of "Intelligent Design" (ID). Although vehemently

[13] Peter Bowler, *Monkey Trials and Gorilla Sermons*, Cambridge, MA: Harvard University Press, 2007, p. 187.

[14] Simon Conway Morris, *Life's Solution: Inevitable Humans in a Lonely Universe*, Cambridge: Cambridge University Press, 2003.

[15] Elliott Sober, *Did Darwin Write the Origin Backwards?*, New York: Prometheus Books, 2011.

denied by its proponents, ID is really a "God-in-the-gaps" argument – invoking divine action to explain gaps in scientific understanding. The problem is that any advance in knowledge which reduces the size of such gaps means less room for God. ID first came to general awareness in the book *Darwin on Trial*,[16] written by a Californian lawyer, Phillip Johnson, explicitly reacting against the naturalism of Richard Dawkins and some rather sophisticated criticisms of conventional evolutionary theory by palaeontologist Colin Patterson and biochemist Michael Denton. The main complaint of Johnson and his followers was not evolution as such, but the assumption that belief in evolution leads inevitably and inexorably to atheism. A scientific case for ID has been claimed by Michael Behe on the grounds that some biological mechanisms and processes are "irreducibly complex" and incapable of evolution by natural selection.[17] Behe's examples have received short shrift from reviewers; they are in fact standard God-in-the-gaps proposals, never mind reviving the classical argument of God as a Divine Watchmaker, periodically adjusting the functioning of His work.

ID has a much wider acceptance in Christian circles than it warrants. The reason for this probably lies in its seductiveness in apparently finding a place for a "hands-on" God, one who is an artificer as well as a creator and redeemer. This is an understandable and laudable ambition, but it portrays a God who is far too small; one who cannot really be understood as sustainer as well as creator (Psalm 104:28–30; Colossians 1:17; Hebrews 1:10–12). We need to recognize that…

---

[16] Phillip Johnson, *Darwin on Trial*, Leicester: IVP, 1991.

[17] Michael Behe, *Darwin's Black Box: The Biochemical Challenge to Evolution*, New York: Free Press, 1996; *The Edge of Evolution*, Free Press, 2007.

> *The God in whom the Bible invites belief is no "Cosmic Mechanic". Rather is he the Cosmic Artist, the creative Upholder, without whose constant activity there would be not even chaos, but just nothing ... To invoke "natural processes" is not to escape from divine activity, but only to make hypotheses about its regularity.*[18]

5. The understanding of evolution in (particularly) North America is further complicated by sociological assumptions under the guise of science. Darwin's contemporary, Herbert Spencer, sought to synthesize biology, physics, philosophy, and sociology into a single entity, which he called "Social Darwinism". This argued that "progress" was inevitable; that whatever existed was "natural" – the rich were rich and the poor were poor because of "natural law". It was an explanation that fitted nicely with Karl Marx's belief that the proletariat would "naturally" come to deserved power one day, and also with a need for eugenics to counteract allegedly inexorable processes of genetic deterioration. Paradoxically Spencer's arguments were also welcomed by industrial leaders, typified by John D. Rockefeller's perception that ...

> *The growth of a large business is merely survival of the fittest ... [Forcing small companies out of business] is not an evil tendency in business. It is merely the working-out of a law of nature and a law of God.*

This "Social Darwinism" horrified the poor – they were now disinherited by God as well as by the often rapacious economic system. It accorded with the assumption that anyone who wants

---

[18] Donald MacKay, *Science and Christian Faith Today*, London: Falcon, 1960.

to succeed, can succeed; but it disadvantaged the yeoman farmer or the struggling employee. It became associated with the idea of inevitable success to those who strived righteously, and was promoted by preachers who emphasized human endeavour leading to success as distinct from the scriptural doctrine of failure needing grace. To those who rejected this sub-Christian set of beliefs, it followed naturally that evolution could not be countenanced. Perhaps acceptance of evolution itself was a sin. Anti-evolutionism became – and remains – linked to conservative theology and thought. Pollsters strengthen this polarization by asking if people believe in evolution or the Bible, implying the necessity of choice between two alternatives.

6. Finally there is a widespread misunderstanding about the possibilities and limits to science. It is not true that science can answer any possible question. Nobel Prize winner Peter Medawar has strongly argued for the need to recognize "that science should not be expected to provide solutions to problems such as the purpose of life or the existence of God". He professes no doubts that "there is no limit upon the power of science to answer questions of the kind that science *can* answer", *but* that science has

> limits is shown by the existence of questions that science
> cannot answer and that no conceivable advances of science
> would empower it to answer ... it is not possible to derive from
> the axioms and postulates of Euclid a theorem to do with how
> to cook an omelette or bake a cake.[19]

Medawar's argument is particularly convincing, because he is not trying to defend a religious position. He records his personal regret concerning "my disbelief in God and religious answers

[19] Peter Medawar, *The Limits of Science*, Oxford: Oxford University Press, 1984.

generally, for I believe it would give satisfaction and comfort to many in need of it if it were possible to discover good scientific and philosophic reasons to believe in God." Notwithstanding, he entirely accepted that "metaphysical (i.e. abstract or supernatural) questions are not nonsense nor bunk; it can be and has been a source of scientific inspiration and of fruitful scientific ideas."

Onwards to maturity with science and Bible

What then is the relationship between scientific knowledge (including evolutionary processes) and divine activity? The most satisfactory solution seems to be that they can be regarded as "complementary", a concept used by the physicist Niels Bohr to account for the paradoxical fact that light behaves as both a wave and a stream of particles. He wrote, "It must be realized that the attitudes termed mechanistic and finalistic are not contradictory points of view, but rather represent a *complementary* relationship which is connected with our position as observers of nature." The words on this page have a purpose in communicating (hopefully) certain ideas, but they can also be described in terms of chemical pigments on a contrasting background: two different but non-competing explanations of the same physical object. Donald MacKay is probably the person who has most explored the theological implications of complementarity. He wrote:

> *What we call physical laws are expressions of created events that we study as the physical world. Physically they express the nature of the entities "held in being" in the pattern. Theologically they express the stability of the great Artist's creative will. Explanations in terms of scientific laws and in terms of divine activity are thus not rival answers to the same*

question; yet they are not talking about different things. They are (or at any rate purport to be) complementary accounts of different aspects of the same happening, which in its full nature cannot be explained by either alone ... To invoke "natural processes" is not to escape from divine activity, but only to make hypotheses about its regularity ... (For example, we cannot settle the validity of our ideas in geometry by discussing the embryological origin of the brain!).[20]

This approach enables us to describe and analyze an event in as quantitative and rigorous a way as possible, but also to acknowledge God's hand in and control of it. An enormous benefit of the complementarity model is that it allows a traditional and robust understanding of God's providence. It permits a God who is outside time as well as space. To picture God outside time is not to imagine Him inactive or uninvolved, but as seeing creation – its complete span of space and time – as a whole. In the context of evolution, it is entirely logical to believe in God as creator and sustainer and simultaneously accept a conventional scientific account.

A good scientific theory is one which explains more than the data that brought it into being and which suggests further ideas. The same applies to faith. This was beautifully expressed by C. S. Lewis, who wrote "I believe in Christianity as I believe the sun has risen, not only because I see it, but because by it I see everything else." There is of course much more to the Christian faith than intellectual coherence, but it is one of the joys and excitements of being a Christian. The testimonies recorded in this book describe the struggles of a mixed group of Christians to make sense of creation. A key test is congruence:

---

[20] *Op. cit.,* p. 10.

do evolutionary ideas help or hinder understanding? Darwin's work brought coherence to many more facts than those set out in the *Origin of Species*. Evolutionary concepts can be regarded as like the string holding together the pearls in a necklace. For the Christian, the awe and respect which creation inspires in us is surely increased by the study of the natural world, and through this the ability, in Johannes Kepler's words, "to think God's thoughts after Him".

Understanding and caring for creation

Christ on the cross reconciled *all things* to Himself, *all things*, whether on earth or heaven (Colossians 1:20). "Creation" and "evolution" are not mutually exclusive concepts. As a wise Christian once said, "When I meet my Maker, He is unlikely to ask me how He made the world; but He is very likely to ask me how I treated it." Our calling is to care for God's creation (Genesis 2:15; Psalm 115:16), not to indulge in interminable myths and genealogies (1 Timothy 1:4). We all have to make up our own minds how best to do this. There is a longstanding tradition that God wrote two books – a book of Words (the Bible) and a book of Works (creation). They have the same author but are written in very different languages. It is a mistake which almost certainly will lead to error if we read only one of them.

Denying evolution is theologically unnecessary and intellectual nonsense. Worse, it is also pastorally and evangelistically counterproductive. Sixteen centuries ago, Augustine of Hippo railed against such an attitude:

> It is a disgraceful and dangerous thing for an infidel to
> hear a Christian, presumably giving the meaning of Holy

Scripture, talking nonsense on these topics [the natural world] ... To defend their utterly foolish and obviously untrue statements, they will try to call upon Holy Scripture for proof and even recite from memory many passages which they think support their position, although they understand neither what they say nor the things about which they make assertions.

Those brought up as Christians are likely to have begun with "stories" about God and His work, stories about a garden, a talking serpent, a flood, a fantastic tower; it is spiritually dangerous to remain unweaned, unable to understand and reinterpret the stories of our infancy (1 Corinthians 13:11; Hebrews 5:12 – 6:8). Let us be transformed by the renewal of our minds. Then – perhaps only then – will we be able to discern the will of God, and to know what is good, acceptable, and perfect (Romans 12:2).

Note

Besides the many works published by either "creationists" or "evolutionists" to justify their own position, there have been a number of attempts to mediate between the two. Writers in the later nineteenth century such as Frederick Temple (*The Relations Between Religion and Science,* Macmillan, 1885) or Aubrey Moore (*Science and the Faith*, Kegan Paul, 1892) were more concerned to explore compatibilities than differences. In more recent times, one of the first to attempt mediation was Bernard Ramm (*The Christian View of Science and Scripture*, Eerdmans, 1954) who argued that God might have used evolution for His purposes. *The Genesis Flood* was produced in part as a reaction against Ramm's work. Dutch zoologist Jan Lever argued similarly but more strongly than Ramm in the same period (*Creation and Evolution*, International Publications, 1958 [Original Dutch edition 1956]). The American Scientific Affiliation followed up Ramm's book in 1959 (*Evolution and Christian Thought*, edited by Russell Mixter, published by Paternoster). IVP published a multi-author book on *Creation and Evolution* (edited by Derek Burke, 1985) in a series "When Christians Disagree", with the two "sides" stating their case and commenting on the other.

A suggested list of recent books is given at the end of this volume for any who want to read further.

CHAPTER 1

He's Still Working on Me

Nick Higgs is a postdoctoral fellow at the Marine Institute of Plymouth University. He was born in the Bahamas but came to Britain for his schooling, going on to read Marine Biology at the University of Southampton, and then to study for a PhD at the University of Leeds in collaboration with the Natural History Museum in London. His research is on the ecology of chemosynthetic ecosystems.

He's still working on me,
To make me what I ought to be.
It took him just a week to make the moon and stars,
The sun and the earth and Jupiter and Mars.
How loving and patient He must be,
He's still working on me.

Joel Hemphill

I begin with a confession. This story is not about a radical change of heart or mind. At no point in my life could I honestly say that I did not accept the truth of evolution; rather it is about how I came to accept evolutionary theory despite growing up around people who were hostile to the very idea of evolution. I suspect that quite a few people experience exactly the same set of circumstances as I did, and I hope that my story may resonate with them.

Childhood perceptions

My childhood was spent on a tiny tropical island, one of the 700 or so which make up the Bahamas. "My" island was inhabited by around 1,500 other people that made up a close-knit fishing community. Christianity was intricately woven into its fabric. Virtually everyone on the island was a professing Christian, or at least believed in the Christian God – atheists were an alien curiosity. Depending on your particular inclination, you had a choice of Brethren, Southern Baptist or Methodist churches. My parents were active members of the last, and I have many happy memories growing up as part of a loving church family. This church environment, and to some extent that of the other churches on the island, shaped my early attitudes to faith, the Bible, and the world around me.

The Bahamas was a British colony until 1973 (my father was a British citizen) and undertones of British Methodism permeated the church culture. That said, the geographical proximity of the southern United States exerted a strong influence, and determined the flavour of the Christianity with which I grew up. All three denominations were pretty conservative in their teaching (the Methodist church perhaps the least of the three) with a wholly literalist understanding of the Bible and a strong emphasis on personal salvation. The Sunday school curriculum and teaching materials were imported wholesale from the American Bible belt. Evolution would have been seen as irrelevant at best and atheistic or wicked at worst. I have no recollection of evolution ever being discussed in my early childhood years, and later events (described below) suggest that my memory is accurate.

One of the great blessings of growing up in this environment was the hearty singing tradition. I grew up with traditional hymns, and many of the words still spring to mind in different situations. When I was a child, one of my favourite Sunday school songs was "He's Still Working on Me". I have no idea why it appealed to me, but it has stayed with me through the years. In many ways it encapsulates the tensions that I later faced when thinking about how evolution related to my faith. The first lines emphasize God's ongoing work in personally transforming my life while the following lines recall God's "week" of creation.

As well as a strong Christian upbringing, my childhood home afforded a close relationship with the rest of God's creation. I spent my early years in the Bahamas immersed in nature, whether chasing lizards, or hunting giant hermit crabs in the bush or watching fish at our dock. Like most men in the community, my father was a fisherman and I spent a lot of time on boats and diving on reefs. I wanted to be a marine biologist for as long as I can remember. This passion was responsible for getting me where I am today. Firstly, it drove my pursuit of a career in the natural sciences, inevitably plunging me into the maelstrom surrounding evolution and the Christian faith. Secondly, it allowed me to fully appreciate evolution when I was introduced to it later on. It seems to me that the better one's grasp of actual organisms and natural systems the easier it is to comprehend why evolution is such an elegant and powerful theory.

At the age of eight, I had no doubt that God created the world, and this took six literal days. But around the age of ten or twelve I noticed that some things in the Bible didn't quite add up. I still have my Youth Explorer Bible with carefully handwritten notes in the back pages highlighting discrepancies that I had noticed between the different Gospel accounts of Jesus' genealogy and also the events of Easter morning in the garden where Jesus was buried. It struck me that in each regard one Gospel must be historically accurate and one not; obviously there was either one angel or two. Perhaps the Bible was not an inerrant factual textbook? Then there was the time when my older brother was told that the Bible was not literally written by God, but by humans inspired by God: "Huh! Well I don't believe any of that," he replied. He was being flippant but I remember thinking that there was a point here: humans are fallible. In addition, what I was reading in English seemed to vary depending on which Bible I looked at: I'd certainly never heard of "the prophet Jeremy" before (Matthew 27:9, King James Version)! There seemed to be more uncertainty in the Bible than I had been led to believe.

Of course, I now know that there are numerous possible explanations for the apparent incongruities. At the time though, none of this caused me to give up on studying the Bible or doubt its authority as the Word of God, nor was I disturbed enough to question an adult about these vagaries. Instead, I mulled these ideas over in my mind. I gradually began to understand that the Bible was a complex compendium of documents, each with a historical context. At some point I realized that when it "took him just a week to make the moon and the stars", it did not need to be taken literally to be meaningful. After all, the persons who wrote the text of Genesis could not have actually witnessed the creation that they describe.

Encountering evolution

At the age of twelve, my life took a different turn. I entered a boarding school in England. The school was located in rural Suffolk, and was surrounded by extensive parkland and woods where we were allowed to play and get our fill of the outdoors. I am thankful for this "right to roam", which maintained my connection with the natural world, albeit in a very different set of habitats from those of my earlier years. The school had been founded by the Methodist Church, which meant a certain amount of continuity in my Christian upbringing. However, few students were practising Christians. The school was a very different environment for me from both the religious and the social point of view. I had to learn how to talk and think about my faith from a new perspective.

My first encounter with evolution must have come during my GCSE year, when we had a few biology lessons on ecology and evolution. I cannot recall them, but I do remember my sixth form biology teacher instructing anyone who wanted to know more about evolution to read Richard Dawkins' book *The Selfish Gene*. The summer following my AS-level exams, I read with fascination and marvel about the intricacies of evolution in that well-crafted book. I was completely ignorant of Dawkins's views on faith, and I am grateful that I was able to read it without prejudice. I wonder if the same would be possible today, given his high-profile atheism. I am also grateful that my teacher (a devout Quaker) did not hesitate to recommend the book.

It is worth pointing out that at this stage, I had no indication that science and faith might be at odds with each other. I had a solid (albeit immature) grasp of the Christian faith, and I was beginning to understand evolution and other aspects of science in earnest, yet there was no conflict in my mind. I suspect this was because the two strands of my thinking were developing in parallel to each other and failing to intersect.

My first introduction to the science-religion dialogue was a rather obscure one. During my A-level course in philosophy and ethics I had to write an essay and prepare a poster on a significant thinker, chosen from a select list. I opted for the Jesuit priest Pierre Teilhard de Chardin (1881–1955), included for his attempts to synthesize evolution and Christianity. The concept intrigued me – I had not considered the two together. Writing the essay and reading about Teilhard's work forced me to realize that my science and my faith were not two distinct phenomena but were actually closely linked. Both must be taken together. This monism, that the physical and spiritual aspects of nature are not distinct phenomena, was at the heart of Teilhard's writings. I was no expert on his philosophy, but I read enough of Teilhard's works to make a lasting first impression that helped me to understand how science, and evolution in particular, impacted my Christian faith.

There was another aspect of Teilhard that appealed to me: his frequent altercations with church authorities. At this time my adolescent liberalism was bringing me into strong disagreements with authority figures in my churches over issues such as female leadership; I felt a sense of solidarity with anyone who "pushed the envelope". Teilhard's thoughts were deemed too radical by the Roman Catholic Church of his time, which led to frequent bans on teaching and publishing his work. This culminated in a 1962 *monitum* (warning) by the papal office on his work "to protect the minds, particularly of the youth, against the dangers presented by the works of Fr. Teilhard de Chardin and of his followers".

Was this not the same charge levelled at Socrates? Teilhard was as much a hero of free thought to me as Socrates. I admired his self-conviction while at the same time maintaining the humility to submit to his superiors. These episodes in Teilhard's life also alerted me to the fact that contemporary Christians might possibly have problems with a worldview that held Christianity and evolution together.

Testing the faith

Anti-evolution attitudes became increasingly obvious to me on my visits back home. Although much of my education was taking place in England, my holidays were spent in the Bahamas; indeed, most of my reading was done working on a fishing boat over the summer. On one occasion a fellow fisherman chastised me for reading Carl Zimmer's excellent book, *Evolution: The Triumph of an Idea*,[1] which he dismissed as "foolishness". I was not quite ready for confrontation and justified myself on the ground that whether I agreed with it or not I had to at least know about it for my undergraduate course in marine biology. I was more candid with some of my friends, who were shocked and perplexed in equal measure. During a discussion about evolution, the age of the earth, and how it all related to the Bible, one friend said to me, "I've always wanted to meet someone who believes in all that stuff." She went on to question me fiercely, seemingly incredulous as to whether I could actually believe that humans had evolved from a common ancestor with the other great apes. Another friend – my closest friend – thought that my acceptance of scientific orthodoxy was a bit wacky but could see my point and respected my "opinion". He later told me that one of the Sunday

---

[1] Carl Zimmer, *Evolution: The Triumph of an Idea*, London: Harper, 2001.

school teachers had considered asking me to teach a class on the topic of evolution, since she knew I was studying science and assumed that I could deliver a defence of literal creationism. She changed her mind, though, when my friend informed her that I was an evolutionist. Perhaps I was a potential danger to the minds of the youth!

It was not only Christians in the Bahamas that seemed hostile towards evolution. A significant contingent of students in the Christian Union at my university in the UK were suspicious of evolution and its perceived atheistic undertones. It was one thing for folk back home to be sceptical, where evolution was fairly irrelevant to daily life, but I was astounded that people studying at degree level (some of them in science) could flatly reject a fundamental tenet of biology. I recall an evening in the pub with men from my local non-denominational church questioning me – "You don't go along with this evolution idea, do you?" – knowing that I was a science student. I tried to see their point of view. I borrowed a "creationist" book, *What is Creation Science?*[2], from the church library in the Bahamas. Rather than providing a coherent alternative explanation to evolution, it just tried to pick holes using spin and unappealing rhetoric. I was so appalled that I did not return it.

At the same time my science course-mates assumed that all Christians were obtuse anti-evolutionists who were intellectually vacuous. I knew that this was a gross misrepresentation, but I could not deny that *some* Christians did resemble their caricatures. I began to strongly resent any association with "creationists", to the degree that I thought I might give up labelling myself a Christian altogether. It came with so much unwanted baggage. Of course,

[2] Henry Morris and Gary Parker, *What is Creation Science?*, San Diego, CA: Master Books, 1987.

we must all be prepared to accept persecution and ridicule for our faith, but I felt that I was taking flack for beliefs that were not my own. For many of my friends, the anti-intellectualism that they associated with Christianity was a complete barrier to the gospel. I could not talk to them about my faith without the issue coming up. How could I claim to be proclaiming the ultimate truth, while associating myself with Christians who were rejecting the most basic elements of common knowledge?

I found myself contemplating a life outside the church. It seemed that I was being forced to choose between my calling as a scientist and my Christian fellowship. I certainly had no intention of betraying my scientific integrity and could not see the point of being part of a body that could be so wilfully ignorant. I was also frustrated by Christian leaders who seemed to tolerate anti-evolution sentiments in an effort to keep the peace or because they felt ill-equipped. My personal belief in God was unshaken though and I intended to continue as a believer, but was uncertain as to how I could work out my faith. I knew that it was entirely possible to be a Christian without attending church, but I did feel the need for fellowship. Luckily, I found some solace attending a Quaker meeting house from time to time, where the congregants were refreshingly open-minded.

By chance I happened to live in a city with an active branch of Christians in Science (CiS), a network for those interested in the interaction between science and the Christian faith. Some members visited one of our Christian Union meetings to advertise their presence and I jumped at the chance to meet others that might be in my situation. CiS was a Godsend. I began to meet other scientists who were Christians, who took both aspects of their lives seriously. They organized lectures by eminent speakers on various topics in the science and faith arena. All of this gave me a sense of affirmation and reassurance, that that showed me I was not foolish for wanting to maintain my Christian and scientific convictions together. I later attended a short course run by the Faraday Institute for Science and Religion in Cambridge, which opened up my mind to the vast body of research and writings in the science-faith arena. I suddenly felt more confident in my faith and could show people that there were rational Christians out there.

In my new-found zeal, I entered a student essay competition for the Christians in Science magazine. Rather like my previous foray with Teilhard de Chardin, the brief was to write about an inspirational figure in the history of science and faith. After some research, I ended up writing a rather flat bio-sketch of Asa Gray (1810–88), Professor of Botany at Harvard for thirty years from 1842. He was an excellent naturalist and one of the earliest supporters of Darwin in the years after the publication of the *Origin of Species*. In retrospect, I wish that I had chosen to write about another personal hero of mine: Philip Henry Gosse (1810–88). At the time I didn't know much about him, except that he was a marine biologist and unshakeable fundamentalist. My distaste for Christian fundamentalism caused me to overlook him for the essay, despite our shared marine interests. While at university I read two publications that changed my mind: the first was Stephen Jay Gould's essay "Adam's Navel"[3] and the second was a wonderful biography of Gosse by Ann Thwaite.[4] Gosse was a passionate zoologist, an effective science communicator, and a correspondent of Darwin. He introduced the concept of the

---

[3] Reprinted in Stephen Jay Gould, *The Flamingo's Smile*, New York: W. W. Norton, 1985.

[4] Ann Thwaite, *Glimpses of the Wonderful*, London: Faber, 2002.

aquarium to Victorian England. Despite his acquaintance and respect for Darwin, Gosse flatly rejected evolution.

Gosse's story is pertinent to my own, so a slight diversion is in order. He was a biblical literalist and had already spent much time trying to reconcile his science and faith before Darwin published his ideas of natural selection. Gosse subscribed to a Young Earth Creationist interpretation of the Bible, leaving him at odds with fellow scientists, who had shown that the earth was much, much older than the few thousand years that he believed it to be. Gosse reconciled this with a theory that the earth just *appeared* to be old. He hypothesized that when God created Adam he would have had a navel, even though he was not born of a woman, because it is a part of being human. Likewise, Gosse maintained that when God created the trees they would have necessarily had tree rings, and in the same way the hills would have different rock strata. His whole book *Omphalos: An Attempt to Untie the Geological Knot* was a litany of examples explaining that signs of antiquity in the natural world were a necessary artefact of a young creation. While seemingly brilliant, it did not catch on and most of the copies were pulped: his fellow scientists found it untestable and irrelevant, while fellow churchmen thought it made God out to be a deceiver. Gosse's sincere attempt to bring believers and scientists together (as embodied in his own life) was a failure.

Lessons learned

I still admire Gosse because of his steadfast belief that God's Word in the Bible and His work in creation could not be at odds, since God is the author of both. Any apparent conflict must be a misinterpretation of one or the other. The idea that the one God has written two books – a book of Words (the Bible) and a book of Works (creation) has helped many. The books are written in very different languages but they have the same author; it is nonsensical to think that God would contradict Himself in His books. I suspect that many anti-evolutionists do not know the quotation from Francis Bacon's *Advancement of Learning* (1605) which Darwin placed at the beginning of the *Origin of Species*:

> *Let no man ... think or maintain that he can be too well*
> *studied in the book of God's words or in the book of God's*
> *works; rather let all men endeavour an endless proficience*
> *in both.*

It is a powerfully simple idea; it is the single most important reason why I never rejected evolution. Gosse's mistake was doggedly maintaining that his acceptance of the authority of Scripture was the same thing as his interpretation of it. For myself, I had known God as creator before I knew anything about evolution and science. I knew that no threat to God could ever come from the study of the natural world; He is behind it.

Nor did I ever see evolution as a challenge to the Bible. Evolution provides a way in which we can understand how the diversity of life came to exist, how God works in the world which He has created, in a way that we could not and should not expect to get from Scripture. Gosse refused to engage with the emerging scholarship of literary criticism in his time that was bringing new insights into how the Bible was constructed and has been passed down to us. This secular analysis of biblical texts (coinciding with Darwin's publications) was perceived as threatening by many Christians, and repelled a faction of ardent conservatives that has persisted to this day. I have no doubt whatsoever that a mature study of Scripture is a critical part of working out the Christian faith. The apostle Paul writes: "When I was a child, I spoke and thought and reasoned as a child. But when I grew up, I put away childish things" (1 Corinthians 13:11, NLT). The tragedy is that too many devout Christians never really engage with Scripture and remain at the level of "Bible stories" and Sunday school songs. The early Christians were chastised for not developing their faith: "you ought to be teaching others. Instead, you need someone to teach you again the basic things about God's word. You are like babies who need milk and cannot eat solid food" (Hebrews 5:11–14; verse 12, NLT). If my view of Scripture had remained unchanged from my early childhood, I might well have felt threatened by evolution, but thankfully I had begun to mature long before coming across it. I can only attribute this to parents who encouraged me to read widely and think critically.

Gosse's story also helped reconcile me to the wider church. It is clear that most Christians who oppose evolution do so out of sincere faith. I share with them a desire to seek God's truth but differ in how we view the evidence. It is a lesson in humility. Even good scientists can be tempted into shoehorning science into their metaphysical assumptions if they are not careful. Just as siblings or parents can be embarrassing at times, yet we still love them, so I could not stop loving other Christians or cut them out of my life, just because they do not share my academic understanding. No one has a perfect faith. As the apostle Paul warns, "If you think you are wise by this world's standards, you need to become a fool to be truly wise" for "Now we see things imperfectly ... but [when the time of perfection comes] we will see everything with perfect clarity" (1 Corinthians 3:18; 13:12, NLT).

So we must move beyond childish reasoning in our engagement with Scripture, but at the same time we must accept the kingdom of God with the humility of little children (Matthew 18:2–4); "while knowledge makes us feel important, it is love that strengthens the church" (1 Corinthians 8:1, NLT). We must also take Jesus' subsequent warning in Matthew 18:6 seriously that "whoever causes the downfall of one of these little ones who believe in Me – it would be better for him if a heavy millstone were hung around his neck". In framing evolution, and science in general as a threat to Christianity, anti-evolutionists may be driving young believers away from faith, as my experience can testify. It is incumbent upon those with a strong faith that can encompass the full majesty of God's Word and God's works to support those for whom science might seem an attack on their faith. In recognizing this I am happy that "He's still working on me, To make me what I ought to be".

CHAPTER 2

Nothing in Biology Makes Sense Except in the Light of Evolution

Emily Sturgess was born in Northampton, and read Biological Sciences at the University of Oxford. After completing her degree, she spent a year as an administrator with her church in Oxford and then moved to the University of Reading for an MSc in Species Identification and Survey Skills. Currently Emily is combining her administrative experience and skill with her love of science in the role of development officer for Christians in Science – an international network for those concerned with the interactions between science and faith.

In 1973, the leading American geneticist, Theodosius Dobzhansky, wrote an article entitled "Nothing in biology makes sense except in the light of evolution".[1] It was his reaction to a petition to the King of Saudi Arabia from the Grand Mufti of Saudi Arabia, Sheikh Abd el Aziz bin Baz, asking the king to suppress the heresies arising from science. The sheikh wrote:

> *The Holy Koran, the Prophet's teachings, the majority of Islamic scientists and the actual facts all prove that the sun is running in its orbit ... and that the earth is*

---

[1] Theodosius Dobzhansky, "Nothing in Biology Makes Sense Except in the Light of Evolution", *American Biology Teacher*, 35 (1973), pp. 125–129.

fixed and stable, spread out by God for his mankind ...
Anyone who professed otherwise would utter a charge of
falsehood toward God, the Koran, and the Prophet.

Dobzhansky was horrified by these assumptions and their implications, firmly believing that science and religion do not contradict each other. In his article he reviewed the evidence that evolution had occurred, and concluded, "Does the evolutionary doctrine clash with religious faith? It does not. It is a blunder to mistake the Holy Scriptures for elementary textbooks of astronomy, geology, biology, and anthropology."

Unfortunately the title of the essay apparently implies a narrow-minded arrogance on the part of scientists. Not understanding the context of the essay's title, it certainly used to mean that to me. My heart sank when I walked into the large zoology lecture theatre for my very first lecture as an undergraduate at the University of Oxford and saw projected up on the screen: "Nothing in science makes sense except in the light of evolution". I was already nervous, convinced that my offer and grades must have been a fluke, and afraid that somebody would realize that I wasn't clever enough to be there. I would never be able to pull through this if they knew I was a Christian *and* an academic stowaway. I was hoping to remain undiscovered, but now I felt there was a neon sign above my head saying, "This girl believes in a creator! She should not be here."

Nobody was actually saying it, but all I seemed to be able to read was: *"Everything in Biology will only be explained by evolution. So put your foolish ideas about God away, Emily, and we'll do some real science."* The crushing weight of how my two non-overlapping magisteria were soon to collide weighed heavily on me, even before the first lecture had begun.

The trouble was, I had come to university with the notion, which I fear is held by many, that one simply could not believe in a creator God and also "believe" in evolution. In my head they were two mutually exclusive religions: a Religion of God and a Religion of Evolution. I had opted for God and I knew the Bible was His Word to me; this meant the Religion of Evolution was necessarily a thing shrouded in cynicism, scepticism, and fear.

Let me be clear from the beginning, in the light of what I am going to say about having to change my approach to God and His workings: I have an enormous respect for those who brought me up and demonstrated to me what it is to love and live for God. During my childhood and teenage years, my parents, friends, and church leaders were (and continue to be) wonderful role models, with passionate hearts for God and His kingdom. They inspired me, pushed me on, and laid the foundation for me really to think about who God is and how He works. I am truly grateful for all that they taught me. The thing is, my upbringing didn't contain many scientists, nor very much to persuade me that evolution was particularly important to the biological sciences.

I committed myself to Jesus at a relatively young age, which is something I will never regret because that foundation sustained me through some demanding teenage years. During the summer that I was thirteen, there were a few of us youngsters in the church who had real encounters with God, including my big sister and my best friend. With some discipling and encouragement we all responded by getting baptized. It was a phenomenal time, and as I write, I am happy to celebrate the ten-year anniversary this very weekend. However, my trust in Jesus took place before I'd decided to be a biologist. At thirteen I was a musician, mathematician, writer, historian, painter, and many other things. As thirteen-year-olds should, I enjoyed a bit of everything, and God underpinned it all. The decision to focus on the biological sciences did not come until a few years later; and issues of creation and evolution never crossed my mind. I was saved, I knew I was loved by the King, and I was raring to live for Him. That was all that mattered.

Aged fifteen, I began working in our local Christian bookshop as a sales assistant. I developed a talent I was particularly proud of: the ability to talk about most of the books in the shop without having read them, or at most, only a chapter or two. The span of my employment was over my GCSEs and A-levels; so along with studying, practising an instrument, learning to drive, doing youth work, and collecting bonus UCAS points for my university applications, the time to actually read the books I was employed to sell was distinctly limited.

I worked every Saturday afternoon, which was normally rather busy, but also helped in weekday shifts through the school holidays. These holiday shifts (at, say, eleven o'clock on a Wednesday morning) tended to be much less busy and left time for shelf-perusal and page-flicking. There was a section that I always came back to in those quiet moments, and would spend my hard-earned wages on: "Science". From this one section of the shop, I actually read the books. There seemed to be a wealth of controversy within this section, even when you only scratched the surface, and I didn't know what I was meant to make of it all. There were persuasive DVDs about elements of creation that "defied evolution" and books that argued that Dawkins and his counterparts were wrong; but I was never sure which of the arguments against them really stood up.

Either way, my interest was piqued, even if I didn't come to any conclusions about what I was trying to understand. At the time I would not have known to give them names, but I know now that the three arguments I was torn between were Young Earth Creationism, Intelligent Design, and Evolutionary Theism. I had no idea whether the stance I thought I was *supposed* to believe was the one that was *correct*.

My parents were interested in this debate too; they landed a little more firmly towards the Young Earth-Intelligent Design end of the spectrum. Occasionally a pamphlet would come through the post that explained how chance and death could never have made such spectacular creatures as those we see in nature. Such literature spoke with wonder at God and His creation, but scepticism at some scientific practice and evidence. Examples such as the intricacy of the eye, and the perfect positioning of valves in the giraffe's neck that stopped blood excessively flooding the brain when they bend to drink were used as evidence against "substandard" intermediate states that (they said) must have occurred if evolution had produced them. The inference was that the natural world showed a multitude of features which could only function if they had been right first time. I could see their point, and I knew that I was in awe of God in many ways already, so in general what they were saying seemed to add up.

However, it is no surprise that the thing that influenced me most at home was not pamphlets, but my evolution-sceptical father. My dad is a brilliant, worshipful, and godly man, with a wit and way with words sharp enough to cut steel; I'm proud to have inherited some of this. While often used only in throwaway humour, discussions on television and radio about how we "all came from the primordial soup", and how animals "decided" to move onto land from water would feel the sharp cut of his words keenly (Bruce Forsyth's jokes suffered similarly). Looking at it now, from the other side of postgraduate study, I share in much of his frustration of how evolution is portrayed in media and entertainment. To my eyes, it is overanthropomorphized, with too much focus on organisms "deciding" to change particular elements of their physiology; the true driving forces of evolution are misrepresented. I suspect to my father's eyes this anthropomorphism represented science presenters glossing over knowledge gaps, not "showing their workings", and presenting unsatisfactory science that would not persuade him that evolution worked.

Disparagement and disregard can be ridiculously contagious, particularly from people you love and respect, and especially when it's funny. Because of the fact that unlike many teenagers, I actually got on with my parents almost all of the time, I saw no reason to rock the boat by disagreeing with the views I thought they held. My parents are genuinely in no way anti-science, and not even anti-evolution *per se*, but I interpreted their wariness of evolution from a plethora of sources that I put two and two together and made five, assuming this must mean they believed it to be completely wrong. So far, what my parents believed had matched up entirely with what I had come to believe, and in the busynesses and naiveties of teenage life I just hadn't thought to question this. I made an assumption and stuck with it.

At school, my interest in biology grew during my GCSEs and A-levels, and I went on to study it at university. I loved learning about how perfectly homeostatic systems held bodies in balance; and what phenomenal mechanisms plants had for detecting day length to infer seasons. It was (and still is!) fascinating to me.

In retrospect, some of the problems I had with evolution came with the modular nature with which all of this was taught at school. Within a module, subjects built upon one another, and sometimes interconnected; but the module itself would be taught, revised, and examined as a separate entity. After that, we would move on to something completely different. Learning the theory of natural selection was just another one of those topics, like knowing the double-circulatory system or the chemical stages of the Krebs cycle, which were memorized, regurgitated for exams, and thrown away when there was something new to learn. The natural selection aspect of the syllabus at GCSE and A-level was not in-depth, barely relevant, and certainly not interesting. It was far from being my favourite module. Nothing was mentioned about the wide-reaching biological significance of selection; how it underpinned all of the other processes that we were learning about, and how it was probably the one thing that ran as a common thread through all of the fascinating but disparate pieces of information we were being taught.

It was this modular, boxed-in thinking that let me carry on believing that natural selection might be something useful in the short term – if you were a camel who needed longer eyelashes or bigger feet in the desert – but it probably hadn't got much significance for everyone and everything else. My mental concept as a GCSE student was that natural selection could make organisms camouflaged, fast, and strong, and that was about it. Every time I wondered about how it might work in a wider context, I felt that perhaps I wasn't being a very good Christian, and so I would put it back on the shelf in my mind. After all, the few famous evolutionary scientists I knew were atheists, so it seemed that the two must go hand in hand.

The accumulation of all of these factors, for a teenager who had plenty else to assimilate, left an academically and theologically confused young woman. Through a plethora of misunderstanding, naiveté and mixed messages, what I had wrongly come to understand was that you could only believe in God or in evolution. I had already chosen God.

This was how I ended up on that first day of university, cowering in the glow of a projector that was telling me that nothing in biology made sense except in the light of evolution.

My early days at university were exhilarating, but sometimes disconnected from God. I never lost my faith or strayed too far from the beaten track, but I initially (and foolishly) felt that God was only at home, and not quite big enough to be in Oxford at the same time. The very first tutorial I attended required an essay about the "Cambrian explosion" – the phenomenon of an abundance of types with new body plans having been found as fossils within a relatively short geological era. The key text for the essay was the *Crucible of Creation* by Simon Conway Morris.[2] As an inexperienced researcher, I ploughed through all the wrong bits of the book for the question I was trying to answer, in an attempt to piece together some thoughts about what might have happened; all the while sceptical about whether an explosion of new body plans could be a legitimate occurrence. If I had known then what I know now, that Simon Conway Morris is both a Bible-believing Christian and a palaeobiologist, I might possibly have got off on a very different foot! If I had discovered that there were professional biologists out there who had reconciled their career with their faith when I was seventeen rather than twenty-

---

[2] Simon Conway Morris, *Crucible of Creation*, Oxford: Oxford University Press, 1998.

two, how I approached that essay and the scepticism of my early undergraduate thinking could have been so very different. But that did not happen, and I spent a lot of time wondering if I was the only one who was confused.

Because I initially felt that God was quite far away from Oxford, it was easy to let all of the things I was learning about evolution at university be part of my "university life", with God remaining part of my "home life". The trouble was that when I laid my scepticism aside, everything that I was learning about evolution was *fascinating*, truly wondrous, and it was quite uncomfortable to think that God might not be on board with all of it. So, for a while at least, I kept evolution and my relationship with God in two separate boxes.

The first shift in my thinking happened at home on one of the holidays during my first year, when my church leader, who had been an engineer and maths teacher, met up with me to chat about how things were going at university. He challenged me particularly about what I was learning, how I was processing it, and what it was doing for my relationship with God. I wasn't sure, and fudged some kind of answer about how it was all really interesting, but that there was a lot that scientists still didn't know (or at least, that I didn't think they knew; I certainly didn't know), and so much that could be the miraculous works of God. He stopped me in my tracks fairly quickly. "So what happens when the scientists work out the bits that they don't know now?" he asked me. "What happens when science has worked out so much that there's nothing miraculous and unknown to ascribe to God any more? Where does God fit into your science then?"

The conversation that followed, in that noisy coffee shop, revealed to me how unhelpful and potentially foolish it was to use "God of the gaps"-style thinking about science. We discussed how if you only let God be in the bits that you didn't understand or that seemed miraculous, God would rapidly get smaller. And why shouldn't you attribute the things you *do* understand to God – does understanding them make them any less created by God, or any less awesome? He then challenged me on my compartmentalized thinking – about how I would answer a question about evolution completely differently in a tutorial as to how I would at church, or to my parents. Where was the integrity in that? I floundered. I had been putting off trying to make any kind of reconciliation between the two boxes, because just getting my essays in on time was taking up enough of my brain space. But in doing so I was walking with double standards: I was discrediting both what I was learning and what I believed in. That conversation was a revelation and conviction for me.

When I finally settled in a church in Oxford, having clocked that God is quite big enough to be in Northampton and Oxford at the same time, I realized that the church I'd chosen was painfully low on biology students. In fact, despite having a reasonably sizeable student population, it turned out that not only was I the only biology fresher, I was the only biology student *at all*. This is not a situation that changed in any of my student years, undergraduate or postgraduate; I flew the biology flag alone in our student work for five whole years. In terms of being able to get alongside other biologists who were Christians, and try to think through things together, this was not the easiest of situations.

I decided in my second year I had to get proactive. I knew, by some kind of statistical reckoning, that I couldn't be the *only* Christian biologist in my year. I started to look out and took note of the people who wore mission-week hoodies to lectures, had vintage WWJD ["What Would Jesus Do?"] bands, or had been overheard saying comments such as "Sorry, I've got Christian Union/church/something particularly godly tonight". It soon became clear that there were some other Christians on the course. Moreover, as biology is a fairly interactive subject, with labs, field trips, and cross-pollination of tutorial groups between colleges, most of us Christian biologists knew at least one or two others by Christmas of our second year. Over that vacation, a few of us hatched a plot via email, all inviting a few more believers we knew to the conversation, and decided that we should try to support each other.

From that we formed a small faculty group, where we would meet to chat about the things we were learning about and what we made of them as Christians. It was the best thing that little group of about eight could have done, creating a forum where we could support each other, pray for each other, and try to work out how we could reconcile this huge process of evolution with our belief in a creator God. We made a conscious decision to meet in the zoology department café, and have our conversations out in the open. It was through those conversations that we began to see how much we had learned, how much our thoughts had changed since we'd started university, and also how different our views were on some matters. That safe and supportive environment where we were able to say, "But what about this? Would that mean God didn't exist? Or isn't good?" allowed us to talk through the contentious questions we weren't sure we would be allowed to ask anywhere else. While we did not solely talk about evolution, many conversations boiled down to the fact that we had learned so much about evolution that it was incredibly difficult to refute it any more.

It turned out that many of us had grown up assuming that the six-day account of creation in Genesis was something we were meant to take literally. As our scientific thinking grew and matured, I had to recognize that my modular pigeon-holing about evolution being dispensable if it didn't fit with my theology didn't stand up to scrutiny. For one thing, Evolution and Systematics was a compulsory second-year module, so we couldn't escape it if we wanted to. But more importantly, I was beginning to see that there could be no façade, no fudging of facts, no scientific wishful thinking: there was a lot of evidence, and evolution was a genuine process that we had a lot to learn about. More than that, and much as Dobzhansky had said, nothing we were learning would make sense without it. It underpinned all of the processes and theories we were researching, and as rational thinkers we had to accept that evidence.

All the while, as my thinking shifted about accepting evolution, my thinking about how to read and interpret the Bible had to shift too. Unless my theological and scientific worlds were allowed to meet, no reconciliation could be made and no peace found. Much of my initial theology was based on the assumption that the Genesis story was written to be taken literally, and that non-literal interpretations of this section of the Bible would lead one down a slippery slope.

My adjustment to all this was like one of those scrambled picture games you play as a child, where you have to move one tile up to move another across, and then another down, to sort the tiles into the picture it was meant to be. I had to shuffle one bit of scientific thinking, then shuffle a bit of theological thinking, and so on, until my scrambled thoughts could progressively rearrange to make sense. Much as there was no one source that had made me originally think that evolution was wrong, there was no single book, conversation or epiphany that shook all the pieces out of the holder and put them instantly into the right arrangement. But, bit by bit, I became more assured and less fearful in my thinking.

Much of the change to my thinking came from coming to understand how Genesis 1 and 2 had been written, and how these chapters fitted with the other Bible accounts of creation. Having come to accept that the world was much older than 6,000 years and that all species didn't appear fully formed in a six-day period, there was space for me to reinterpret how I read the beginning of the Bible. One tile moves up.

Another important strand to my thinking was about trust in God and His goodness. I feared that if one thing I had learned about God was not as I'd thought, then perhaps all the other things I knew of God would be shaken too. However, during those months at university, God repeatedly confirmed to me through various situations that His character is completely unchanging and unfailing. He never deserts people who need Him (even if, like Job, it sometimes feels as if He does), He never stops loving, He never stops being good and faithful. I came to see that my changing understanding of Him did not actually change Him. Another tile moves across...

Recently, I was asked by a student friend whether it is theologically justifiable to read the Bible through scientific eyes rather than reading science through biblical eyes, the implication being that faith in the Word ought to have precedence over faith in science. I could understand where he was coming from. When we profess to put God above all and trust the Bible as the Word of God, surely it should be through those eyes that we interpret the rest of the world, rather than the other way round.

The understanding I have come to, though, is that God has revealed Himself to us in two books: a book of Words (the Bible) and a book of Works (creation); we need to read them both – and use the wisdom and insight that we have to understand them. They have the same author, even if they are written in very different languages, and we therefore have to read them differently. God has given us the earth to steward, investigate, understand, and find delight in; but He is not a deceiver, and science is not an intrinsically ungodly pursuit. Proverbs 25:2 says "It is the glory of God to conceal a matter; to search out a matter is the glory of kings" (NIV). *The Message* translates the same verse as: "God delights in concealing things; scientists delight in discovering things." We need a true humility in our task of discovering God's mysteries in the world. In Proverbs 3 we are told that "[Wisdom] is a tree of life to those who take hold of her; those who hold her fast will be blessed" (verse 18, NIV), but immediately afterwards we are informed that, "By wisdom the Lord laid the earth's foundations, by understanding he set the heavens in place; by his knowledge the watery depths were divided, and the clouds let drop the dew" (verses 19–20, NIV).

It follows that the wisdom that we are encouraged to pursue and cling to, and which will bless us, is the very same that brought forth the creation of the world. God has given us the opportunity and privilege to delight in seeking out His wisdom through His creation as well as through Scripture. So, when we find things in nature that do not fit our interpretation of the Bible, we must accept that it comes from our misunderstanding – either of what the text is saying, or how we are interpreting what is happening in nature. His wisdom is written deeply through both the Scripture and the world. It is not that we read the Scripture through the eyes of science, trying to squeeze it to fit what we want it to say; our task is to dig deeper into what is the true meaning of the text. When my understanding of science seemed to show creatures evolving over large periods of time, my understanding of God as creator shifted into a longer timeframe than reading the six-day Genesis account at face value might initially suggest.

More and more, these small assurances of how I approach both evolution and creation have caused my thinking to become less confused, with the tiles much more resembling a real picture, rather than the scrambled mess I started with.

When this book appears, I will be twenty-four years old. Several more years may pass before you read it. My prayer is that by that time, my journey with God as a scientist may be vastly deeper, more mature and with a great deal more understanding than at present. For now, I know that I am still trying to answer lots of questions about how God has done things, and what various bits of evolutionary history mean in terms of biblical history and of God's plan for the world. I cannot yet set out all the answers; but, hopefully, I can encourage you that letting go of a literal six-day view of creation does not mean letting go of God as creator, or designing a god for yourself, different to the God of the Bible. I do not worship a "God", who I have reshaped to fit with some science I have been persuaded by. I worship The Lord, and He remains "The Lord, the Lord, the compassionate and gracious God, slow to anger, abounding in love and faithfulness, maintaining love to thousands, and forgiving wickedness, rebellion and sin" (Exodus 34:6–7, NIV). And, funnily enough, I have started to see that nothing in biology makes sense except in the light of evolution.

CHAPTER 3

From Belief in Creationism to Belief in Evolution

Professor Sir Colin J. Humphreys, CBE, FRS, FREng, Hon DSc, FIMMM, FInstP, FCGI, FRMS. Educated Luton Grammar School and Imperial College, London. Director of Research, Department of Materials Science and Metallurgy, University of Cambridge since 2008. Goldsmiths' Professor of Materials Science, University of Cambridge since 1992–2008; previously Professor of Materials Engineering, Liverpool University, 1985–89. Director, Rolls-Royce University Technology Partnership in Advanced Materials since 1994; Director, Cambridge Centre for Gallium Nitride since 2000. Fellow, Selwyn College, Cambridge since 1990.

"Give me a child until he is seven and I will show you the man" was supposedly said by the founder of the Jesuits, Ignatius Loyola. It represents a basic belief that something firmly fixed in the mind by the age of seven is unlikely ever to go away. It does not apply in my case.

Both my parents were Christians and both believed that God created our universe in seven days. My father ran the junior Sunday school at Ceylon Baptist Church in Luton. We used to go to church two or three times every Sunday; it was a normal part of my upbringing. My father was born in Leicester, the son of a gardener. He had worked as an engineer in Leicester but was made redundant; he moved to Luton to seek work. He met my mother there, and I was born in the town. We were quite a poor family. We had no bathroom and only an outside lavatory. We kept a large metal bath outside the house. Once a week my father would bring it indoors and it would be filled with hot water boiled in a kettle (it required many kettles full!). I would get in first, then my mother had a turn, and finally my father, all using the same water. My parents had to sit in the bath with their knees pulled up to their chin because it wasn't big enough to stretch out. The bath would be emptied by repeatedly dipping a large jar into the water and pouring the contents down the kitchen sink.

We lived in a small terraced house in Dale Road, Luton, until I was nine. Our home had very few books; one year I was given the single-volume edition of *The Children's Encyclopaedia* by Arthur Mee, which I read so avidly that it fell apart. The chief reading material in the house was Christian literature, including small booklets and tracts sent to us at regular intervals by a creationist society my father belonged to. I used to love reading them. Although they were written for adults, I remember being fascinated and totally convinced by them. I was a voracious reader and regularly borrowed books from the local library. One reason for this may have been that I had problems with my feet and had to wear leg irons up to the age of twelve (rather like Forrest Gump!). This severely restricted my ability to take part in any sport.

My parents were great friends with Dennis and Louise Parker, who also went to Ceylon Baptist Church. At the end of the evening service, we would frequently go to the Parkers's house, which was much larger than ours and in a "posh" part of Luton. I liked going there because Louise made delicious cakes. I used to play with their son while our parents dissected the sermon they had just heard. Visiting preachers would be assessed as to whether they were "sound" or not. Anyone believing in evolution would certainly not have been classified as "sound"! I listened to their discussions with fascination, and increasingly joined in with my own comments.

My father and Dennis Parker were lay preachers. They would often go out to local churches, usually small village churches, conduct the service and preach. I would sometimes accompany my father and sit in the congregation. Occasionally he would ask me to announce the next hymn to be sung. Sometimes at Ceylon Baptist Church there would be a midweek speaker, occasionally on a creationist theme. I used to go to these; I was totally convinced by all that I heard.

The above may make my parents sound like rather narrow people. This would be wrong. If I said that I did not feel well or did not want to go to Sunday school or church, then that was fine and I would not be pressed to go. At one time, my parents wanted me to join the Boys' Brigade, a Christian youth organization which met in Ceylon Baptist Church. I went a few times and thought it a waste of time. So I said I did not want to go and my parents did not insist.

Dale Road, where we lived, had a street gang, of which I was a member, and we regularly had fights with other street gangs in the neighbourhood. Unlike street gangs of today, we would never dream of pulling a knife and stabbing anyone. But we did use our fists. Some members had air pistols and air rifles which would shoot pellets. I remember being hit a number of times, which was quite painful. The pellet would not usually break the skin, but it would bring up a painful hard lump. Looking back, I can see that if a pellet had gone into one's eye, it could have been serious. The primary school I went to was also extremely rough, with many fights in the playground.

My father was a great believer in education. He had gone to evening classes in a local technical college in Leicester and had obtained engineering diploma qualifications. These qualifications plus his work experience enabled him to become an Associate Member of the Institute of Mechanical Engineers. He was very proud of this and regularly wore his AMIMechE tie. When I was about nine years old he decided that he wanted us to move to another part of Luton where there was a better school (and no street gang). So for the sake of my education, we moved house. I vividly remember my father taking me to the local primary school there and sitting with him in the headmistress's office. She said that each year-group in her school had three classes: top, middle, and bottom. She said that since I had come from Denbigh Junior School I had to start in the bottom class. My father insisted that I went into the top class. The headmistress then asked me some questions. I could not answer any of them. She told my father that this was exactly what she expected; pupils at Denbigh Junior School were significantly behind pupils in her school, and I had to go into the bottom class. I remember being both embarrassed and proud of my father saying that he would not leave her study until she had agreed to give me a month's trial in the top class. Eventually and probably to get rid of us, she agreed. I remember struggling in this class and indeed being bottom in the initial tests. However, I gradually moved up into the top third of the class and subsequently passed the 11-plus examination and entered Luton Grammar School.

An early interest in biology

As a child, mechanical things did not particularly interest me. One Christmas my father bought me a substitute Meccano set. My mother told me that real Meccano sets were very expensive, but my father had found this one much more cheaply and it was just the same as a real Meccano. I used to play with it, but never really took to it. However, I found living creatures fascinating. One day, when I was about eight years old, I was taken to London as a treat. Our route took us along the Strand where we passed a shop called Watkins & Doncaster. In the window were the most amazing butterflies and moths I had ever seen. There was a moth called the Atlas moth which had a wing span of almost twelve inches. I dragged my parents into the shop and asked the shopkeeper from what part of England these wonderful moths came. He replied that the moths on display were exotics from all over the world, and the large ones came from tropical countries. He said that I could buy moth eggs from him and hatch them at home. I desperately wanted to do this but my parents said no. However, I took away various catalogues from the shop and read through them from cover to cover. I managed to persuade my parents that I really wanted to breed exotic moths like the amazing Atlas moth. My parents gave in and nobly agreed that I could try, and I wrote to Watkins & Doncaster with a cheque from my father ordering some eggs of a giant silk moth. The firm also sold equipment for hatching such eggs and breeding cages for containing the caterpillars as they grew. Since we could not afford such equipment, I made it myself. I remember thinking that to hatch the eggs out I had to simulate a steaming tropical jungle. So I fitted an electric light bulb in the bottom of a large cardboard box, put some dampened blotting paper on a piece of cardboard above the light bulb, plugged the light bulb into the mains, switched it on, and, hey presto, steam rose up from the blotting paper. I had created my artificial jungle! (It never occurred to me that I had also created a fire hazard.)

When the eggs arrived, I set them out on the wet blotting paper. A Watkins & Doncaster leaflet that came with the eggs suggested suitable food plants for the caterpillars. We had a privet bush in our front garden and an apple tree at the back, and a neighbour had a plum tree. I put leaves from these trees on the blotting paper. Amazingly, the emerging caterpillars ate their eggshell and then some of these leaves – and survived. This was only the beginning. I acquired more species. I would go to the library and look up the food plants of caterpillars in their native land, and then look for a related plant that grew in the UK. I would then cycle out into the countryside and try to find one of these plants; nearly always the caterpillars would eat the leaves of this plant. I remember that some of the caterpillars were huge, over six inches long, and almost an inch across.

When the adult moths emerged, they would fly at night, flapping their wings and circling around my room. They used to fly all over our house. In the daytime they would rest, frequently hanging from net curtains in our front room, with their wings between the curtain and the window pane. Sometimes, people would gather outside our house looking at these magnificent specimens, and even knock on our front door asking if we knew we had such amazing insects in our house!

I started breeding these moths when I was in Dale Road, and continued when we moved to our new house. I was interested in British butterflies and moths as well as overseas exotics. I read that a good way to catch British moths was to paint a mixture of rum and molasses on tree trunks, which would attract moths flying at night. Both my father and my mother were strict teetotallers, but I asked them if we could do this in the interest of science. They readily agreed, and my father went shopping and brought back a bottle of rum. We heated this with molasses (dark brown sugar syrup) in a large pan until the mixture had the consistency of paint – and emitted a most wonderful smell. In the evening my father and I then set off on our bikes to a nearby wood, where I painted the rum/molasses mixture onto the trunks of trees. We then stood back and waited. Before long moths started to appear, hovered by the tree trunk, and drank the intoxicating liquid. This made them drunk and they fell to the ground, where I could easily collect them. I knew the Latin names of a large number of butterflies and moths from an early age.

At Luton Grammar School there was a history teacher called Dr John Dony who was an expert amateur botanist. He wrote two standard reference books, *Flora of Hertfordshire* and *Flora of Bedfordshire*, which are still available today. When I was twelve years old, he told us during one of his history lessons of his interest in wild flowers, and asked if any boys would like to come with him on one of his expeditions into the countryside. Nobody volunteered; we all thought this was a rather sissy occupation. However, when he told us that we would have to climb over fences with barbed wire on the top, wear wellington boots and wade through marshy bogs, it seemed that it wasn't sissy at all. At that stage, I volunteered with three other people in the class.

Doc Dony, as we called him, was wonderful. He would drive the four of us into the country every weekend, and we would indeed climb over and under barbed wire, and wade through treacherous marshy bogs, in the search for both common and rare wild flowers. He had amazing eyesight, and as we were walking along grassy chalk downland, for example, he would throw himself headlong onto the ground saying, "Look at this." He had spotted some tiny flower or an unusual leaf which none of us sharp-eyed schoolboys had seen. I became engrossed and when Doc Dony was not taking us out into the countryside, I frequently went out on my bicycle looking for wild flowers, with or without my parents. The other three boys and myself entered a national wild flower competition which was held every year to spot the largest number of wild flowers in flower in the UK. The four of us won this national competition for two years running, identifying almost 1,000 different wild flowers. I knew the Latin names of nearly all of them.

My encounter with evolution

I was first introduced to the theory of evolution in biology lessons at Luton Grammar School when I was twelve or thirteen. I thought evolution was nonsense and said so. I was supported by a classmate called Basil Allsopp, who was a Christadelphian (a small, non-Trinitarian group). In the class, we questioned our biology teacher closely on the subject and won most of the arguments. Looking back I can see that I had considerable knowledge both of plants and insects. I remember asking our biology teacher if he could give the class one example of a fossil plant which was intermediate between two species, and finding he could not. I then asked him if he could give one example of a butterfly or moth which was intermediate between two species. He started telling us about industrial melanism in the peppered moth, *Biston betularia*. Originally, peppered moths rested where light-coloured lichens covered the tree trunks.

Nearly all the moths had light-coloured wings so that they were not seen by predators. However, in the industrial revolution the atmosphere became polluted and sulphur dioxide started to kill the light-coloured lichens on the trees. This exposed the dark bark of the tree trunks, making the light-coloured moths an easy target for birds. A darker-coloured form of the moths then took over in the polluted areas. It turned out that I knew more about industrial melanism than our biology teacher, and I pointed out to him that no new species of moth was produced. Industrial melanism was simply evolution within a species but not between species.

I then asked our teacher if he could name any intermediate fossil between major different groups of animals. He told us that *Archaeopteryx* was a fossil which was intermediate between birds and reptiles. I still remember asking him how he defined a bird. He said that a bird was defined by its feathers. Basil and myself immediately told him that *Archaeopteryx* had feathers and was therefore a bird. It was not an intermediate form at all. Basil and I won the debates with our biology teacher, strengthening my belief in creationism.

It is often said today that the evolution/creationism controversy should not be mentioned in school science lessons but only taught, if at all, in lessons about religion. I disagree. The biology lessons in which we debated with our teacher were extremely popular with the rest of the class and became widely talked about in the school. Biology became the most popular science subject among my classmates because it was the only science subject in which we really debated the issues. Although the detailed questioning of our biology teacher was initiated by Basil Allsopp and myself, the whole class got involved and we had some really lively biology lessons. Belief in creationism certainly did not turn Basil or myself away from science. On leaving Luton Grammar School, Basil got a BSc and a PhD in chemistry from Imperial College, London, and then went to Africa where he researched tropical diseases. After Luton Grammar School, I obtained a BSc in physics at Imperial College, London, followed by a Cambridge PhD. So I have very positive feelings about the merits of debating creationism and evolution in biology classes in our schools.

Doubts about creationism

When I entered the sixth form, I started to have doubts about creationism, but perhaps rather oddly, not on biological grounds. I was challenged by physics. We learned about radioactivity and radiocarbon dating. I had heard of radiocarbon dating from the creationist pamphlets at my parents' house, which asserted that such dating methods were very inaccurate and could not be relied upon. However, I discovered that radiocarbon dating can be cross-checked with dating using the decay of radioactive forms of other elements, such as uranium and potassium. Using such cross-checks establishes that radiocarbon dating methods are not inherently unreliable, giving dates accurate to about 10 per cent. Although radiocarbon dating is not as accurate as once thought, it is not wildly out provided that sample contamination is avoided. All this made very clear to me that the creation of our earth was very much earlier than about 4,000 BC, as Young Earth Creationists believed. The fact that my belief in Young Earth Creationism seemed to be wrong, forced me totally to question not only creationism, but the whole of my Christian beliefs. In my final year at the Grammar School, I was very busy taking

A-level examinations; I decided to have a major rethink when I got to university.

In my first year studying physics at Imperial College, I spent much of the first two terms reading and thinking about evolution and creationism. Once I had decided that the earth must be very much older than 4,000 BC, it was only a small step to realize that the early chapters of Genesis were not meant to be taken literally. It was clear that I didn't have to believe in creationism at all. What then struck me, which I had never seen referred to in creationist literature, is that the Adam and Eve creation story is not referred to at all in the Old Testament after the first few chapters of Genesis. Moses and the exodus from Egypt are referred to many times, as is Abraham. In contrast, Adam and Eve are never mentioned. For creationists, the first few chapters of Genesis are absolutely essential to their beliefs, their thinking, and their literature, but to the Jewish people who wrote the Old Testament this appears not to have been the case. I then realized that Jesus only referred to Adam and Eve in passing, as defining marriage, although he talked about Moses and about Abraham. I also learnt that first-century AD Jews such as the historian Josephus appeared to believe that the early chapters of Genesis are allegorical, and the third-century AD Christian scholar, Origen, explicitly stated that events in the early chapters of Genesis were not meant to be taken literally.

By the end of my first year at Imperial College I had moved from being a creationist to accepting that evolution was the mechanism God used to create the universe and life on earth. More importantly, I had thought through and fully regained my Christian faith. Interestingly, creationism was something which I never again discussed with my father. I knew that he would not change his mind and I did not wish to upset him. I suspect that he knew that I had changed my mind and he did not wish to upset me. When we met we often talked about Christian matters, but never about creation and evolution.

I left Imperial College to do a PhD in Cambridge, after which I went to Oxford, first as a postdoc and then as a lecturer. In Oxford I became friends with a Roman Catholic nuclear physicist, Peter Hodgson. Peter instigated a series of booklets for school sixth forms called *Studies in Christianity and Science*; they were published by Oxford University Press. Peter wrote the first in the series, on nuclear power. I volunteered to write the second in the series, on creation and evolution. I did this because I felt it important to give school pupils the facts about creation and evolution from both a scientific and a religious viewpoint. In particular, I thought it important to provide good scientific information and also accurate information about what the Bible really says. My booklet was widely used in schools; it sold over 20,000 copies and I know it was photocopied many more times from the requests I received from school teachers.[1] The publishing of my forty-eight page booklet in 1985 by OUP marked the final stage of my conversion away from creationism and to believing in evolution. I wanted to set out the evidence for others.

The concluding paragraph of my 1985 booklet was:

> *There are a number of arguments which very strongly suggest that creationism is wrong. That is why most scientists who are Christians reject creationism and instead believe in both evolution and creation. They believe that God chose to create everything by a process of evolution.*

---

[1] The booklet is called *Creation and Evolution*. It is out of print, but copies sometimes turn up in secondhand bookshops.

There is a continuous evolutionary trail from the Big Bang to our galaxy, to the Earth, to single-celled animals, to fishes, to reptiles, to mammals and to man. In a sense, God's plan and purpose for mankind were encapsulated in the original Big Bang. He was active in the whole evolutionary process and continues to sustain the world now. What brilliant creative genius to produce the Universe, and life in all its complexity, diversity and beauty, by evolution from a single small beginning.

I gladly and positively affirm these sentences written thirty years ago.

CHAPTER 4

Connecting Heart and Mind: A Journey Towards Wholeness

Darrel Falk was brought up in a Christian home in British Columbia. He is a molecular biologist, with a PhD from the University of Alberta; he is now Emeritus Professor of Biology at Point Loma Nazarene University and a senior advisor (former president) of the BioLogos Foundation. He is the author of *Coming to Peace with Science: Bridging the Worlds between Faith and Biology* (Downers Grove, IL: IVP, 2004).

I have two clear memories from when I was four years old. One is a high-speed trip to the hospital for emergency surgery to repair the source of what seemed like excruciating abdominal pain. The other is a fairly detailed recollection of the events surrounding a much different sort of pain, one associated with the agony of guilt followed by the liberating experience of forgiveness. The fact that it was so important to me says a great deal about that which dominated my life as a young boy raised within the Wesleyan-holiness tradition in western Canada.

The latter event took place in early August – peach season in British Columbia. My parents' finances were tight and they couldn't afford to purchase fresh peaches, at least not as the season was beginning and prices were still high. My mother took my brother and me to the grocery store and we came upon the display for fresh peaches. Ogling their enticing appearance, I asked her to buy some, but she replied that we couldn't afford them right then. As she walked away, I realized that the only thing between a juicy peach and my pocket was a reach of my hand.

Within my Christian tradition there was considerable emphasis on the two internal voices "whispering" to our will – the voice of Satan and the voice of God. As I looked at the peaches, I heard one of those voices say "Take the peach, take the peach." Unwilling to resist, I obeyed that voice, stuck the peach in my pocket, and successfully carried out my first crime. Later that afternoon, sitting on the front stairs of our house, I took it out of my pocket and began to eat. My sister, who was nine, saw me eating it and asked how it was that I happened to have a peach.

"Tell her your mommy bought it for you," it seemed the voice in my head said this time. So I did; I told a lie. My first lie and my first theft: I was four years old, and although it was unlikely that I had yet heard the story of Eve in the garden, there I was in my own garden, taking a bite out of my own forbidden fruit and finding myself trapped into attempting to cover up my shame.

Not surprisingly, everything went downhill from there. My sister, knowing that our mother would never have bought a peach for me without also buying one for her, proceeded into the house to straighten matters out. By the time the day was over, I became poignantly aware that I had listened to the wrong voice, and that I needed to tell God of a heartfelt desire to listen to Him rather than Satan. With that, and with the tears flowing down my young face, and at the strong but loving guidance of my parents, I knelt beside our living room chair asking Jesus for forgiveness and inviting Him into my heart. I promised that I would now live for Him and not for Satan any more.

As one of my two first memories, it stands out as being the single most important event in my childhood, the moment when I committed to live for Jesus knowing that in that life I would experience security, safety, forgiveness, and love.

My brother and I had a picture in our shared bedroom showing Jesus as the good shepherd holding a staff in one arm and a lamb in the other. Sheep were following them, all looking to the good shepherd as they followed his path. We knew well that each of us was like the lamb being held by Jesus and that our loving parents had entrusted our lives and their own to His care.

So at the age of four, I chose to abandon my life of sin and allowed Jesus to direct my path. My parents were exceptionally kind and the home they provided was a place where we felt safe and thoroughly loved. Our church was the same. I grew up living within what seemed to me to be the idyllic life of faith. I can hardly recall a time ever again in my childhood where I set out to do what I knew was wrong. I was following Jesus. My every day would end with my kneeling beside my bed in quiet prayer. Indeed, my parents used to say, it wouldn't be unusual for my brother or me to peacefully fall asleep kneeling in prayer by the side of our beds. When that happened they would come in, get us up off of our knees and into bed, nicely tucked in – safe and sound.

Outside of family members and church friends, I can recall knowing essentially no one else at school or in the neighbourhood who we thought of as Christians throughout my childhood years. This was western Canada where church attendance was fairly sparse, but another reason was that our view of what it meant to be a Christian was pretty narrow. By the time I was about eleven,

I began on occasion to question this assumption of privileged truth. "Could it really be, that of all the religions in the world, I just happened to be born into the right one?" I wondered. Could it really be that everyone around us was wrong, and only we (and our small circle) had it right?

It was also about that time that I began to develop some questions about the Bible as it relates to science. I can recall only one Sunday school lesson about the days of creation, and no sermons on evolution or the importance of believing in a global flood. It was not that my church or my family were anti-science. It was just that any possible disconnect between science and faith was largely ignored – the important doctrinal issues were related to living a holy life and to loving God with our whole being.

At about that time I made a commitment to read the New Testament through from Matthew's genealogy to Revelation's last word. As I got near the end, I was especially struck by a verse that indicated that the angels came from the four corners of the earth. It seemed to me that the author really thought the earth had four corners. It precipitated into doubt as to whether this really was God's Word. Surely God would have been able to get this right, I reasoned. I mentioned my concern to my sister, but she was not bothered by it at all. "That's just what they thought in those days," she said. That may have been fine for her, but it didn't work for me, not with my understanding of God being the author of all Scripture. Still, I pushed the matter aside, preferring not to think about it too much; I was far too happy within my idyllic world of following Jesus to let it be destroyed by inconsistencies... at least, most of the time.

Then came seventh grade. Here I took a course in social studies, the curriculum of which included a discussion of physical anthropology, complete with a description of fossil finds and the suggested progressive changes which led to modern humans. My doubts were rekindled. Were my parents – together, of course, with our extended family and church members – the only ones who had it right? Was my teacher, the authors of the textbook, and the many scientists who believed otherwise really wrong, or was it us that had it wrong? I did my best not to think about this because I didn't want to lose the only life that seemed available to me – a life where I was comfortable and a place where I felt safe. I found it difficult to sort through this as a twelve-year-old boy and I don't recall seeking help. I think I would have been too ashamed.

I certainly don't recall anyone within my church or home emphasizing anti-evolution views at that time, or even mentioning them. The discordance was one I sensed; if the Bible was God's Word, then all these smart people were wrong. My father emphasized compatibility between science and Scripture in a way that took the science seriously. For me, though, when I was by myself, I felt that the Bible spoke pretty clearly to the issue of the mechanism of creation, and I was suspicious of any other way of reading the Scripture which forced compromises, that attempted to make the Bible say something that it really wasn't saying. It seemed that twisting its words to make them fit with science was a little like continually patching an old garment because you don't want to let it go, when really what you need is a whole new garment. Deep down I thought that the Bible may well be an ancient document that didn't hold up to modern scrutiny.

Most of the time, though, I cast those suspicions aside and refused to consider them. I loved the secure and very beautiful life I enjoyed in home and church, and never wanted to see it end. I continued living the Christian life assuming it was true, and expecting (or at least hoping) that someday the dissonance would disappear.

When the doubts did creep in, they plagued me. I remember in particular lying in my bed before getting up one morning and looking at the cherry tree outside my window. I asked God if He would make His presence real to me in a way so clear that it would have no other explanation. Looking out at the cherry tree on that wind-less morning, I asked God if He would wiggle a particular cherry tree leaf for me. That, I reasoned (and told God!), could be a lifelong signal to me. From that I would know He was real; it would erase my concerns about the seeming disconnect between modern science and the Bible. The leaf never wiggled, though, and I was left in that state of refusing to think about the dissonance, in order to have peace of mind.

Unlike many of my fellow evolutionary creationists, I was never really a Young Earth Creationist. Rather, I was a person who strongly suspected the science was correct and lived in hope that some day the disconnect between the Bible and science would be explainable. In the meantime, I lived with the dissonance by pushing it to a corner of my mind that I just didn't visit very often. But I knew it was there and was haunted by its presence.

This went on through high school and into college. Since biology created the greatest dissonance, I steered clear of it until I went to university. Once I reached there, though, and planning on becoming a physician, I was forced to take biology courses. Although I continued to be perplexed by the disconnect, as I peered deeper and deeper into the marvellous beauty of life, I rejoiced and wondered at it all, and worried less about scriptural inconsistencies. As time went by, in later graduate school years and then early in my postdoctorate studies, I began to feel at home in other communities outside of my churches, and the dissonance seemed to diminish, not because I didn't think it was real, but rather because I didn't care about it. Increasingly it seemed I didn't need the Bible, or even a personal relationship with God any more.

Soon after entering into my postdoctorate years and as our two daughters moved out of babyhood and became full-fledged toddlers,[1] I began to wish that they might experience the security I had known when I was a child. But I also longed for it myself again. I was twenty-seven years old and a couple of years into a new environment, heavily grounded in the naturalism associated with doing experiments and studying genes. None of this provided the rich meaning I had known through relationship with Christ and members of His Body in earlier days. I longed for that again. Eventually, for the first time in years, I knelt down by a bed again, this time calling upon God to re-enter my life – if He was really there. I still had doubts, many of which were uncomfortably rooted in the disconnect between science and the Bible, but I knew the beauty of that earlier life, and I longed to experience it once more. My prayer, remembered these many years later was, "Lord, I don't know for sure if You're real, but the Bible says that we can come to You in faith and ask You to come into our lives. It is in that faith that I ask You back into my life." I went on to tell God that I would reassess the situation in a couple of years, but for now I would cast all doubts aside and live by faith.

With that I began to walk down His pathway once again. He was the good shepherd and what I wanted most of all was to trust

---

[1] My wife, Joyce, whom I met at our denomination's Bible college, and I were married while I was an undergraduate. Our two girls, Cheryl and Shelley, were born during my graduate school years.

His wisdom. As I did this, I began to experience His presence with such vitality that I reached the point that I was about as certain of His existence as I could ever be about anything. My times with Him and our relationship grew to become dynamic and fulfilling. My Christian reading played a major role in all this. My father, who loved to read, pointed me to Malcolm Muggeridge, whose perspective on life's purpose played a key role in getting a new life of the mind started for me (e.g. *A Third Testament* and *Jesus Rediscovered*). From him and then others,[2] I learned that people much smarter than I had made the same journey I was embarking upon. With that, I discovered that there was a deeper, more intellectually satisfying side to Christianity that I had missed earlier. This led me to riches that I never dreamed existed in my youth, when I only knew how to read Scripture in two dimensions, and for some reason was stymied from looking deeper.

As the reality of my Christian faith became intellectually exciting and more spiritually fulfilling, the surface discrepancies between the Bible and science evaporated. Christianity had become so coherent that any seeming inconsistencies between the Bible and my discipline of biology were likely due to the fact that the Bible was a much more nuanced narrative than I had ever imagined as a child and teen. I didn't yet know how they connected entirely, but I chalked that up to my ignorance rather that the Bible's inadequacy.

---

[2] For example, Dietrich Bonhoeffer for his theologically brilliant and profound call to discipleship (e.g. *The Cost of Discipleship*, Prentice Hall & IBD, 1963) and Leo Tolstoy for his visionary imagination (e.g. *Resurrection*, Dodd, Mead, 1900). Other fine minds that led me into this new dimension included C. S. Lewis (e.g. *Mere Christianity*, Geoffrey Bles, 1952) and Søren Kierkegaard (e.g. *Purity of Heart is to Will One Thing*, Harper 1938).

Still one very significant concern remained. I wanted our little girls, indeed our whole family, to live within the church-centred family setting I had known as a child. The people in the church community of my youth had been individuals who took the Bible very seriously. Their lives emphasized a radical life-changing revolution that comes from living life in relationship with Jesus. They cared deeply about each other and they devoted much time and effort to a life grounded in Christian community. They knew biblical living on its highest plane, and now that I had gained an academically fulfilling faith that no longer depended on the literality of the Bible, I longed for the same sort of environment once more.

The road back into that environment seemed potentially tortuous. I was now a professional biologist, certain of evolution and seeking to read and understand the Bible for all that it had to offer as the Word of God. I missed – desperately missed – the sort of church environment in which I had grown up, and I wanted the same for my little girls. But I felt there would be little room for someone like me in churches like that. On one occasion, only a year or two after the bedside re-conversion experience, we went to a beach in Orange County, California and happened to park close to a bus from a church of the same denomination in which I had grown up. I assumed that it was some type of youth gathering of the sort that I had experienced as a teenager. Later that afternoon, as I watched our two- and four-year-old daughters playing on the sand in front of us, I recall thinking that they would never be able to experience the Christ-centered sense of community that I had experienced in church picnics, camps, and other activities that had been the centre of my life. It seemed to me that my life as an academic, a person firmly ensconced in evolutionary biology, would automatically be excluded from meaningful full-fledged acceptance into such community.

Soon after that, I completed my postdoctoral studies and accepted a position in the Department of Biology at Syracuse University in upstate New York. Determined not to give up on churches of the sort that both my wife and I had experienced in our youth, we sought evangelical churches. We spent several months attending one in particular, but realized that the members' view of the Bible would never be able to make allowance for an evolutionist like me, not if I wanted to be a fully engaged member of the community. Following that we moved on to non-evangelical churches where belief in evolution would not constitute a problem. However, those churches were equally unsatisfying to us for a different reason. Evolution was not an issue, but that was because the Bible as the Word of God was not an issue either. Along with that, Christ-centred community was absent too. So, much to my frustration and after much time searching, we had come very close to confirming the conclusion I had reached on the beach in California: life in Christ-centred community would not be available to someone like me and my family. We would be on our own. Worse was a realization that bothered me even more: it seemed that a Christ-centred life does not carry effectively from one generation of a family into the next without church involvement.

It was with that feeling of last-ditch desperation that I ventured out by myself to the far side of Syracuse one October Sunday morning to visit a church that, as we saw it, would be our last attempt before giving up on church for the rest of our lives. It proved to be one of the most defining moments of my adult life. I could tell immediately that this particular church was so focused on Christ-centred community that even a biological scientist would be welcomed with open arms and heart. My certainty about evolution would not be a barrier that would block full-fledged acceptance into the community. We would be welcomed just as we were. The next Sunday the whole family came with me; our girls quickly found dear friends, and Joyce and I felt loved and respected. Before long, I was asked to teach Sunday school (a little risky in my opinion, since I was still just figuring out how I fitted theologically), asked to serve on the Church Governing Board, and finally, within a couple of years, I was asked to be the director of the Sunday school.

The question of evolution and my thoughts about it seldom came up and it is likely that few would have agreed with me on it. However, it was relegated to the category of being an insignificant detail compared with the overwhelming significance of simply living a Christ-centred life in a manner that fully respected the Bible as God's authoritative word on salvation and a life centred in Christ.

So positive was that church experience that I responded to what I felt was a call to leave the secular university setting after eight years and to spend my life working with Christian young people in a Christ-centred university setting. From that teaching experience, and after many conversations with students, I decided there was a need for a book to help my students (and others) to understand why evolution was true, and why there need be no conflict between accepting what I considered to be the fact of evolution and a life centred in the reality of the resurrected Christ.

The book, among the first by a biologist in North America, generated much controversy when it was circulated in draft form.

Many of my earlier fears about my acceptance in the evangelical community resurfaced for a while, as some in churches of my denomination claimed that I was undoing all that they had taught their children in Sunday school. In the end, however, I came to see that I was not alone any more. There were hundreds just like me, and even though the uproar over the draft of my book extended to the upper echelons of evangelical Christianity (e.g. James Dobson of Focus on the Family and Phillip Johnson, founder of the Intelligent Design movement), I realized there was a need for ever more people just like me in evangelical circles. Unlike that Sunday afternoon on an Orange County beach twenty-five years earlier, I knew I was not alone in my acceptance of biblical authority and its harmony with mainstream science.

As the controversy brewed about my manuscript (and before it was even published), one of America's most eminent scientists, Francis Collins, agreed to write a foreword. That led to a friendship that has significantly influenced the course of the rest of my life. It led to my having the privilege of working alongside Karl Giberson, Syman Stevens, and Francis in the public launching of BioLogos. This organization – initially because of the Christian spirit and high scientific credibility of Francis Collins, and now, under the leadership of Deborah Haarsma – has come to play a significant role in helping evangelicals worldwide to understand that there need not be a conflict between science and Christian faith.

I've had the opportunity over these years in the classroom, and now more recently on public platforms, to reflect on my own personally tortuous journey where only God and I knew of the turmoil of doubt I occasionally experienced. The question for me was always biblical authority – could the Bible be trusted or not?

Science brought this into question. Ultimately, I had to take a step of faith. From there God, through people such as Bonhoeffer, began to show me how very flat my reading of Scripture had been. I had missed so much by thinking that the Bible was making inaccurate statements about a four-cornered earth or six creation days, 6,000 years ago. Still what mattered most in my life was that simple prayer of a four-year-old boy – "Jesus come into my heart, and make me clean" – and the later equally sincere prayer, "Lord, I'm not sure if You're there, but I want to ask You back into my life again; by faith, I'm going to live for You and will reassess, but not until the journey has commenced again." I passed the fortieth anniversary of that second prayer last week. Never could I have imagined how fully God would have answered it.

Even now, though, there is a sense in which I am still that four-year-old boy praying the first prayer for the first time. As important as it is to get the details right and to grow in appreciation of the depth of Scripture and the richness of the Christian life, that simple prayer, prayed under the guidance of a set of wise parents, is also the most profound of all: "Change my heart O God, make it ever true; Change my heart O God, may I be like you."

CHAPTER 5

Fossils That Inform[1]

Stephen J. Godfrey is Curator of Palaeontology at the Calvert
Marine Museum, in Solomons, a small community in Maryland
on Chesapeake Bay, south of Washington. He has a PhD
from McGill University and considerable experience as a field
palaeontologist.

I am told that my grandfather declared soon after my birth, "We'll
make a scientist out of this one." I don't know if (or how) his hopes
influenced my interests, but for as long as I can remember, I have
had an insatiable fascination with the natural world. As a child
growing up in Canada, I loved going to natural history museums.
I began my own collection of natural objects – pine cones, sea
shells, fossils, even animal skeletons – until my bedroom became
a miniature natural history museum. Fishing trips turned into
hunts for fossils; stops at rest areas along highways were an excuse
to gather pine cones or scour outcrops for fossils.

I was raised in an evangelical Christian home. Because
of this, it was virtually inevitable that I would seek answers for
the diversity and origin of life from Genesis, rather than from

[1] This essay is largely based on the author's account of his questioning and
disillusionment with Young Earth Creation in a book *Paradigms on Pilgrimage:
Creationism, Paleontology and Biblical Interpretation* (Toronto: Clements
Publishing, 2005), written jointly with his brother-in-law and biblical scholar,
Christopher Smith.

scientific theory. We considered evolution to be a rival to the Bible's explanation; it was equated with human attempts to deny the existence of God. We were taught that evolution proclaimed an a-teleology – an absence of purpose in the natural world. By implication, anyone who affirmed a belief in evolution must have abandoned belief in the existence of God and have an entirely naturalistic and mechanistic view of the universe. The appeal of evolution to the atheist lay in its apparent ability to absolve humankind of its moral responsibility to an almighty God who had created all that there is; for my family and me, God was the omnipotent creator of the world and its biological diversity.

My first encounter with an evolutionist was in grade one at school. Our teacher stated that we had evolved from the apes. I was shocked. Over dinner that evening, we concluded that the teacher's claim could not possibly be true, because if it were, then apes would be turning into humans today – and we knew that was not happening.

My dad had an interest in origins and owned a hardbound copy of John Whitcomb and Henry Morris's book *The Genesis Flood*.[2] I recall reading some of the text and looking at the pictures and being very impressed with its claims and conclusions. As I grew, I continued to read literature and books from Morris's Institute for Creation Research (ICR), and I received their newsletter, *Acts, Facts and Impacts*, for a number of years.

Our church taught us to read the creation account in Genesis literally, and this led us to adopt a young earth paradigm in which the earth and universe were no more than 10,000 years old, and perhaps only 6,000. It maintained that our world had been created in six consecutive 24-hour days, in a "mature, fully

---

[2] First published in 1961.

functional" state, its appearance of greater age notwithstanding. If objects looked old, that was only an illusion. God's creation was, in effect, instantaneous. There was no possibility of the earth being formed through currently operating natural processes, for there was insufficient time for this to have happened. We dismissed estimates of the earth's age based on the decay of radioactive elements because such dating methods, we were assured by the Institute for Creation Research, were subject to so many imperfections that their results were of no value whatsoever. We were taught that the sedimentary rocks that held the fossilized remains of once-alive animals were deposited as a result of Noah's flood. This flood was understood as having been worldwide in its scope and proportions, so that all terrestrial life was swept into the ocean, and vast quantities of churned-up sediments entombed the bodies of these creatures, creating the fossils I loved to collect.

How was the great diversity of life forms – my lifelong fascination – to be explained? The answer given was simple: "microevolutionary" changes could occur within so-called "Genesis kinds", but mutations were the only possible source of "macroevolutionary" variation. However, mutations were the result of human sin and were always bad. This meant they could never result in the creation of a new "kind". On the contrary, they produced degradations of the genome, causing much of the pain and suffering seen today.

I was content with this Young Earth view; it seemed very believable. Growing up, I had never seen any evidence of evolution with plants or animals, so it seemed reasonable that species were created instantaneously. But this teaching was not inviolable, and from time to time cracks appeared in my apparently solid belief system. Walking home from school one day in my late teen years, I observed that one could easily make out horizontal layers within the large accumulation of snow. I knew that not all the snow had fallen in one storm; days or weeks could pass between snowfalls. Along the road, I could see layers made up of snow that was hard and grey. These layers constituted, by analogy, a troubling counter-example to one of the creationists' claims. If all the sediment at the end of Noah's flood had been redeposited within a year or so, the vast majority of rocks should be relatively uniform in composition. I could not help wondering why there was such a great variety of sedimentary rocks in the world. It seemed more likely that they had been deposited the way the snow had been – on many different occasions.

After high school and college, I enrolled to study biology at Bishop's University outside Montreal. It was not long before I became worried about some of the things I learned; about predators and prey, carnivores and herbivores. Why were predatory organisms so well suited for hunting, capturing and killing their prey, and prey organisms just as remarkable for avoiding, hiding or running from predators? These were fundamental differences in anatomy and physiology, not simply behavioural differences which might easily be modified. This question troubled me, because I knew from my creationist reading that no animal had died on earth before Adam and Eve ate from the Tree of Knowledge. Before the Fall, organisms must have been either autotrophs which make their own food (such as green plants) or herbivores (i.e. plant-eaters). Dinosaurs, sharks, cats, and web-spinning spiders: had not God designed them? And why would an animal need an immune system? No microorganism could have killed it if there was no death. Why did animals need to be able to sting or bite? They would not have had to do this as part of the original creation. Where did these remarkable designs come from, and when were they created? One question led to another.

Around this time, I attended a creationist seminar led by Duane Gish, a well-known Young Earth Creationist from the ICR, whom I greatly admired. He mentioned that many organisms may have become carnivorous when Adam and Eve sinned, although he had to admit that the Bible was silent on the matter. If the Bible had nothing to say on this purported divinely orchestrated transformation, where was I to turn to get light on this fantastic and profound change in the biology of life? As part of my undergraduate degree, I carried out a literature review on the Jurassic Period *Archaeopteryx*, which creationists referred to as a bird because it preserved feathers, but which palaeontologists described as the first-known feathered dinosaur – morphologically intermediate between dinosaurs and birds – a poster-child for macroevolution. Although I did not believe that evolution had occurred, I was impressed by how similar its skeleton was to some of the small theropod dinosaurs. Indeed, it was much more like many meat-eating dinosaurs than they were to other dinosaurs. I decided to study vertebrate palaeontology in graduate school to find out if there was a conspiracy to "fix" the fossils so as to give the appearance of an evolutionary sequence. This decision was crucial because my confidence in the reliability of the Christian faith at that time rested on my literal reading of the Genesis creation account. In 1981, I began doctoral research in the Redpath Museum of McGill University.

My strict creationist position began to unravel the following summer on a geological expedition to quarry fossiliferous rocks near Garnett, Kansas. Besides the fossils we were seeking, we exposed many layers with fossilized animal footprints. I don't think anything else I have ever seen so profoundly affected my thinking. If all sedimentary rocks and their fossils were the result of the flood, how, I wondered, could these fossil footprints have been made? Apart from the animals in the ark, all living land-dwelling animals were supposed to have been drowned in the flood. I started to collect literature on the occurrence of trace or track fossils in other parts of the world. I discovered that such remains are found at countless levels throughout sedimentary rock formations all around the world. It was one of the final nails for me in the coffin of "Flood Geology". Even worse, different kinds of tracks appear at different levels in the geological column. If I knew only about trace fossils and had no other evidence for the earth's antiquity, I would still have to conclude confidently that the world's sedimentary rocks are not the product of one gigantic year-long flood.

If trace fossils disproved Noah's flood as responsible for the formation of fossil-bearing sedimentary rocks, how old was the earth? Could it be as old as "evolutionary" geologists claimed? I remember thinking that Young Earth Creationists could not help me to satisfy my questions any more than the Flat Earth Society could help someone calculate the spherical volume of the earth. Years later, as I read more widely about the history of geology, I found that some nineteenth-century geologists had suggested that the flood had been a quiet one, leaving no significant geological effects. It made me realize that much of what is often presented as biblical teaching is not actually in the Bible. There is no way a Young Earth Creationist can know *from the Bible alone* when fossils formed. Why had the flood become so central to the young earth paradigm, which is supposed to be based firmly on scriptural teachings? Could it be that creationists did not want to opt for the two alternatives – that God created the world with fossils already in the ground, or that the earth was more than 6,000 years old?

Once I entertained the notion that the earth might be old, I had to question all the rest of the "scientific creationist" paradigm. It all seemed to be based around one single lynchpin about the age of the earth; pull out that pin and the whole system would crumble. In my case, the pin had been pulled. It was time to see where that led me.

What made my shift in understanding particularly difficult was that eternal matters were on the line. Did the truth of the whole Bible hinge on the scientific accuracy of a literal rendering of the first chapters of Genesis? My narrow creationist river of 10,000 years had broken its banks and time was spreading far, far out over the flood plain. There was no telling how far it would go. Trace fossils enabled me to know something because I had seen it with my own eyes, not because someone with impressive credentials believed it, not even because I had read it. Footprint fossils spoke to me as silent witnesses to the great antiquity of the planet. But on top of this, I was distressed because it showed that creationists in general would highlight scientific discoveries when they suited their agenda, while heaping scorn on the same scientific endeavours when the findings did not mesh with their expectations. I found this uncomfortably disturbing because I had greater expectations of those who were "of the faith".

My doctoral research focused on the anatomy of *Greererpeton*, a member of an extinct order of amphibians. I came to realize that wherever "my" animal occurred, a similar suite of extinct animals also occurred with it – but the remains of other animal fossils were not present. Different kinds of organisms are found only with certain other organisms; they are not scattered randomly throughout the fossil record. I had been taught something completely different – that all the different kinds of organisms that had ever lived were together on earth right up until Noah's flood. Since those early days I have done a great deal more palaeontological research, both in the field and in literature, but I have never found a fossil which would pose a threat to the evolutionary paradigm by being out of place in the stratigraphical column. I have tried and failed to account for this on creationist expectations. My knowledge of fossil deposits increased significantly when I worked on contract for the Royal Tyrrell Museum in Drumheller, Alberta. There I worked on strata containing fossils preserved in their "life position", i.e. preserved right where they once lived and died, with different suites of fossils stacked one above another in different layers, with their characteristics indicating whether they lived in fresh, brackish or salt water. I knew now that different kinds of organisms had lived at different times on earth.

Trace fossils had convinced me that Noah's flood could not be credited with forming the vast majority of the geological column; my experience in Alberta had persuaded me that the earth's animals had changed through time. These two "geological facts" forced me to conclude that the earth was more than 6–10,000 years old. I was happy to let go of my belief in a young earth. I realized the age of the earth and the theory of evolution were not inextricably linked; that it was not the theory of evolution that had forced me to accept a great age for the earth. But I was not ready to admit that the diversity of life through successive geological periods was the product of evolution. To my thinking that would have removed God from the creative loop. Moreover, many Christian scholars accepted that the earth was old, but insisted that God had, at unknown intervals throughout these vast expanses of time, created specific kinds *ex nihilo*.

The domino effect of a crumbling paradigm brought forward another problem: how many times had God created new kinds of organisms, and when had He done so? Was the creation account in Genesis actually a re-creation after one or more cataclysms as some Old Earth Creationists supposed (the "Gap Theory")? I did not know any evidence for this. From what I knew of the fossil record, there had never been a time when all living beings had become extinct, even during times of mass extinction, such as at the end of the Permian Period (252 million years ago) or the Cretaceous Period (66 million years ago). No matter how great the catastrophe, life in one form or another had been on the planet continuously from the day God had first introduced it. I might have been content to believe that God had miraculously created every species instantaneously at different times in the geological past, but I could not help but notice the lines palaeontologists drew so as to describe evolutionary lineages. I knew from my own thesis research that the oldest four-legged vertebrates (from the Devonian Period) were more fish-like that any other known tetrapod. But were the most ancient tetrapods really more similar to an entirely extinct group of Devonian fish that evolutionists considered to be their ancestors? Had I been duped by the power of suggestion? I concluded that they were really more similar, when I realized that had tetrapods became extinct at the end of the Devonian Period and if God had not introduced any others (except, of course, humans), then on the basis of overall similarity, we would group Devonian tetrapods with lobe-finned (elpistostegid) fish. And the same for birds. From my waning creationist perception, I could not think of any reason why the oldest known tetrapods would have had to appear when they did in the fossil record, resembling a contemporaneous group of fish in so many ways. Indeed, God could have introduced tetrapods at a time and with an anatomy so unlike any other living organism that no one would have dreamed of any evolutionary connection between them.

Feathered dinosaurs and ancient fish-like amphibians are not exceptions to patterns in the fossil record. They are simply rather good examples of a clearly displayed pattern, once one acknowledged that the record had been laid down over a very long period of time. I am constantly amazed how the full impact of some knowledge can be shrouded for years. I had come to accept that different species of organisms characterized different sections of the stratigraphical column, but the pattern within the record is even more telling. In retrospect, it surprises me that it took me so long to appreciate the significance of the fact that two anatomically similar species are much more likely to occur close together in time than to be far removed from each other in the column. The non-random distribution of anatomically similar organisms in time is so obvious. Why did I not recognize it more quickly? True, God could have created similar species close together, but why do it so consistently?

But perhaps I was seeing no more than mere variation within a created "kind" (Genesis 1:24–25), rather than evolutionary change. It might be that a "kind" could encompass all the species we classify within a taxonomic family. In other words, evolution might operate within a "kind", but "kind" boundaries would not be crossed. This left me wondering whether God really created similar species at about the same time geologically speaking, or did He only create "kinds" from which descendant species arose as a continuous genealogy? If, as I was willing to grant, the earth was very old, how long might a given "kind" have existed? Could I distinguish between evolution within a "kind" and the origin of a new "kind"? This brought another problem: if I accepted evolution within a species (so-called microevolution) but also that new species could arise within the limits of a created "kind", had I not accepted the central tenet of evolutionary biology? What part of the evolutionary process was still the sole domain of God, if everything could have happened naturally? What part of evolutionary theory did I really object to?

On top of all this, there were burning questions of biblical interpretation. Were there biblical prohibitions of genetic change beyond that within a "kind"? What did the phrase "according to its kind" (NIV) actually mean? Was it simply a way to keep God involved in the process by which new creatures were introduced? As I read Genesis, it seemed to say not that God had created "kinds" with a certain but unspecified degree of genetic variability, but rather that God was very pleased with *everything* He had made, just as He had made it. No matter how I explained them, I had already had to acknowledge two facts: there are bridging morphologies between major groups of organisms, such as dinosaurs and birds; and secondly, similar organisms are more likely to occur together in time than be separated. These two realities pushed me in the direction of admitting that there was a reasonable cause to look for a natural mechanism to account for them. When I added bridging morphologies and adaptive radiations, I was forced to admit that life looked evolutionary in its overall expression. Could God have used natural processes to bring about life and all its diversity? It was an idea that had never been presented to me as a credible option.

Most of my objections that biological diversity could have resulted from continuous, long-operating processes vanished when I was working on dinosaurs in Drumheller, but I shed the final vestiges of the old paradigm because of a simple analogy that occurred to me at that time. The Bible states clearly that it was God who sent rain, at least in ancient times, on the land of Palestine. In other words, the Bible attributes to divine action something which we currently and unreservedly understand to be the result of natural processes. That being the case, why would it be wrong to consider the possibility that biological diversity, which the Bible also attributes to the action of God, could similarly come about as a result of naturally operating processes?

I had been deeply disappointed by Young Earthers when I realized the implication of the existence of trace fossils. As I searched the Bible's references to God sending rain and pondered on the science of meteorology, I became angry and frustrated, both with creationists and myself, for our lack of consistency in biblical interpretation. In the days when I espoused the creationist paradigm, I did not object to the science of meteorology! But I should have, because there can be no doubt that it is God who "[sends] rain on the face of the earth" (Darby) (Genesis 7:4; Leviticus 26:4; Deuteronomy 11:14; 1 Kings 17:14; Job 5:10; Psalm 147:8; and many other places). Deuteronomy 11:14, at least, seems to indicate that the rains are natural and expected and not the result of a miraculous intervention: "[God] will give the rain for your land in its season, the early rain and the later rain, that you may gather in your grain and your wine and your oil" (ESV). We are content to let natural processes account for precipitation, but firm Bible believers that we are, remain adamant that no natural processes could – or ever would – be found to account for biological diversity, something else that the Bible attributes to the actions of God.

Thanks to the science of meteorology, we now have a remarkable understanding of the natural processes involved in the formation of rain. But what has been the response of fundamentalist Christianity to these findings, in view of the fact that the Bible claims that it is God who sends rain? As far as I know, none! But aren't meteorologists discovering the mechanisms by which we can account for the natural origin of rain in the same way that biologists continue to work on resolving the mechanisms whereby we can also account for biological diversity? I know of no court battles over demands by "Biblical Meteorologists" for equal time in science classes to teach that God alone sends rain. Why should we take exception to attempts to discover and describe the natural processes by which God creates organisms, but not object to the study of natural processes whereby He sends rain? It is no excuse to object that the mechanisms of evolution are different because they are complex; it just means that we have to work harder at figuring them out.

Unfortunately the Bible does not provide a road map to this end. We have to figure it out ourselves. But just because something is complex, this does not mean that it cannot happen naturally. From a scientific perspective, rain formation is ateleological. That is, the mechanisms that cause it to rain do not have the foresight to know what they will accomplish. And so it is with evolution. I have come full circle to one of the original condemnations to evolution that used to be presented to me.

Once the idea had occurred to me, I continued to meditate on the rain and meteorology analogy. There seemed no barrier to taking seriously the thesis that life in all its complexity and historical diversity could be the result of many variables and interactions in nature. Evolution, in other words (contrary to what I was taught and believed while growing up), wasn't devised specifically to deny the existence of God, any more than the science of meteorology was. Over the past 200 years, palaeontologists have given us a much clearer picture of the many bizarre and wonderful organisms that have lived on earth during the course of its 4.5-billion-year history. I now rejoice in being able to have a part in the studying of God's work through studying fossils. For me, the question of biological diversity no longer carries with it any theological baggage. It is simply a scientific question. Put another way, the question of origins is only as theological as the origin of rain.

I will remember my years in Drumheller as having marked the time in my life when I laid aside the anti-evolution tenets of Young Earth Creationism. But a major problem remained: what was the Genesis creation account about if it was not a literal telling of how things came to be the way they are? I sought the help of my brother-in-law, Chris Smith, who is a biblical scholar and retired minister. Chris was brought up to accept Young Earth Creationism, in much the same way as me. He attended Harvard, and was president of the Christian Fellowship there in his final year. After Harvard (and marriage to my sister), he went to Gordon-Conwell Seminary. A watershed for him was a lecture on the interpretations of Genesis by Meredith Kline, and the recognition that interpreting the Bible meant taking it on its own terms, respecting the literary conventions according to which it was written rather than our own preconceptions and theories.[3] Chris has described the implications of this and of his understanding of God's creating work in his chapters in the book we wrote together (*Paradigms on Pilgrimage*), and also in a commentary he wrote on *Genesis* (IVP-USA, 2010). His contribution to my ability to look afresh at Genesis and bring together my scientific and biblical interpretations is an essential part of my story – but my account here is about my personal foundational paradigm shift over many years, not the exegesis of the biblical accounts.[4]

My shift involved much emotional turmoil, derived mostly by mistaken understandings and expectations (propounded by well-meaning parents and the Protestant churches within which I was raised) about the creation accounts in Genesis; ongoing differences of opinion with Young Earth Creationist-minded parents; and church (i.e. institutional) pushback. To suggest that I was *persecuted* by Christians for adopting a naturalist view of the universe would be too strong, but it would not be stretching it to say that that view was not welcomed with open arms by the Christian churches within which I moved; indeed, it was greeted with opposition and subsequent avoidance of the topic: how could I have sided with the enemy; wasn't evolution the foundation and bastion of all things atheistic? When church small talk turned to what I did professionally, inevitably I would be asked how I had

---

[3] Some of Meredith Kline's understandings are set out in "Space and Time in the Genesis Cosmogony", *Perspectives on Science and Christian Faith*, 48 (1996), pp. 2–15.

[4] There are some excellent accounts by conservative scholars. Besides Chris's commentary, see John Walton, *The Lost World of Genesis One,* Grand Rapids: IVP USA, 2009; Melvin Tinker, *Reclaiming Genesis*, Oxford: Monarch, 2010.

worked my way through the creation/evolution debate. Upon learning that I profoundly opposed Young Earth Creationism and was a methodological naturalist, reaction ranged from those who wanted to know more, to those who were disappointed and puzzled: wasn't Young Earth Creationism well-substantiated scientifically?

Individually, church acquaintances are wonderful people, and for the most part genuinely curious about my pilgrimage. But institutionally they don't want to know. They are driven by fearful leaders (those toeing the party line with a "let's not upset the congregation" mentality) and constrained by their individual church or denominational constitutions (and everyone knows that you don't amend a constitution!). That I might be qualified to speak on the topic is completely disregarded; they just don't want to hear it. I am condemned within fundamentalist/evangelical circles, the overseers having been inoculated to react strongly against any hint of an evolutionary worldview. The keepers of fundamentalism would, of course, say that I was duped by or was a willing mouthpiece for Satan.

Trying to effect change from within is nigh impossible when one is not given a voice and when fundamentalist/evangelical media presentations imported from nationally known groups are presented as authoritative bulwarks stemming the tide of evolutionary/atheistic creep that church members and adherents can trust as scientifically accurate at its highest level (a tragic false sense of security). As an *intensely* frustrated observer, I grieve at how Young Earth Creationism has made it so easy to ridicule Christianity by association within scientific circles.

Young Earth Creationists should not rejoice when their views are opposed, as proof of the truth of the position they hold. Opposition to Young Earth Creationism does not simply come from atheists; objections come also from Christians who know that creationist claims are wrong! Some would argue that because the cosmology of the Bible is out of date, so too is its spiritual validity. Its cosmology roots the composition of the Bible in a time and place; so yes, it is out of date in its descriptions of the universe. But justice, mercy, forgiveness, hope, and love have not been replaced with something better. The Bible never makes the claim that its descriptions of the physical universe are good for all peoples for all time, whereas it does make definitive pronouncements about being a guide to whoever has an interest in being right with God.

CHAPTER 6

Learning to Hear God's Message

Husband and wife Scott and Grace Buchanan came to read
the creation stories in the Bible (and their implications) in
different ways and at different rates. Both grew up believing
in the inerrancy of the Bible. They tell their stories about
their struggles as they changed their understanding of the
Scriptures without altering or diminishing their confidence
and trust in biblical authority. Scott is a chemical engineer;
Grace is a teacher. They have three children.

Scott's story

Early faith

Around the age of twelve, I began to read the Bible, and found
appealing wisdom in the Old Testament book of Proverbs.
That pulled me into giving serious consideration to the Bible as
a whole. When I read the Gospels, I was impressed with Jesus'
wholeness and authority. At home one night, after hearing in a
vacation Bible camp of God's offer of forgiveness and fellowship
through Jesus, I said "Yes" to Him.

In my first few years of being a Christian, I did not encounter
any problems over the Genesis creation story. Knowing what I
did about science, it seemed clear that it was not 100 per cent

physically correct, but it seemed much more realistic than the creation accounts of other ancient Near Eastern religions. I was impressed with how close the story came to what we now know of the epochs of the earth's creation, despite being written millennia before modern science. My intuition was that it was no big deal if the Genesis story was not literally accurate. It was still majestic and inspiring.

Encounter with Young Earth Creationism

When I got to college in the early 1970s I met dogmatic Young Earth Creationism. At my university there was a strongly conservative Christian fellowship which invited Dr John Whitcomb to speak during my freshman year. John Whitcomb was a devout and learned man and a co-author of *The Genesis Flood*, which made a case for the literal accuracy of the six 24-hour-day Genesis creation, and for "Flood Geology" – the interpretation of the earth's geology in terms of Noah's flood. It was a very influential book in the 1960's and 1970's.

In his lectures and book, Dr Whitcomb argued that the mainstream scientific understanding of the earth's age was incorrect. He presented evidence about polystrate fossils, supposedly older rock layers resting atop supposedly younger rocks, and recent lava flows where radioactive dating methods gave spuriously old dates. He pointed to a lack of transitional fossils, and to the lack of transformations from one major life form to another evident today. It was naturally appealing to me to believe that the rock layers confirmed and demonstrated the truth of God's revelation in the Bible. Moreover, the literal story of a beautiful, idyllic Garden of Eden in recent times seemed more comforting and sensible than the evolutionary picture of millions of years of cold-blooded animals eating each other. I became a believer in Young Earth Creationism, although it was never a big focus of my faith.

Different views of Bible interpretation

After graduation, I attended an academically rigorous and relatively conservative seminary, Gordon-Conwell. I took an Old Testament class under Meredith Kline. He argued that the two triads of the six creation days in Genesis 1 indicate a thematic, rather than chronological, framework for the creative acts of God: days one, two, and three involve the formation or structuring of day/night, sky/sea, and finally water/land, while days four, five, and six provide occupants or rulers for these realms, in the same order: sun and moon (for day/night), birds and fish (for sky and sea), and land animals on day six. The earth was initially (Genesis 1:2) "formless and empty" (NLT). These two deficiencies are corrected in the next six days, as the earth is "formed" (structured) in days one to three, then "filled" in days four to six. There is a pleasing, symmetrical logic to all this. This point of view offered me a way to acknowledge that the Genesis account is not chronologically accurate, while maintaining a high view of biblical inspiration.

Another significant classroom interaction occurred in a New Testament exegesis course. Comparing accounts in two Gospels, I found events that I could not reconcile between them. I went to the professor to try to get some help on this, and found he did not have a nice pat answer. I finally asked him point-blank, "Do you believe that there are actual discrepancies in the Bible?" He looked at me and hesitated for a few seconds, weighing what to say. Finally he said, "Yes." I was scandalized. I did not want to accept this. It was only later when I had calmed down that I reflected that my professor seemed to be as good a Christian as I, and maybe he knew something that I didn't. That helped release me from the fear that my whole faith would go down the drain if there were any inaccuracy in the Bible.

Old Earth Creationism

After a year in seminary, I changed my plans. I went back to college for a bachelor's degree in chemical engineering and then a PhD. I picked up enough hard science to realize that the earth was in fact several billions years old, and that the rock layers were laid down over millions of years, not in a single global flood. But I still could not stomach evolution.

By the 1990s I was reading and accepting the views of Hugh Ross, author of many books and founder of the Reasons to Believe ministry. Ross defends the Big Bang as a singular, non-recurring event, seeing it as evidence for a creator who lies outside of this universe. He teaches a form of Old Earth Creationism, where the "days" of Genesis 1 represent long geological ages, described in correct chronological order. To do this, he has to employ some strained interpretations of the Genesis story to make it fit what is known of the geological history of the earth. While endorsing the conclusions of mainstream astronomy and geology, Ross rejects macroevolution and sees Adam and Eve as supernaturally created.

Into the fray

Sometime around 2004 I had a conversation with a work colleague which had a strong impact on me. I had conceived all genetic mutations being merely substitutions at various points along the DNA strand. That seemed to offer no way for the increase in information content in the genome necessary if life were to evolve from simple bacteria to full-fledged animals. I told my chemist friend this was a major reason that made me sceptical about evolution. He listened to me politely, and then informed me about other types of mutations, including ones where whole sections of DNA can undergo duplication and get inserted into a new DNA strand. This means, for instance, that an extra copy of a gene may be added to the genome. (This was new to me; my last exposure to genetics had been in high school in 1970.) It was immediately clear to me that gene duplication offered a viable pathway for an increase in genetic information and dissolved my strongest mechanistic objection to evolution.

I became more deeply engaged in the creation/evolution debate as a result of an encounter at a church men's retreat. A participant there led a workshop in creationism. He was a committed Young Earth Creationist. He presented slides and handed out written material claiming that all the evidence for the earth being very old was mistaken, and also that evolution was scientifically impossible. I was not prepared to counter the examples he gave, but felt obliged to stand up and say that there was more than one point of view among Christians on these issues.

The speaker urged me to get on board with Young Earth Creationism. We started corresponding, and sent each other some books. With my background knowledge, and with help from websites such as TalkOrigins and Old Earth Ministries,[1] I was able to point out where the geological evidence he presented for a young earth was flawed. But without a biology background, I was

---

[1] http://www.talkorigins.org/origins/faqs-youngearth.html; http://oldearth.org/youngministry.htm (accessed 3 July 2014).

at a loss on how to respond to the claim that all known mutations are harmful, and that genomes are necessarily deteriorating with each generation. He sent me a copy of *Genetic Entropy* (2008), written by retired Cornell professor John Sanford. This book makes the case for the inexorable accumulation of deleterious mutations over time. The implication is that populations could not evolve positively or even maintain their fitness for millions of years.

Having found that the arguments against an old earth were inaccurate, I became motivated to settle, at least for myself, the question of evolution. In order to determine the truth about these matters, I spent hundreds of hours studying genetics and reading original papers in the field. Some helpful resources were the BioLogos website, an article "Evolution for Christians" by a professor at Berea College, and "29+ Evidences for Macroevolution" at TalkOrigins.[2]

I found that all the objections advanced against evolution were unfounded. There are plenty of examples of beneficial mutations, and plenty of evidence within our genomes of common ancestry with chimpanzees. Furthermore, the fossil record is broadly consistent with evolution, if one looks at the fossils that have been found instead of merely complaining about those that have not yet been found. It is intrinsically unlikely to find fossils of the actual ancestral transitional forms, since (from elementary population genetics) a new species is most likely to develop in some small, isolated population.

Furthermore, the old earth/anti-evolution interpretation cannot account satisfactorily for all the fossils in the older rock layers. If these fossils do not represent organisms that slowly

[2] http://biologos.org/; http://community.berea.edu/scienceandfaith/essay05.asp; http://www.talkorigins.org/faqs/comdesc/ (accessed 3 July 2014).

evolved over time, where exactly did they come from? The only consistent answer is that God must have arbitrarily and miraculously created hundreds of new species every million years or so, in a sequence which just happened to mesh with evolutionary expectations. That seems unpalatably deceptive.

I wrote up my findings on geology and genetics in the form of several long letters to my creationist correspondent. Having put all that effort into these letters, I decided to make them more widely available. With help from my daughters, I started a blog called "Letters to Creationists" in 2009 and posted our interchange as "STAN 1" through "STAN 4".[3] I have since added occasional articles on other Bible/science topics, such as the age of the Grand Canyon, the "Cambrian explosion", and "junk" DNA.

Hard questions and cold shoulders

As I started to get closure on the scientific issues regarding the formation of the earth and its biosphere, I was left with some disturbing questions. If all Scripture is inspired by God, and God cannot lie or make a mistake, then it would seem that all Scripture must be inerrant. But then, how could the Genesis creation story, affirmed as it is in the New Testament, be factually inaccurate? Was this a slippery slope, leading to the denial of the historicity of the resurrection?

Besides my own inner turmoil, I had to contend with the reactions of my family and friends. My non-Christian friends could not relate to my concerns over the Bible while nearly all my Christian friends were so committed to biblical inerrancy that I could not readily talk with them about my problems. The few

---

[3] http://letterstocreationists.wordpress.com/ (accessed 3 July 2014).

times I brought it up, the conversation got so chilly so fast that for the sake of ongoing relationship, I had to quickly drop the subject. My wife, Grace, and I get along quite well in general, but when the topic of Genesis came up, a defensive anger would rise up in her.

I live in the north-east United States, where fundamentalism is poorly regarded on the whole. Most of the people who attend my church are college-educated professionals. Notwithstanding, they are nearly all hostile towards evolution. Since my wife and I assist in the ministry to youth, this has caused some difficulties. Knowing it to be controversial, I generally avoided bringing up the subject of creation with the church youth. However, there were times when a boy would confidently pass along some scornful remark about, say, the Big Bang, and other heads would nod in agreement. Presumably they had heard anti-science comments at home. Since they were airing falsehoods, I felt obliged to let them know that there were differing opinions on this subject among Bible-believing Christians, and that I found all the physical evidence to show that the Big Bang and evolution were the means through which God had chosen to form today's world.

A few months ago the pastor of children's ministries sat my wife and me down and told us that there had been complaints from some parents; if we wanted to continue serving, we had to agree to not discuss the subject of evolution with the youth. Under the circumstances, we did consent. I could sympathize with the pastor's desire to avoid controversy over a non-core issue.

What to make of the Genesis story?

It took me some time to find an interpretative approach to Genesis that could hold up in light of the physical facts about the age of the earth. Fortunately, by the time I started to dig into these issues, a number of relevant books by evangelical Christians had appeared. These included Darrel Falk's *Coming to Peace with Science* (2004), Gordon Glover's *Beyond the Firmament* (2007), and Denis Lamoureux's *Evolutionary Creation* (2008).

All of these books argue that we must recognize that the ancient Israelites had their own notions of the physical universe, and that God accommodated His revelation to the science of that day. People in the Middle East in the time of Moses "knew" that the earth was immovably fastened to its foundations; the sky overhead was a solid dome, and that animals reproduced strictly after their kind (no evolution). God could have corrected this ancient science, but chose not to. This was not a mistake or scriptural "error". Rather, God wisely and graciously accommodated His spiritual revelation to the contemporary physical understanding, in order to facilitate communication of vital spiritual and relational concepts. It would have been pointless and confusing if, for example, the ancient Israelites had been given a creation account in terms of today's science (Big Bang, supernovae, plate tectonics, dinosaurs, etc.). The Genesis account provides a means to communicate powerfully key concepts about God, humans, and the world. In contrast to the quarrelling, greedy gods of the pagans, the Genesis story depicts the Hebrew God as sovereign, calmly, freely and gladly choosing to create the universe, and granting humans a dignified and responsible role in the earth.

The pre-scientific Genesis creation account effectively accomplishes what 2 Timothy 3:15–17 says is the purpose of the Scriptures. It vividly conveys a high doctrine of God's goodness and power, and His authority to give moral direction to humankind. It is thus "profitable for doctrine, for reproof, for correction, for instruction in righteousness" (KJV). Retaining the ancient physical concepts (instead of trying to correct them) was essential in accomplishing this divine purpose for the people to whom this revelation was given.

That said, it still bothered me that the Genesis story was not factually true. Upon further study, I found that telling stories which didn't really happen was a well-established device for the Israelites, especially when the occasion involved calling someone to account for their sin. For instance, in 1 Kings 20 a prophet wants to rebuke King Ahab for sparing an enemy king. The prophet does so by disguising himself with a headband and telling a made-up story about having let a captive escape. After he got the king to agree that that sort of irresponsibility deserved judgment, the prophet removed his headband and revealed that this story was really about the king's actions. The story itself, like the Genesis creation narrative, was not literally true.

When the prophet Nathan confronted King David over killing Uriah and taking Uriah's wife Bathsheba, he started off by telling a story about a rich man robbing a poor man of a lamb. He presented it as a true story, even though it was not.

Likewise, Jesus' primary mode of communication was to tell stories that never really happened: "With many similar parables Jesus spoke the word to them, as much as they could understand. He did not say anything to them without using a parable" (Mark 4:33–34, NIV). To argue over whether there really was a good Samaritan is to completely miss the point of the parable. The same goes for arguing over the historicity of Genesis.

For most of Jesus' parables, the hearer is expected to figure out that the story is not really *about* some son who ran away and fed pigs or *about* some unfortunate traveller who got mugged on the way to Jericho. The hearer needs to enter into the story and see that he or she is represented by one or more of the characters in it; that was the point of the parable, not whether the story itself ever actually happened. I have come to think this is true also with the Eden narrative. After first reading it as a story about someone else, and clucking over the arrogance, faithlessness, and blame-shifting exhibited by the first couple (and maybe indulging in blaming them for our sorry state), the reader should realize that "*I* am that man and that woman – I have done the same things, and I, too, am in need of divine covering." We are all Adam ("Adam" in Hebrew means "man" or "mankind"), choosing to doubt God's goodness and to blame others for our mistakes.

The Fall and original sin

The passage that I found most difficult to reconcile with evolution was Romans 5, where Paul links the representative righteous work of Christ with the unrighteous, consequential acts of Adam. Tim Keller has written, "If Adam doesn't exist, Paul's whole argument – that both sin and grace work 'covenantally' – falls apart ... If you don't believe what he believes about Adam, you are denying the core of Paul's teaching."[4]

These are serious issues. It is clear that Paul assumed the Genesis 2–3 narrative to be literally true. That is what any pious Jew or Christian of the first century believed: that is what they had all been taught, and they had no reason to think otherwise.

Paul did receive some special revelation regarding the unfolding of God's plan in Christ (e.g. Galatians 1:11–16; Ephesians 1:9–10) and he faithfully transmitted the teachings of

[4] http://www.christianitytoday.com/ct/2011/june/historicaladam.html (accessed 3 July 2014).

the earlier apostles, but Paul was not omniscient (Acts 23:5; 1 Corinthians 13:12). Since I had no grounds to assume that God gave Paul knowledge of science beyond the understanding of his age, I had to accept that Paul would share the beliefs of those around him regarding the origins of the physical world, whether or not those beliefs matched reality.

This perspective provides an understanding of what Paul wrote in Romans 5. In verses 15–19 Paul compares and contrasts the work of Adam and the work of Christ. The statements here about Christ ("those who receive the abundance of grace and of the gift of righteousness will reign in life through the One, Jesus Christ"; "through one act of righteousness there resulted justification of life to all men" NASB), go to the heart of the gospel.

The question then becomes: are the statements about Christ only true if the statements about Adam are true? The answer is, "No". Paul does not make the truth of these redemption statements contingent upon the truth of the statements about Adam. He merely believes both sets of statements to be true, and proceeds on that basis to draw rational parallels between them. His teachings here about Christ's work of redemption stand on their own, being backed by dozens of related passages in the New Testament. Thus, the contention that "if there was no historical Fall, there is no need for a historical atonement" is false.

The same considerations apply in 1 Corinthians 15:21–49. In this passage Paul sets out the future resurrection of Christians. Believing the Genesis 1–3 narrative to be literally true, he quite reasonably draws on it for comparisons between death coming via Adam and life coming via Christ. Again, Paul's statements regarding the reality and effectiveness of Jesus' resurrection stand on their own. He never makes them logically dependent on the historicity of Adam.

Adam's fall being responsible for our present sinfulness and God's dealing with us covenantally through Adam are mentioned in the New Testament only in the passages discussed above, and are merely add-ons to the points Paul was making anyway. Paul develops the universality of sin in Romans 1–3 with no mention of original sin. He moves from, "The wrath of God is being revealed from heaven against all the godlessness and wickedness of people, who suppress the truth by their wickedness ... although they knew God, they neither glorified him as God nor gave thanks to him" (1:18–21, NIV) to "all have sinned and fall short of the glory of God" (3:23, NIV) without introducing Adam. In all of the gospel proclamation to both Jews and Gentiles recorded in the book of Acts, there is not a single reference to Adam's sin.

The Fall is never mentioned by Jesus. On the contrary, Jesus directed people away from religious speculations or blaming others, and towards a consciousness of their own transgressions and their personal need for mercy.

The image of God

Another concern I had was whether evolution threatens our status as bearers of God's image. I was offended at the thought that we came from apes, but I realized the biological reality is even more humiliating. I came, not from a monkey, but from a tiny single-celled egg formed in my mother's ovaries. This is true of all humans now living, and their parents and grandparents. How God physically made the first human bodies (whether from dust or from other primates) is completely irrelevant to the status and value of us today as human beings and bearers of the image of God. Moreover, it cannot be the case that God simply assigns

119

a soul to an egg as soon as it is fertilized: identical twins result from the division of an egg after it is fertilized, yet presumably they each have their own soul. I think it wise to remain humbly agnostic on this matter.

Grace's story

Continuing the story, I am Grace, the other half of the Buchanan marriage. You may know the saying, "Underneath anger is fear." Well, that has certainly been true in my experience. I know Scott's story and think he is admirable, a man with such a passion for truth and a willingness to spend the hundreds of hours he spent to educate himself and research to such a depth.

However, most human beings I know are more like me: a complex mix of insecurities and fears and guilt and shame. We tend to use thinking more to defend our own emotional fortresses than to examine all sides of an issue dispassionately for the sake of arriving at truth. That has been my experience.

Growing up, I was lonely and ashamed for not being perfect. My mother would take me to church as a child and prayed with me every night before sleep. I always believed God was real, but I wanted more. I desired to know God personally and wished God would talk to me.

When I was a freshman in high school in 1970, a friend told me one night at a party that Jesus loved me. I remember crying as she spoke to me. Soon after, there was an invitation in the school daily announcements for people to come to a lunch meeting to talk about Jesus. When I saw that invitation, a silent scream of joy welled up in me; I was so hungry to know God better.

I went to the meeting and students told me not only that Jesus loved me and died on the cross so I could be forgiven, but that God does indeed speak to us today. I started going to Bible studies and prayer meetings and reading the Bible like a starved person. I would wake up at four or five in the morning and devour the Scriptures. My heart has been progressively healed by God and I have never looked back; ever since then I have been learning to hear God's still small voice day by day.

It was Scott who put the notice in my high school daily announcements. At the time we unreservedly accepted the Bible as the inspired Word of God, and believed with all our hearts that every word had been dictated by the Holy Spirit through the pen of the writer. We never thought about the human involvement. To be fair, no one ever told us anything else. All the Christians we knew spoke of the Bible as the infallible Word of God, to be embraced unquestioningly. I memorized Bible verses regularly and intensively.

Eight years later, Scott and I married. I became a teacher. In church settings I helped children learn Bible stories and memorize Bible verses through music and crafts. I did not stumble over the six-day creation account in Genesis. I never liked science in school, and avoided it in my college coursework as much as possible. The Big Bang theory seemed to fit nicely with Genesis 1 and that was as much depth as I wanted. Since God can do anything, my superficial consideration of creation allowed me to gloss over any problems with the facts of the natural order. I simply dismissed the entire subject.

Scott's early attempts to justify a young earth perspective fitted my bent exactly. When he started to find contradictions between the findings of geology and the writings of Young Earth Creationists, I listened to him uncomfortably; it felt that the very basis of my faith was being challenged. Indeed, I was enraged that someone was taking away my comforting view of a personal God who had downloaded the Bible for us without human partnership or error. I had taught the Genesis story as literal fact to children for over twenty-five years. How could I be forgiven for deceiving them and/or possibly causing them to lose their faith when they later got to science classes that convinced them they had been lied to in Sunday school?

I was not worried about science per se, but I did care about Scott as he wrestled with his understandings. My own cognitive dissonance concerning the Bible was another matter. Frankly, I felt like shooting my husband when he rocked my comfortable psychological boat. But relief came, not as a single blinding revelation, but through a series of keys that one by one unlocked successive doors to my prison of fears.

In a graduate course on the Wisdom books of the Bible, I learned there was a great deal of human thought and planning involved in many biblical writings; many of the psalms and proverbs followed the elaborate literary devices of the Hebrew poetical forms of the day, including acrostics and very specific poetic patterns. "Wait a minute," I thought, "that means that a human being filtered those thoughts through an educated mind and had to work hard over a long period of time to craft his writings!" How did that fit with divine inspiration? Writing the Bible was clearly more of a partnership between writers and Holy Spirit than I had realized.

A hinge point came when we took a trip to celebrate our thirtieth wedding anniversary and Scott was writing up what he had learned about biblical interpretation. He noted the widespread use of figurative language in the Scriptures. I read his quotes from giants such as Augustine, Calvin, Galileo, and others.

Augustine had a huge word of warning on science and the Bible in *The Literal Meaning of Genesis* (AD 408):

> *Usually, even a non-Christian knows something about the Earth, the Heavens, and the other elements of this world, about the motion and orbit of the stars and even their size and relative positions, about the predictable eclipses of the sun and moon, the cycles of the years and the seasons, about the kinds of animals, shrubs, stones, and so forth, and this knowledge he holds to as being certain from reason and experience. Now, it is a disgraceful and dangerous thing for an infidel to hear a Christian, presumably giving the meaning of Holy Scripture, talking nonsense on these topics … If they find a Christian mistaken in a field which they themselves know well and hear him maintaining his foolish opinions about our books, how are they going to believe those books in matters concerning the resurrection of the dead, the hope of eternal life, and the kingdom of heaven, when they think their pages are full of falsehoods on facts which they themselves have learnt from experience and the light of reason?*[5]

Calvin wrote in his *Commentary on Genesis* that God accommodated His revelation to the limited physical understanding of its ancient hearers:

> *Nothing is here treated of but the visible form of the world. He who would learn astronomy, and other recondite arts, let him go elsewhere. Here the Spirit of God would teach*

---

[5] Augustine, *The Literal Meaning of Genesis*, Mahwah, NJ: Paulist Press, 2004.

> *all men without exception; ... it is the book of the unlearned*
> *... It must be remembered, that Moses does not speak with*
> *philosophical acuteness on occult [obscure] mysteries, but*
> *relates those things which are everywhere observed, even by*
> *the uncultivated, and which are in common use.*[6]

In matters of astronomy and geology, it was easy for me to concede the truth. When it came to biology and evolution, my emotional objections made accepting the facts more difficult. What helped me most was distinguishing physical mechanisms for the development of bodies from worldviews about how human beings are made in the image of God. This distinction as to how human beings are so distinct from other animals in their level of consciousness, language, and spiritual capacity to know and relate to God remained – it still remains – a huge mystery worthy of total awe. Notwithstanding, the value of anything is determined by the price that is willingly paid for it. Jesus Christ expressed our value to God when He shed the last of His blood for our redemption.

I grieve to hear Christians lash out against the discoveries of evolutionary mechanisms. What they are doing is confusing biological mechanisms with the meaning of life, with the worldview about the value of human beings in the sight of God. It amounts to a failure to apply logic. The media conspire in this by equating evolution with materialistic determinism as a philosophy of life. Unthinking Christians have swallowed this confusion without analyzing the difference between biological mechanisms and that for which material sciences (including biology) have no explanation.

I came to peace in realizing Scott's view of God and

---

[6] John Calvin, *Commentary on Genesis*, Edinburgh: Banner of Truth Trust, 1965.

Scripture is actually higher than that of the average Christian. Scott has a deep appreciation for the incredible complexity and sophistication of God's creative ability over billions of years, as well as a healthy humility about the fact that God has made man in God's own image in ways no one can even begin to explain. This is more and not less marvellous, and marvel we do!

For all the years I was fighting him tooth and nail, Scott exhibited tremendous kindness and tolerance, and was so gentle in letting me express my fear and anger – I can't say enough about how patiently he endured my reactions to his maturing views on nature and Scripture. Every time the subject came up, Scott got the brunt of my visceral response. He endured until finally I learned enough about how Scripture was written that the facts of the science no longer threatened me.

I have a deep compassion for Young Earth Creationists. I completely understand why they feel they are being disloyal to God if they question the literal interpretation of Genesis. For biblical literalists, the loyalty to that interpretation of Scripture is akin to loyalty to God. They sincerely believe they are helping God out by holding on to a very simple view of divine inspiration. I know because I used to be right there too.

If your core value is serving God and you believe that anything but a literal interpretation of the Bible is disobedient to God, *you can't hear any of the scientific arguments.* That was the way it was with me. Until I learned to separate loyalty to God from loyalty to a particular understanding of the Bible, I could not proceed to the science. The fact is that even now I don't like the pain of this new reality; the history of life on our planet is far more complicated than I would ever choose. But the crucial fact that makes it all bearable is that God is good, and God's love as expressed through Jesus Christ is more than adequate for every complexity, every pain, and every messy fact of a world that I can't and never will understand completely. I no longer fear unanswerable questions – but dealing with that fear was a process that took decades, and continues to evolve.

CHAPTER 7

Reflections

Lisa (née Orchard) Goddard took her first degree in the natural sciences at the University of the West Indies, followed by a PhD in biochemistry from the University of Cambridge under Sir Hans Kornberg, supported by a Commonwealth Scholarship. She then turned to theology, acquiring a BA from Oak Hill College in London and a second PhD (this time in theology) from Liverpool University. She subsequently taught "science and theology" to ministerial students, but is presently recovering from a long-term illness. She is married to the Revd Simon Goddard, and they live in rural Cambridgeshire. She enjoys observing wildlife and reading detective novels.

I have been a six-day creationist, an atheistic evolutionist and supporter of Intelligent Design; and all before my twenty-fifth birthday. In those years, I lost my Christian faith and re-found it (or rather God found me), enthusiastically pursued a scientific career and abandoned it, and left my beloved home in the Caribbean to live in England. These were turbulent years in which the creation-evolution debate played a major role in my life, but if there was some wisdom gained from my experiences which could help others, then I would be content.

I describe myself as a Creole. Although my parents are of European descent, I was born in the Caribbean and grew up deeply embedded in its culture. So, for instance, Creolized English is my first language and still my instinctively preferred one, especially if I am surprised, excited or annoyed! God-talk is also common in the Caribbean. At a very early age, I became a Christian with a faith strongly focused on the person of Jesus. I loved Jesus with the ardency and vulnerability that is natural for children but very difficult for adults. I recall vigorously arguing with my teacher that Jesus would never throw out a man from a banquet just because he was poorly dressed (a misunderstanding of Matthew 22:11–13).

I don't know, however, exactly when or how I came to understand the Christian faith – there is no single instance or person that stands out. It was not in the home, as my family were not religious; we never prayed or went to church (except occasionally at Christmas). I did go to a Catholic convent school which taught religious education and, as I said, God-talk is common, and many West Indians, especially among the poorer black community, have a deep faith in Christ. No doubt I just picked it up.

During these early years, the intensity of my faith was matched by my determination to study the sciences. Again, there are no role models or particular events that fed my interest. I was, and still am, fascinated by the world that science explores. Even now, when I browse a scientific journal, I feel myself undergo a personal transformation – I become, almost paradoxically, both enthused about life and serene. I have tried, without complete success, to determine exactly why this is so. The best I can say is that the world of science, particularly at the molecular level, inspires awe and excitement in me. And the careful reasoning and logic of a scientific study well done is restful and even beautiful.

Science, even when it produces more questions than it answers, also brings a kind of clarity to the world. While the forward thrust towards new discoveries and theories inspires an almost childlike excitement, the experience of awe, beauty, and clarity have a calming effect on my soul. So, strange as it may sound, science contributes to my personal happiness.

If only these two passions in my life could have coexisted peacefully; but sadly it was not so. When I was eleven, my eldest brother told me about evolution and the emergence of species over long periods of time. This conflicted with the biblical six days of creation that I had been taught. Both science and faith mattered too much for me to ignore this apparent contradiction. One of them must not be true; I was devastated. My mother recalls that I cried for about two weeks until she despaired of what to do. Eventually, she took me to see the nun in charge of the convent school who listened sympathetically but said nothing then to answer my problem. A few weeks later she came into my class and interrupted the lesson to announce – to my somewhat bewildered classmates – that even if evolution is true, someone must have started off the process. I felt lied to – they had told me that God created in six days, but now were telling me that it was not so. At that moment, while still standing by my school desk as we did when a teacher entered the class, I chose to abandon my faith. My heart felt as though it was breaking. I have experienced many losses in my life since, but none so heart-rending as when I turned away from Christ.

How might things have been different? Perhaps if the nun was sufficiently confident to speak to me directly, I might have been reassured about the integrity of the Christian faith. Or maybe if there were some resources – people or books – to help me deal with such questions? If I had more carefully read Genesis for myself then this too would have helped. Genesis 2:4 says "in the day that the Lord God made the earth and the heavens" (KJV), using the term "day" to refer to the creative acts of all six days. It is clear in this literal reading of the text that the writer employed the term loosely. Sadly, this clarity is lost in some modern English versions where "in the day" is translated "when".

That Genesis need not be problematic was poignantly brought home to me a few years ago when I read a book by Francisco Ayala, a renowned biologist. Ayala was educated by Jesuits, who themselves had been influenced by the evolutionist priest Teilhard de Chardin. Ayala wrote:

> It was an unexpected turn of events for me, coming from conservative Spain, to discover that there was in the United States a strong creationist current that saw Darwin and the theory of evolution as contrary to religious beliefs ... I first heard about evolution in the Catholic grammar school and high school I attended in Madrid. My first science class, in sixth grade, was taught by Father Pedro, a gentle soul, who would catch fire when explaining science. That the theory of evolution might conflict with the teachings of the Catholic Church ... was never mentioned.[1]

How different his story is to mine!

It would also have helped if I had had a more reasonable expectation of references to the natural world in Scripture. We should not be surprised, for instance, that Scripture depicts the sun as moving across the sky (e.g. Psalm 19:4–6; Joshua

---

[1] Francisco Ayala, *Darwin's Gift to Science and Religion*, Washington (DC): Joseph Henry Press, 2007, p .2.

10:12–13). Even in our scientifically literate society, we still speak of such things as sun*rise* and stars *coming out* at night. They are conventions derived from the way things appear to us, and perhaps occasionally from ancient cosmological ideas. No doubt, if an extraterrestrial visited our planet and observed the way we commonly speak and write, even in scientific texts (unless they are technically concerned with the subject), they would assume we have a completely disordered cosmology. But they are handy expressions to which not even the most obsessive of pedants would object. To say that whenever we use such idioms our statements are necessarily untruthful, is surely wrong. Yet, we often apply this standard to Scripture, and judge its truthfulness on these terms; a standard that not even scientifically informed moderns keep.

Back now to my story: I had lost my faith, but my interest in science continued. My school, however, didn't teach any of the natural science subjects at secondary level. So, with much effort, I persuaded my parents to send me to a boarding school, which they did. When I arrived I found that the school offered biology and a very occasional chemistry teacher but no physics – to my great disappointment. The school was willing to enter me for the physics O-level on the condition that I taught myself. I tried reading through a physics textbook but decided against doing it on my own. I have always regretted not doing physics.

During these years, I also attended the compulsory church service on Sundays and special occasions (unless I successfully hid in the toilets). But it made no impact on me. In truth, the only thing I can remember of the services was the beautiful blue sky through the church window; I never took in a single word. I was equally indifferent to the conversions and charismatic experiences that happened to some of my friends. I did resent, however, my class having some Scripture lessons from a visiting priest. I summarily informed him that I was an atheist. Not surprisingly, my school friends told me recently that they had decided that I was the least likely person to become a Christian. There were certainly few moral remnants of my previous faith either – I was not a pleasant teenager. Although popular among my peers, I was rude and arrogant, and much disliked by my teachers (very different to primary school where I had been a favourite). The only reason I wasn't expelled, according to the headmistress, was that they expected my exam results to benefit the school's prestige.

During these secondary years, I visited a campus of the University of the West Indies (UWI). Watching the students walk by, I thought how wonderful it would be if I could attend. Remarkably, my dream came true, and I began a natural sciences course at UWI in the late 1980s. Now, for the very first time, I was taught by people who were enthusiastic about science. I very quickly became fascinated with molecular biology and genetics, although inorganic chemistry was a competing favourite. For me, the very idea that we can understand and study the processes at such a fundamental level is one of the marvels of science! Inevitably we dealt with evolution as part of our biology course. I can't recall my classmates voicing any disagreement over the issue, but perhaps I wasn't listening.

There were now two of us in my class who were confessed atheists. (I later became a Christian and he became a Rastafarian.) To make this open declaration is very unusual in the Caribbean, where many are religious and nearly all have a deep respect for faith, even if it's not a personal commitment. But we weren't ostracized in any way. Even though some of my friends were very "religious" and regularly attended Christian student meetings, I remained indifferent and would just drift away whenever the conversation turned to Christian things. With those I felt able to challenge, I argued strenuously that evolution disproved Christianity.

Then one day, which began like any other, I was leaving my inorganic chemistry class when I had a sudden realization. Walking along a narrow veranda with its dappled sunlight from the trees nearby, I realized that I would not find the answers to life, which I instinctively sought, in science. I was by now a nihilist of sorts. Although I didn't articulate it as such, I saw life as having no ultimate meaning, devoid of real goodness, and without any full and lasting fulfilment of hope and love. I expected science somehow to fill this void. Perhaps I tacitly thought that its mesmerizing clarity, simplicity, and beauty would lead eventually to some form of transcendent reality. As I walked along that veranda, I suddenly knew that this wouldn't happen. I experienced some disenchantment with science, but I had no thoughts at the time of returning to Christianity. Months later, my boyfriend talked to me about prayer and I laughed and mocked him. Nevertheless, later that night I remembered the joy that I'd known as a young believer, a joy which was simply no longer there. I prayed that if there really was a God, He would give me back my joy.

Very slowly, things began to happen. Twice I experienced a profound sense of the presence and reality of God. The first time, I was overwhelmed with awe, and just kept repeating to myself, "There really is a God!" On the second, I experienced an unspeakable joy; one that eclipsed all other thoughts and feelings. For the very first time I had a sense of really being alive, as if all my previous life had been lived in the shadows. There were also unlikely answers to prayers. On one occasion, I caught the bus outside my house with the intention of going to a particular charismatic church. I had no idea where the church was. In fact, it was in an obscure location and I knew almost nothing of the island's roads and geography. But despite this, I was somehow confident that I would get there. On the bus I found an acquaintance who was also going to the church – as it turned out, she was the only person I knew who went to that church – and she was only catching the bus because her car had broken down that morning!

My life began to change. I gave up smoking and drinking – I had started getting drunk at about age twelve, and by then it was a regular occurrence. I now swore a lot less, and God began working on my arrogance; that, however, is still a divine work in progress. My life was being "redeemed" or "bought back", but with the difference that my new faith was focused on "God". Although I fully accepted that Christ died for my sins, I was hesitant over – even repulsed by – the person of Jesus. I still had moments of wariness in my worship of Him, and found it much easier to think of Him as the Son of God. Obviously, I was reluctant to return to the Jesus I'd known in my youth. So, the shadow of the creation-evolution debate still lingered on in my life. It has finally lifted – but only now, and rather wonderfully as I write this chapter. So if these words accomplish nothing else, they have been healing for me.

In the meantime, I graduated and began work as a chemist in a research and quality control laboratory for the sugar cane industry. Like other friends, I also applied for various scholarships for further study. But I didn't really want to leave the Caribbean, especially now that I was part of a lively, growing, charismatic church. The church, which was excellent in many ways, taught that a literal six days of creation was the only tenable understanding of Genesis 1. They strongly opposed evolution as intrinsically ungodly. I felt torn between the joy of my renewed faith and my scientific education. It caused me much confusion and doubt. My thoughts during this period alternated between thinking that I was insane to return to Christianity and really needed a psychiatric appointment, and that I was the most doubting Christian in the whole of Christendom.

But I couldn't return to the nihilism that I had recently left. So I finally accepted, with many misgivings, the six-day account. It involved rejecting science, at some level, and meant I was very reluctant to take my scientific career any further. So I refused the offer of a scholarship for postgraduate study in chemistry at an American university. When I was awarded a Commonwealth Scholarship to do a PhD at Cambridge University, I was utterly shocked; but once again some amazing answers to prayer made it clear this was God's will for me.

Arriving in England on a rainy, dark October day was dispiriting. My whole first year was a culture shock. Added to this, doing a PhD in molecular biology meant I couldn't avoid the clash between science and faith. So I went to the Christian bookshop and bought some Young Earth Creationist books. (Interestingly, I can't recall seeing any Christian evolutionist books for sale.) I was very disappointed at the quality of the science in these young earth books. I didn't keep any of them, and I can only vaguely recall their contents, which seemed largely about the errors in fossil dating. I found them useless for the task of defending a six-day creation among my fellow scientists.

Even less compelling was their suggestion of a conspiracy in science to undermine Christianity. Science doesn't work like that. Theories are robustly tested and criticized; and a strong competitive spirit (not the nicest side of science) at least ensures that every aspect is properly assayed, contested and alternative explanations explored. Truth in science is hard won. Furthermore, most of the scientists that I knew were ordinary people; some were Christians and the others, for the most part, were either indifferent or politely respectful towards Christianity. Only a few were like Richard Dawkins. A conspiracy was not credible. So I felt at a loss to defend my faith and avoid its nihilistic alternative, which made me even more aggressive and militant in my arguments against evolution. My reaction to evolutionists, particularly Christians, relied mostly on rhetoric and claims of anti-theism rather than reason.

But, if I knew Christian evolutionists, why didn't this persuade me that the two views were compatible? There were several reasons: partly because the idea of conflict was by now so deeply ingrained. Also, Christianity in England seemed very different to the Caribbean, and in ways which didn't engender my respect. It lacked the same zeal for evangelism and personal holiness. It was also compromised: on matters of faith, for example, by holding liberal ideas about the authority of Scripture and the uniqueness of Christ; and on matters of morality, as Western Christians got drunk, smoked, and danced in clubs, all of which were completely inconsistent with a genuine commitment to Christ. (Of course, this is a rather simplistic view of religious expression in both places, but it's how it appeared to me.) So, persuading me about their views on science wasn't going to be easy. If anything, their apparent laxity in other areas meant that their acceptance of evolution was just one more compromise.

Nonetheless, I couldn't avoid the issues of science and faith. So, during the first year of my PhD, I rather reluctantly accepted an invitation to attend a Christians in Science (CiS) meeting. I found this worthwhile and became a regular attendee. It appeared that the vast majority of CiS members were evolutionary creationists. Although I remained unconvinced about evolution, I was at least impressed by their faith – they were serious about Scripture – and by the quality of their thinking in science-faith matters. I was also beginning to revise my early impressions of English Christians. One instance stands out: I wrote a rather troubled letter to Oliver Barclay, a senior member of CiS, about a question of science-faith (evolution, I think), and received back a very lengthy response. He had obviously taken much time and thought over his reply. The arguments he gave in support of theistic evolution were not new, but the concern he showed meant a lot. I gradually began distancing myself from the anti-evolutionist stance.

My initial opposition to evolution brought me into contact with supporters of the Intelligent Design (ID) movement in Cambridge. ID books, questioning the validity of Darwinian evolution, were just beginning to circulate. Some of the arguments were already familiar, such as the improbabilities of biological life emerging from a primordial "soup" by chance, especially given the incredible complexity of even the simplest cell. Indeed, the overall tendency towards increased complexity in evolution seemingly contravened the second law of thermodynamics which states that natural processes tend to disorder (increased entropy). There was a new emphasis on genetics, such as the improbability that natural processes generated the relationship between DNA and proteins; the two are entirely dependent on each other for their existence, but seemingly evolved separately. It was unlikely also that chance could produce the variations in the genetic code which defined various basic forms of plants and animals. There was no issue with the minor variations produced by evolution which made related species differ slightly from one another, such as the variations among Darwin's finches on the Galápagos. Instead, the problem was whether the random-mutation process of evolution could produce sophisticated innovations that distinguished different types of species (such as the differences between, say, birds and dinosaurs).

For the most part, ID supporters accepted the old age of the earth and the fossil record as revealed by science. But they drew attention to the rapid emergence of some species in the fossil record, at times in "explosive" events where many different types appear suddenly together; as well as the apparent stasis (unchanging body form) of other species. This was interpreted as contravening the notion of gradual, continuous evolutionary change, and evidence of special acts of creation. ID advocates have gone on to develop these arguments since those early days.

Some very brief responses, however, are worthwhile. The fossil record is incomplete (understandably, as fossilization is a rare event) but the discovery of new finds continues, especially in places such as China. Further, the so-called rapid emergence of species in the fossil record is a relative term. It may still involve very long periods of time – many thousands of years. In the "explosive" events, the likelihood is that one or more crucial environmental conditions changed at the time, and some genetic innovations produced key adaptive features which permitted the evolution of new biological forms. These species then diversified (relatively) rapidly to take advantage of the available food sources and habitats. This diversification might be especially rapid and expansive if it followed a period of major species extinction – as there would be room and food enough for plenty. Some species, especially those that are more versatile, can survive pretty well unaltered over time. Also much work is being done on fine-tuning the conditions under which the basic molecules of life formed, and on the intermediary role of RNA (ribonucleic acid) in the DNA-protein relationship – RNA has both "DNA-type" structure and can have "protein-type" function. We now have a better understanding of the genetic mechanisms involved in evolution such as gene duplication – when a gene doubles and its "twin" can mutate and may eventually develop new functions. Surely we should marvel at the Creator's genius!

Further, improbabilities are not the same as impossibilities; and God works through both. Indeed, divine action is seen biblically in those things that are: seemingly inevitable (e.g. the sun coming up, Matthew 5:45); highly unlikely (e.g. the spear that kills the king of Israel, 1 Kings 22:17, 28ff); and miraculous (e.g. Jesus heals the man born blind, John 9). We need to recognize that ID divides the happenings of the natural world into two categories: special acts of divine intervention and natural processes in which God has little or no part. Biblically, this is unsound. The example of the sunrise shows that God is equally involved in the natural events as the supernatural ones (see Psalm 104). And what about Genesis 1? Many ID supporters accept an old earth, and consequently reject a six-day creation. My understanding, back then, was that they saw the days as referring to long geological periods of time. So what did the text really mean?

Resolution came when I switched from science to studying theology at an evangelical Church of England college. I'd previously had very little theological input and it was a delight to think about my faith in an academic way. Paradoxically, engaging with the challenges presented by liberal scholarship strengthened my evangelical faith. I think a constant nagging fear, which I'd probably carried since childhood, was that Christianity was not rationally credible. No matter how much I wanted it to be true, it wouldn't hold up to scrutiny. Only by doing just that – scrutinizing my faith – was there true conviction of the glorious relevance of Christ, and inner peace.

I could now look again at the arguments for and against evolution, and at Genesis 1 in particular. I found the "literary" (as against "literal") interpretation of the text by far the most convincing. The days are patterned after the statement in Genesis 1:2 that the world was "formless" and "void/empty". In the first three days, God gives "form" to the universe, and in the next three, He "fills" it with stars, land, and creatures. Further, each of the "forms" created by God are "filled" in the same sequential order. So: day one – separation of light and dark, day two – separation of sea and sky, and day three – separation out of dry land (from sea); corresponds with day four – filling the heavens with stars to rule light and dark, day five – filling the sea and sky with fish and birds (sky creatures), and day six – filling the land with its creatures. The writer's point was that *all things*, every "form" and "filler", are God's creation. There is, of course, much more that can be said about the text, and there are now many good books on evolution and faith.[2]

This literary understanding of the text meant that I was free to acknowledge the findings of science. Not surprisingly, I eventually made a partial return to science. I chose to do another PhD, this time in theology and the biosciences, looking at the morality of self-giving from biblical and evolutionary perspectives. And now, when I teach a Christianity and Science module, I always tackle the evolution debate very early in the course. For many students, it is their stumbling block with modern science. I am content if I communicate not just the findings of science, but that biblical faith does not require six days of creation. Still, it is a painful subject and some feel, as I once did, that the only alternative to a literal six days is atheism.

The science-faith debate goes on. While on holiday this summer, my husband and I got an urgent message – my great-nephew in the Caribbean was deeply distressed. He had just learned in science that the whale is a mammal, but the Bible describes it as a fish in the story of Jonah. Which was telling the truth?

We reassured him that they didn't use modern classification systems back then.

---

[2] Such as Denis Alexander's *Creation or Evolution: Do We Have to Choose?*, Oxford: Lion, 2008 (revised edition 2014). Perhaps the most accessible, requiring no prior scientific or theological knowledge, is Ernest Lucas's *Can We Believe Genesis Today?*, Leicester: IVP, 2005.

CHAPTER 8

Escaping from Creationism

John McKeown (PhD, Chester) was a research associate at Leicester University. Later he worked for Christian environmental charity JRI (The John Ray Initiative), as an associate lecturer in history for the Open University, and as a module leader for the University of Gloucestershire's Open Theological College.

I was a creationist by default. As a student at university, I became a Christian and joined a subculture in which I was encouraged to read the early chapters of Genesis in a way that conflicted with mainstream science. It was some time before I realized that there were other ways of understanding the creation narratives, even within Christianity. My unconscious creationism turned into a conscious rejection of it – and a heightened awareness of God's calling to care for His marvellous creation.

Geography was my favourite subject at school. We had a wonderful teacher who used map-based games and numerical simulations to illuminate topics such as the River Nile's floods, cattle herders in the Sahel, and the effect of unpredictable rain on farmers' choices. Then on a sixth-form field trip to the Jurassic Coast in Dorset, the spectacular sites at Lulworth Cove and Durdle Door made the concepts of geology, stratigraphy, and "deep time" come alive. But I found some aspects of geography deeply disturbing and distressing: pollution, Amazon deforestation, species extinctions, soil erosion, overpopulation, and poverty. Part of me wanted to shut such things out of my mind. Outside school I found some consolation in the first *Gaia* book by James Lovelock.[1] His big-picture systems approach suggested that life on earth would continue in some altered form, even though civilization in its present form might not survive.

My youthful reaction to all this was a feeling that activism was hopeless, and I tended to escapism. A post-apocalyptic BBC TV series titled *The Survivors* affected me, and in real life I expected the great collapse would come soon. I read science fiction and liked the *Cyberiad* by Stanislaw Lem, especially the short stories about the godlike engineer Trurl who constructs a series of miniature worlds with intelligent inhabitants: some run amok; all the worlds turn out to be unsatisfactory and are destroyed by Trurl. I was also designing fantasy campaign worlds and rules for their operation, as well as collecting historical military simulations. It was probably due to this escapism that, against advice from my teachers, I chose to study medieval history at university.

As a child I never attended church, but I wondered whether Christianity might somehow give hope and meaning to life, so at university I began to attend Christian Union (CU) events. I remember becoming startlingly aware that a loving creator governed the world. All things looked brighter afterwards. One result of that was an unthinking acceptance of my chosen subculture's understanding of biblical authority that lasted many years. My allegiance as a new Christian was in the Universities and Colleges Christian Fellowship (UCCF), and I became secretary

---

[1] James Lovelock, *Gaia: A New Look at Life on Earth*, Oxford: Oxford University Press, 1979.

of the Christian Union, responsible for ensuring that visiting speakers formally accepted the UCCF doctrinal statement. During this time, I attended a church near Brighton affiliated with the Fellowship of Independent Evangelical Churches (FIEC), a conservative Reformed type of church.

Beliefs about the origins of life on earth were not emphasized, but I became aware that Christians had ideas on the subject that differed from mainstream science, and I was happy to accept them. As far as I can remember, these came through conversations and recommended books (I administered the CU lending library so I encountered many of the popular books circulating among members) rather than from the pulpit. Sunday sermons were always part of a series working through Bible passages verse by verse; ideas about origins rarely featured systematically. The preachers were rigorous expositors and would avoid commenting on science in the pulpit, whatever their views outside it. By contrast, midweek talks for young people were often thematic, as were presentations at the Christian Union by visiting speakers, so I probably heard creationism expounded. In any case, once I had taken into my system from CU small-group Bible studies interpretive methods based on literalism, many aspects of creationism simply and inevitably followed from reading the first three chapters of Genesis.

Retrospectively, I acquired a collection of ideas and assumptions from this time which can be labelled "creationist". Some of these ideas were obviously expected of any sound Christian, while others were optional. It went without saying that Adam and Eve must have been historical individuals created by God directly from the dust of the ground; they certainly did not evolve from earlier forms of life. They were originally immortal, but after they sinned (the Fall) they became mortal. The earth and all living creatures were created perfect, with no disease, no death or decay. The humans' original sin caused the whole earth and all creatures to also fall into a degraded state, cursed by God. Thorns, wasp stings, infections, plagues, and degenerative diseases were all results of the Fall and not God's original design. Noah's flood was global, and the birds and land animals saved in the ark were the only survivors of their kinds. Jesus could redeem human souls but our bodies were still fallen and afflicted (we disagreed with charismatics such as John Wimber who emphasized physical healing), as was the earth and all nonhuman creatures. At some unknown date in the future (possibly quite soon) God would burn the fallen earth and create a new eternal home for us.

I cannot remember any emphasis on a specific chronology of origins, but some (and I now realize, false) historical ideas were part of the teachings that I picked up: the Bible was the first book, Hebrew was the oldest language, and creation was probably thousands rather than millions of years old. A little latitude in biblical interpretation was permissible. The six "days" in Genesis 1 might possibly represent long spans of time, rather than 24-hour periods. There was also an interpretation called the Ruin-Reconstruction or Gap Theory which envisaged an earlier creation (or even creations) which were destroyed before the second verse of Genesis; Genesis 1:3 introduces and describes the present creation, thus allowing a "gap" of unknown duration. The Gap Theory provided ample room for any cosmological timescale, as well as finding a place for dinosaurs and other extinct forms as relics from an earlier time. I did not (even then) find these options entirely convincing, but they allowed me to shelve any concerns I had about the incompatibility of science and faith.

My creationist beliefs were challenged when I began work on a project at Leicester University to develop computer-based learning materials for geography undergraduates at UK universities. A module on Biogeography and Ecology included some evolutionary concepts; and a module on Quaternary Environmental Change looked at methods of dating materials and determining historical timescales through tree rings, pollen, lake sediments, ice cores, and Milankovitch cycles. This work coexisted uneasily alongside how I understood Genesis. I am still embarrassed by a memory of a visit to a university in the north of England and chatting with a geographer about a theory I had just read and was hesitating over: that a meteor caused the biblical flood by hitting the globe diametrically opposite the location of Noah's ark so the waves cancelled out before they hit the boat. What a mad idea.

Whilst I was at Leicester, Philip Stott, an engineer from South Africa and an evangelist for creationism (not to be confused with the Philip Stott who is a British Professor of Biogeography and frequent broadcaster) spoke at a meeting organized by the Christian Union. The event filled the university's largest auditorium. Stott argued persuasively (so it seemed to me) against evolution, for dating creation to 6,000 years before the present, and extraordinarily, for a universe that revolved around a stationary earth. I was ready to believe him: after all, this was an address sponsored by the Christian Union. I bought his book *Vital Questions* and I briefly wondered if I could help spread his message – perhaps by developing online materials from his book.

Stott's claims brought me to a crisis. A friend in the chaplaincy asked what I thought about the talk, and my reply was that I was 90 per cent convinced about the biology, and 50 per cent convinced about a young earth, but only 10 per cent sure about geocentrism. Stott had advanced various evidences for his claim that the earth was stationary at the heart of the universe, but this was to prove too much for me. I respected astronomers. As a boy I had lived next door to an amateur astronomer with a sliding shed telescope. Astronomy had been my favourite part of A-level physics, and I had joined the Astronomy Club to look at the night sky in meetings on the school grounds.

Once doubting geocentrism, I began rethinking other issues. Stott had not explained how the Ice Ages fitted in his chronology, but I had seen glacial landscaping with my own eyes so I had no doubt they had occurred. The speaker's case for a young earth, created a mere 6,000 years ago, had depended on arguments about the power source of the earth's electrical and magnetic fields, oil pressure in wells, and helium-3 in the atmosphere, all of which involved complex physics and chemistry beyond my comprehension. Instead I considered some dating techniques easier for me to understand: tree rings and layers in ice. Extrapolating from living trees to older dead wood by matching known sequences that overlap went back more than 6,000 years; layers in ice cores extended over 100,000 years. These were data I trusted. They contradicted Stott's claims and pointed to a much older earth than he allowed.

Suddenly at this time any interest I had in creation and origins was submerged by the realization that my concern about environmental degradation could be integrated with Christian faith. Looking back, my youthful interest in ecological issues had revived soon after I became a Christian. I had discovered a new pleasure in walking in the countryside, although I had not recognized creation-care as integral to faith: it was a separate compartment of life. I participated in work camps run by the British Trust for Conservation Volunteers and attended training days: on woodland management (I remember fascinating maps of tree species recolonizing Britain after the last Ice Age) and heathland conservation (with sadness at hearing of the loss of Large Blue butterflies from Britain). Learning again of the decline of wildlife due to human development encroaching on small islands of habitat recalled my earlier pessimism: fallen humankind would slowly but surely destroy God's creation. I enjoyed practical conservation but regarded it as futile: only a hastening of the triumphant return of Christ could save the world.

Then in 1997 I discovered a lively online discussion forum hosted by the Evangelical Environmental Network (EEN) in the USA. The participants (almost all American) were theologically conservative and argued vigorously about creation-care and its biblical basis. Most were environmentalists, but a few supported the anti-environmentalist Calvin Beisner and his cornucopian idea that the earth is divinely designed to accommodate unlimited growth in economies and populations.[2] The EEN forum made a strong impression on me (I still have printouts of the discussions). Through it I became active in EEN-UK and then its successor, the John Ray Initiative (JRI). I was happy to join the creation-care movement and to set aside my uncertainties about origins as unresolved. To integrate my ecological concern and my faith was a more attractive and immediate project.

At first sight, the creation-care movement seemed to be neutral on questions of origins and evolution. Many of the forum debates were about Adam and Eve and the Garden of Eden, and

---

[2] See, for example, Calvin Beisner, *Where Garden Meets Wilderness*, Grand Rapids, MI: Eerdmans, 1997.

contributors talked about the six days of creation, Adam's original sin, and the flood (I was theologically unsophisticated: later I realized that some people might use biblical terminology without necessarily considering it historical). I found an American creationist website also teaching creation-care. I visited a church in Surrey and talked enthusiastically about JRI to a man there. He was interested in creation-care but when I used the word "biodiversity", his immediate response was "I don't believe in evolution"; I reassured him that it was not a requirement for looking after God's creation. I learned to keep my doubts about creationism quiet.

I was more interested in eschatology than origins, but even so was reluctant to concede that disease, decay, and death were features of God's original plan. If the death of so many newborn and young creatures in all species (including humankind until recently) was by design an inevitable result of nature's pattern of excess reproduction to provide fuel for natural selection, what did that say about the designer? And would accepting nature's pattern as God's plan lead to indifference to animal suffering? As for the fallen world, I abhorred Beisner's notion that humankind alone has been lifted from the Fall leaving nonhumans behind and so justifying the humanization (or "taming") of wilderness. Beisner's approach effectively reversed the classic Christian understanding of the Fall by moving the locus of fallenness from Adam to the "cursed earth". Instead I affirmed it was primarily humankind that was fallen but, given the human office and calling as governor, especially as ruler and leader of the animals, I considered it likely that human fallenness had negatively affected the character of animal species, especially those which had been in contact with humankind.

The diversity of opinion about biblical interpretation, and the controversy surrounding particular words in the Bible led me to begin studying biblical languages with the idea of better discerning the truth. In retrospect this was hopelessly naïve and foolhardy given my weakness at foreign languages. I attended Greek and Hebrew classes at the East Midlands School of Christian Ministry in Loughborough in 1998–99, and then (after we moved near to Cheltenham) took a postgraduate Biblical Studies course at the University of Gloucestershire that included a Hebrew module. All this led ultimately to me enrolling in a PhD that initially had the overambitious goal of compiling ecological wisdom from selected verses of the Old Testament.

My acceptance of evolution was linked to my rejection of fundamentalism, and that happened through biblical studies and history. In 2006 I read *Darwin's Forgotten Defenders*,[3] a book showing that some of the Christian leaders encountering Darwin's theory in the nineteenth century were open to accepting evolution as God's method of creation. I also learned that "Creation Science" as we know it originated in the 1970s and could be understood as a sociological and political phenomenon. The book impressed on me that Darwinism was compatible with mainstream Christianity. Around that time, I attempted a reading of Genesis echoing theistic evolution as part of my PhD work:

> *Genesis, commentators agree, is structured by phrases using the word toledot which function as headings and organize the book into eleven parts. The noun* toledot *derives from a verb meaning "to give birth, to beget". It refers to subsequent offspring, not to ancestors.* Toledot *"must refer to that which*

[3] David Livingstone, *Darwin's Forgotten Defenders*, Grand Rapids, MI: Eerdmans, 1987.

is born, or produced … [and] can only refer to that which is generated."[4] The expression "These are the generations" or toledot occurs eleven times in Genesis, and introduces new sections of the book. It occurs in 2:4, 5:1, 6:9, 10:1, 11:10, 11:27, 25:12, 25:19, 36:1, 36:9 and 37:2. The first section heading at 1:1, unlike the others, does not have a toledot and this difference is significant. God does not generate or give birth to the world, but rather creates. There is an absolute ontological difference between Creator and creation. Compared to this all other differences between various kinds of creature are less significant. The first toledot (2:4) indicates that Adam and Eve, whose story is told in this section, are offspring of "the heavens and the earth". God creates the world and He endows the earth and sea with generative capacities. The parallel of indirect and direct creation in vv.20–21 (Let the sea bring forth … and God created) and again in vv.24–25 (Let the earth bring forth … and God made) indicates that these are equivalent. There are secondary causes, and all is God's work. He forms the man from the ground (2:7) and also from the ground He forms every beast and bird (2:19).

After two years' part-time study, the direction of my PhD narrowed to the text "be fruitful and multiply and fill the earth" and I abandoned the earlier efforts, including that part in which I had been trying to make the Bible support evolutionary biology and expecting Genesis to anticipate modern science. I do not dismiss the value of modern "readings" of biblical texts in support of evolution, environmentalism, or whatever: Christians

---

[4] Victor P. Hamilton, *The Book of Genesis Chapters 1–17*, Grand Rapids, MI: Eerdmans, 1990, p. 5.

through history have found inspiration and edification in a great variety of figurative "spiritual" interpretations of various biblical texts. But those homiletic uses should not be confused with the "original meaning" of texts which are best explored in writings by traditional Old Testament scholars, for example by Gordon Wenham[5] and John Walton.[6] I read other commentaries rejecting the Gap Theory and arguing that the six days of creation were (in the narrative) just days, not long epochs. Slowly I realized that the early chapters of Genesis are theology not science. I was ready to accept the peaceful world depicted in the first two chapters of Genesis as an ideal vision, as eschatological hope projected back into a legendary or unknown past.

Creationism is a pastoral issue. Young people in church will usually accept creationism because they trust Christian books, but later they may (depending on their career path, and the wideness of their reading) find these beliefs unsustainable. In particular, claims for a creation less than 10,000 years old and for geocentrism are easily falsifiable and likely to disintegrate. My experience is that when this happens it damages trust. The creationists I have known were all kindly, well-intentioned people, and most adherents, it seems, go through life happily unharmed by the ideology. However, for some personality types, creationism may end up damaging faith. Pastors should not just ignore creationism: since church members are likely to encounter it through Christian TV, websites, and books, I urge pastors to occasionally arrange for teaching and discussion about differing views of how Genesis 1–3 relates to prehistory and science.

---

[5] Gordon Wenham, *Genesis 1–15 (Word Biblical Commentary)*, Waco, TX: Word, 1987.

[6] John Walton, *The Lost World of Genesis One*, Downer's Grove, IL: IVP, 2009.

CHAPTER 9

Living with Darwin's Dangerous Idea

Karl Giberson is a physicist (PhD, Rice University). He was Professor of Physics at Eastern Nazarene College 1984–2011, during which time he also headed the Forum on Faith and Science at Gordon College for three years. He has written and spoken widely on faith and science. He is now on the faculty at Stonehill College where he spends most of his time teaching and writing about science and religion. This chapter is based on his chapter "The dissolution of a fundamentalist" in *Saving Darwin: How to Be a Christian and Believe in Evolution* (New York: HarperOne, 2008), selected by *The Washington Post* as one of the "Best books of 2008").

Introduction

In 1975 I left my home in the Bible belt of maritime Canada to attend Eastern Nazarene College, a Christian institution on Boston's historic south shore. Among the prized possessions I took with me were dog-eared copies of Henry Morris's classic texts of scientific creationism and Christian apologetics, *The Genesis Flood* and *Many Infallible Proofs*. Morris, who died in early 2006, was one of my boyhood heroes. It was he who inspired me to master the art of Christian apologetics – to be, in Paul's words, "[not] ashamed of the testimony of our Lord".[1] He was a giant of American fundamentalism and profoundly influenced religion in twentieth-century North America and beyond.

My childhood experiences of playing baseball convinced me that there was no future in the game for me. Likewise, the gulf between Gordon Lightfoot's guitar-playing and my own persuaded me that I would never make a living in music. But I was good at maths and science – and arguing. Perhaps I might follow in Morris's footsteps and become a Christian apologist. I was enamoured with Morris's scientifically informed defence of the Genesis creation story and his clear-headed refutation of Darwinian evolution. I planned to major in physics, get a PhD, and then join Morris's recently created Institute for Creation Research in California, to become one of his valiant warriors storming the ramparts of evolution and rescuing the Genesis story of creation.

Like many young people raised in fundamentalist churches, I had been captured by the promise of scientific creationism, which Morris had launched in the early 1960s with his remarkable book *The Genesis Flood*. In that classic work, Morris and his co-author, Old Testament scholar John C. Whitcomb, argued persuasively that the Bible and the Book of Nature agree that the earth was created in its present state about 10,000 years ago. The 518-page volume, which has sold over a quarter of a million copies, had enough footnotes, graphs, and pictures to convince any intellectually orientated fundamentalist that there was no reason to take evolution seriously. Readers could rest assured in the knowledge that Darwin's theory was deeply flawed, without empirical support, and on the verge of collapse.

---

[1] 2 Timothy 1:8, KJV.

A few celebrated and highly publicized defections from the evolutionary camp suggested that this was an opportune time to join the war against Darwin's evil theory, and drive it back into the sinister precincts from where it had been summoned by the forces of darkness. In stark contrast to the failing fortunes of evolution, Whitcomb and Morris argued persuasively that the biblical creation story was becoming increasingly credible as scientific evidence accumulated.

My first year at college, which wasn't the fundamentalist haven I had anticipated, was troubling. Away in a strange new city, homesick for the rolling hills I had left behind in New Brunswick, and without close friends, I struggled. My Bible professor suggested that Genesis should be read as poetry rather than science, a liberal heresy for which Morris had prepared me. The science faculty – despite claiming to be Christians – accepted evolution. Even my fellow students, at least the scientists, had limited interest in the creationist cause to which I had heroically dedicated myself.

These experiences steeled my resolve to stay the course. My reading in fundamentalist apologetics and scientific creationism – and my enthusiasm for argument – gave me confidence I was right. I could quote worthy biblical scholars who were clear that Genesis was much more than poetry and that Christian theology would come apart if it was not read literally. I had books on my bookcase by real scientists not blind to God's truth, refuting evolution with solid arguments. Strangely, my professors did not seem to know these works.

In my first year I attended an event at Boston University where Duane Gish, the premier and highly polished creationist debater, humiliated his opponent, who utterly failed to defend evolution. A vision of myself in that role, perhaps a decade hence, further inspired me. Later that year I had the good fortune to meet Henry Morris himself at a local church where he was giving a seminar on creationism. He encouraged me to contact him at the Institute for Creation Research for a possible research position when I had earned a PhD in physics. He signed my well-worn copy of his manifesto, *Many Infallible Proofs* (Creation Life Publishers, 1974), inscribing 2 Timothy 1:7–9:

> *For God hath not given us the spirit of fear; but of power, and of love, and of a sound mind. Be not thou therefore ashamed of the testimony of our Lord, nor of me his prisoner; but be thou partaker of the afflictions of the gospel according to the power of God; Who hath saved us, and called us with an holy calling, not according to our works, but according to his own purpose and grace, which was given us in Christ Jesus before the world began* (KJV)

Dangerous ideas

Scientific creationism was an integral part of the fundamentalist worldview that inspired me as a teenager. I understood God to be the *author* of the Bible, and the "writers" little more than scribes. This meant that the Bible had a wonderful unity of perspective; it was entirely without error and wholly trustworthy. Its scientific statements were completely accurate and its historical references utterly reliable. I quoted Scripture constantly, rarely introducing it with anything other than "the Bible says" or "God says". Complex arguments could be developed by lifting bits of text from disparate books of the Bible and combining them, just as geometrical proofs can be constructed by combining axioms and theorems. If God wrote the entire Bible, then it is one long coherent message, neatly divided into numbered verses to be shuffled about into whatever argument was needed.

This was my creed, learned at my mother's knee, reinforced in Sunday school, and preached by my father from his Baptist pulpit.

It followed that the Genesis creation account must be reliable scientific history: that God created a perfect world, with no sin, no death, and great harmony between His creatures and Himself. Under the temptation of Satan, the first human couple, Adam and Eve, sinned – of their own free will – bringing death, suffering, and destruction into the world. If they had not sinned, they would still be alive, listening to music on their iPods and enjoying millions of great-grandchildren. This is the clear meaning of the text. I took it at face value.

The first appearance of sin in a perfect creation was a catastrophic transformation, like a crack in a magnificent glass window or a beautiful vase. Sin completely changed the *physical* as well as the *moral* structure of the world, introducing a major "break" in natural history. Women's bodies were altered so childbirth would be painful. The ecology changed so growing crops would be hard work. Plants developed thorns, and helpful bacteria turned into sinister parasites, inflicting disease on their hosts. The Bible tells us that all creation "groans"[2] under a universal curse that an enraged God placed on the creation because of the sin of Adam and Eve. Like many scientific creationists I was quite ready to identify this curse with the physicists' famous second law of thermodynamics, the mysterious insight that nature constantly grows ever more disordered as time passes. What

[2] Romans 8:22, NASB.

better explanation for the origin of this law than the sin of Adam and Eve?

At the end of the creation story in Genesis, God rests. Whatever processes were used to "create" shut down on the sixth day of creation and no longer operate. Science has no access to these processes and is limited to studying the stable, *status quo*, post-creation patterns of nature. It follows that there cannot be any "science" of origins, and we should not expect to understand the various mechanisms – all of them supernatural – that God used to create the world. Secular scientists err in attempting to understand origins by inspecting the fossil record and geological history. The record that the geologists and palaeontologists are reading to recreate the natural history of our planet is not the story of our origins; it is, in fact, nothing more than the residue of Noah's great flood.

Morris argued that the flood story was the key to understanding the past. Genesis says that the human race, about 4,000 years ago, had become so wicked it had to be annihilated. The cataclysm reshaped the surface of the earth, laying down the fossil strata we find today and contouring the surface features of the earth, from the Grand Canyon to Mt Everest. Tectonic activity thrust up mountains. Receding floodwaters carved canyons grand and small. The flood scoured away any prior earth history, like a bulldozer removing an ancient forest to make room for a parking lot.

The Genesis Flood marshals lots of evidence for this interpretation, arguing that it provides a better explanation for the fossil record and the surface geology of the earth than the conventional scientific account, since that comes from the false assumption by misguided scientists that the earth is billions of years old. *The Genesis Flood* also argues that the Bible intends us to take the flood story literally and understand it as a global, rather than local, event. After the floodwaters receded, God promised Noah that He would never again flood the earth. He placed a rainbow, for the first time, in the heavens as a signature of His promise. The laws of physics changed at this time – about 4,000 years ago – to enable rainbows.

The Genesis Flood sets out the ways that the scientific and biblical witnesses to these historical accounts fit perfectly together. So why, I wondered, does the scientific community not agree? How can it be that the entire academic community of geologists reject the worldwide flood of Noah and claim the earth is billions of years old? Why are biologists so blind to the simple truth that God created the world in six days? Why do physicists and astronomers propose so many ideas – from radioisotope dating to stellar evolution and the Big Bang – that suggest the universe is ancient? Why do so many biblical scholars – who claim to be Christians – reject the biblical witness to all of this? Why do theologians say that none of this matters? These questions haunted me as an undergraduate.

Creationist answers to these questions are admirably simple. Human beings are fallen, sinful, and easily deceived by Satan. Blind to God's truth, secular scientists and liberal scholars of religion are unknowingly doing the work of the devil. The existence of such a widespread conspiracy to destroy the simple truths of Genesis demands nothing less than a comprehensive condemnation. Satan has deceived the scientific community, and a great many Christians as well.

I wasn't the only person convinced by Morris's arguments. Polls continue to reveal that about half the population of the

United States accepts the biblical creation story, many of them embracing the exact version Whitcomb and Morris presented a half-century ago. The alarming thing is that this position is at odds with almost *all* the relevant scholarship of the past century. Today I would describe this view as sophomoric in the most literal sense of that word (a combination of wisdom and stupidity), which it certainly was for me as I saw it wilt over the course of my second (sophomore) year in college. By the middle of that critical year, I was sliding uncontrollably down the slippery slope that has characterized religion since it began the liberalizing process over a century ago.

A largely discredited concept in evolutionary biology is that *ontogeny recapitulates phylogeny*. Originally proposed in 1866, this idea argues that the development of the embryo of a species – its *ontogeny* – is a fast-forward version of its entire evolutionary history – its *phylogeny*. The sequence of developmental steps through which it passes as it matures is a mirror of the developmental steps through which the species has passed in the course of its evolution over thousands or millions of years. It certainly describes the process I went through in my sophomore year as I evolved rapidly from the simple intellectual life-form called *Homo fundamentalis* to something more complex, passing rapidly through the various intermediate forms that emerged in the decades since Darwin.

As I studied science and mathematics, I began to realize that science could not possibly have got everything as thoroughly wrong as the creationists suggested. The simple physics of radioactivity, widely used to date rocks, is one example. Many different ways exist to date the earth, and all of them agree that the earth is billions, not thousands, of years old. If the earth was a few thousand years old as the biblical genealogies seemed to indicate, why would God plant evidence to trick us into thinking it was billions of years old?

Just as my counterparts in the eighteenth and nineteenth centuries struggled to reconcile the new geology of their day with the Bible, I tried at first to play with different, but still literal, readings of Genesis. Maybe I could salvage the Genesis story by reading the "days" of creation as long periods of time. But this didn't seem reasonable. The Bible says, "In the beginning God created the heaven and the earth" (KJV) while science says the earth appeared some 10 billion years *after* the universe began. Furthermore, God created the sun on the fourth day, *after* the vegetation, which presumably needed the sun to survive. If the third day was a billion years long, the vegetation would have been long gone before the photosynthesis of the fourth day ever got started.

Each new question made things more complicated, and I have still not fully figured out how to make sense of it all. A billion-year-old earth, for example, demands that we reinterpret "the Fall". As long as Adam and Eve appeared in the same week as everything else, it was at least possible that their "sin" brought unintended death and suffering into the world. But now it appears that death and suffering had been present for a billion years with entire species going extinct long before humans appeared. Why would God create species only to have them go extinct long before Adam even had time to name them? Was this the same God who would later *preserve* every species on the planet by having Noah build an ark to rescue them from the flood? If extinction was normal, why did we need an ark? What, exactly, were the implications of the Fall?

The acceptance of an ancient earth brings other troubles. The geological record confronts us with human-like fossils in rock strata more than 100,000 years old. Furthermore, these fossils look as if they belong to a species that evolved from similar, earlier species. If we line up all these species in historical order, we have what certainly looks like a compelling narrative of human evolution from subhuman ancestors. Where in this history do we place Adam and Eve? No logical place appears in the unbroken sequence of human evolution for the famous residents of the Garden of Eden. And where, exactly, *was* the Garden of Eden? The Genesis story says that God placed an angel at the entrance to keep people out, which certainly implies that it was to continue even after Adam and Eve were expelled. We have no record of God closing it down. If God didn't destroy Eden, where is it now?

I began to have doubts about the historicity of Adam and Eve and the Garden of Eden. I found it increasingly hard to read the creation stories without asking unsettling questions. I discovered to my dismay that fundamentalists in the midst of theological breakdowns look in vain to contemporary biblical scholarship for help. My freshman Bible professor had offered many helpful suggestions just a year earlier, bless his heart, but I had rejected all of them. They now came rushing back to haunt me. I found myself in a sort of alternate reality that was a strange and darkened mirror image of the fundamentalist world I had inhabited for my entire life. I was on the Damascus Road but going in the wrong direction.

I missed the satisfying harmony between science, as I had understood it, and the Bible, as I had interpreted it. They had reinforced each other and made the whole greater than the sum of the parts. But real science, which I was studying in college, and contemporary biblical scholarship, which religion majors were studying, seemed to conspire in such a way that the whole was *less* than the parts. The Genesis story of creation apparently had no contact with natural history. It began to look strangely like an old-fashioned morality tale that might teach a lesson, but certainly makes no claim to historicity.

Disturbing revelations came one after the other, once I opened my mind to real scholarship. I learned, for example, that the word we translate as "Adam" in our English Bibles simply means "man" in Hebrew. And "Eve" means "woman". I began to wonder how an old story about a guy named "Man" in a magical garden who had a mate called "Woman" made from one of his ribs could ever be mistaken for actual history. And yet this was exactly what I had believed one year earlier. Talking snakes, visits from God in the evening, naming all the animals in one day – the story takes on such a different character the moment one applies even the most basic literary analysis. The literalist interpretation I had formerly embraced and defended so vigorously began to look ridiculous, as did the person I had been just one year earlier.

I would have liked to find some simple alternative reading of Genesis to replace the literalist interpretation but, if one existed, I couldn't find it. I turned hopefully to scholars of religion but found they had little to offer me. Some of them strangely insisted on the historicity of *some* portions of the Genesis story, while allowing that much of it was not historical. The Fall, for example, was sometimes an important part of elaborate theological systems, serving the critical function of getting God off the hook for a creation filled with so much suffering. So even though Adam and Eve were not actual characters themselves and Eden was not a real place, they at least represented *something* historical. Once upon a time, human beings did *something* to ruin God's perfect creation, and this is where it all went wrong.

I was now wearing scientific spectacles almost all the time, and these explanations looked too convenient. Some theologians, for example, liked the way that Paul's reference to Jesus as the "second Adam" drew a provocative connection between the Fall and redemption (1 Corinthians 15:45). The first Adam made the mess; the second Adam cleaned it up. I could never see – and don't to this day – how theologians could be so comfortable with a mythical interpretation of Eden, but insist on an important historical role for its first resident. Paul's "first Adam" was indeed the original sinner, but he didn't live in the Garden of Eden, he didn't name all the animals, and he may or may not have been married to Eve.

Further complicating my struggles, the theologians I consulted were quite accepting of evolution. An Old Testament scholar assured me that "Genesis was never intended to be read literally". He and his colleagues had made their peace with evolution, apparently as toddlers, and had been at peace about it ever since. They were surprisingly disinterested in the struggles of those who, like me, were trying to hold on to some version of their childhood faith, while portions of its foundations were slowly removed, like the pieces of a Jenga tower that may or may not come crashing down as the tiny logs are extracted.

The universal acid of Darwinism

Tufts University philosopher Daniel Dennett describes evolution as a "universal acid". With undisguised glee he outlines how evolution, which he calls "Darwin's dangerous idea", eats through and dissolves the foundations of religion. For him, the theory of evolution, which he thinks is the greatest idea anyone ever had, destroys the belief that God created everything, including humans. "Darwin's idea", he writes with approval in his classic *Darwin's Dangerous Idea*,[3] "eats though just about every traditional concept, and leaves in its wake a revolutionized worldview."

Acid is an appropriate metaphor for the erosion of my fundamentalism, as I slowly lost my confidence in the Genesis story of creation and the scientific creationism that placed this ancient story within the framework of what I thought was science. Dennett's universal acid dissolved Adam and Eve; it ate through the Garden of Eden; it destroyed the historicity of the events of creation week. It etched holes in those parts of Christianity connected to these stories – the Fall, "Christ as second Adam", the origins of sin, and nearly everything else that I counted sacred. I discovered, however, that this was about where Dennett's acid ran out of steam (or whatever acid runs out of when it stops dissolving everything). The acid of evolution is not universal, and claims that evolution "revolutionizes" our worldview and dissolves every traditional concept are exaggerated. My slide down the slippery slope towards unbelief began to slow.

For starters, what exactly does evolution have to do with belief in God as creator? It rules out *certain* mechanisms that God might have used to create the world, but others remain. God apparently did not create the entire universe and everything in it over the course of a few busy days 10,000 years ago. Neither Rome nor the universe was built in a day. But saying that Rome

---

[3] Daniel Dennett, *Darwin's Dangerous Idea*, London: Simon & Schuster, 1995.

was not built in a day does not imply that Rome was not built or that Rome did not have builders. The acid of evolution – and several other sciences as well – dissolves the claim that God created the world a few thousand years ago, but does nothing to the claim that God may have taken billions of years to create or that God even continues to work as creator.

I took refuge in what should have been a more prominent part of my faith: creation is a *secondary* doctrine. The central idea in Christianity concerns Jesus Christ and the claim that He was God incarnate, truly divine and truly human. This extraordinary idea implies the strange notion that the creator of the entire universe entered the human race in the person of an itinerant preacher from Galilee. From its beginnings Christianity had to defend itself against charges that this was a ridiculous idea.

Most thoughtful Christians, myself included, wonder about exactly how it could be that God entered the human race in the person of Jesus – the historical event called the incarnation. Over the centuries many have been simply unable to believe that this claim was even sensible. Today, thinking Christians everywhere struggle with this belief and what it means. Many have asked God for more faith, to keep doubt at bay or re-establish a foundation for belief. Darwin's theory of evolution adds *nothing* to the complexities and challenges of believing in the incarnation. It didn't take Darwin to make Christianity complex and intellectually challenging. The arguments against the incarnation have been around for 2,000 years, which is why Christianity is described as a *faith*, not as the conclusion of a logical argument.

Christianity merges the incarnation with the belief that Jesus rose from the dead. Christ's resurrection offers hope that we too can have eternal life and one day be united with God. I took great comfort in this hope a few years ago as I stood beside my mother's grave. Human scepticism regarding these claims is hardly new (prominent evolutionary biologist and atheist Jerry Coyne mocked me as superstitious for hoping to "meet my dead relatives in the sky"). The contemporaries of Jesus also found this hard to believe, and many of them, including the infamous "doubting Thomas", had to be convinced by more than hearsay.[4] Human beings, including Jesus, may have evolved over billions of years, or they may have been created a few thousand years ago. The resurrection is equally implausible by the lights of either. Dennett's universal acid of evolution does nothing to eat away at this central Christian belief. The "acid" of logic and reason was hard at work on this before the New Testament was even penned.

Christianity, as its name suggests, is *primarily* about Christ. To be sure, different ideas about Christ exist across the spectrum of Christian belief. But these beliefs, rather than creationist assertions, are the heart and soul of Christianity. And these beliefs are not threatened by Darwin's dangerous idea. Evolution does, however, pose two challenges to *secondary* Christian beliefs: the *Fall* of humankind, and the *uniqueness* of humankind.

Clearly, the historicity of Adam and Eve is hard to reconcile with natural history. The geological and fossil records make this case compellingly. Nevertheless, scholars have proposed many convoluted and implausible ways to resolve these tensions. One could believe, for example, that at some point in evolutionary history God "chose" two people from a group of evolving "humans", gave them His image, and then put them in Eden,

---

[4] John 20:25–29.

which they promptly corrupted by sinning. But this solution is unsatisfactory, artificial, and certainly not what the writer of Genesis intended. Nor does any historical evidence suggest this interpretation. This modification also does absolutely nothing to support the idea that death did not exist in the world before sin. We must concede that the acid of evolution has indeed eaten away the literal part of this story, but I would argue that the most important part of the story remains untouched, and this is why I think Christianity can survive the eventual disappearance of scientific creationism.

The idea at the centre of the Fall is *human sinfulness*. Human beings are sinful creatures, and many of us are really quite dreadful. Even the best of us dare not lay claim to anything even approaching perfection. G. K. Chesterton once quipped that the sinful nature of humans was the only Christian doctrine that we could confirm empirically.[5] The classic story of the Fall is best understood as a powerful statement that we are, when all is said and done, sinful creatures. Exactly how we got that way is not so important.

But what, exactly, does it mean to be *sinful*? Various theological interpretations exist, some more compelling than others. But when the rubber hits the road, *sinfulness* is mainly *selfishness* and I am quite content to simply equate the theological term "sin" with the psychological term "selfishness". We put ourselves ahead of others and ahead of God. We advance our own agenda as if that is all that matters. And sometimes we do this in the most horrific ways.

Evolution says some interesting things about selfishness. Selfishness, in fact, drives much of the evolutionary process.

[5] G. K. Chesterton, *Orthodoxy*, London: John Lane, 1908.

Unselfish creatures died, and their unselfish genes perished with them. Selfish creatures, who attended to their own needs for food, power, and sex, flourished and passed on these genes to their offspring. After many generations selfishness was so fully programmed in our genomes that it was a significant part of what we now call human nature.

But an interesting tension exists in human nature. As incurably selfish as we appear to be, we also possess an innate *altruism*. Human beings are easily capable of actions that benefit others at their own expense – from taking a pie to a new neighbour, to giving money to charities, to risking one's life to save a child. Although altruism is scientifically harder to understand than selfishness, it remains clear that humans are a powerful mix of selfish and unselfish tendencies.

So where does sin originate? In the traditional picture, sin originates in a free act of the first humans: God gave humans free will and they used it to contaminate the entire creation. (I should add here that this claim is so fraught with conceptual difficulties that even the fundamentalists can't agree on what it means.) Freedom was the risk God took in creation. But now we have a new and better way to understand the origins of sin.

We start by enlarging our own troublesome "freedom" to include nature. In the same way that we possess a genuine freedom to explore possibilities, nature has freedom as well, although not a conscious freedom, of course. Physicists enshrine this insight in the Heisenberg uncertainty principle, which accords a degree of genuine "freedom" to particles such as the electron.

If nature is "free" to explore pathways of possibility, then the evolutionary process would predictably lead to creatures with pathological levels of selfishness. Creatures inattentive to their own needs would not have made it. By these lights, God did not "build" sin into the natural order. Rather, God endowed the natural order with the freedom to "become", and the result was an interesting, morally complex, spiritually rich, but ultimately selfish species we call *Homo sapiens*. This is a reasonable theological speculation, at least by my amateur standards. It brings the Christian doctrine of the Fall into the larger picture of an extended creation. Humankind did not appear all at once, and neither did sin.

Once we accept the full evolutionary picture of human origins, we face the most difficult problem of all: human uniqueness. The picture of natural history disclosed by modern science reveals human beings evolving slowly and imperceptibly from earlier, simpler creatures. None of our attributes – intelligence, upright posture, moral sense, opposable thumbs, language capacity – emerged suddenly. Every one of our remarkable capacities must have appeared gradually and been present in some partial, anticipatory way in our primate ancestors. This provocatively suggests that animals, especially the higher primates, ought to possess an identifiable moral sense that is only *quantitatively* different from that of humans. Not surprisingly, current research supports this notion.

Scientists who have spent enough time with primates, especially in natural settings, are continually struck by their social sophistication. In his remarkable books on primates, Emory University primatologist Frans de Waal describes primate behaviours that, were they associated with humans, would suggest a well-defined sense of right and wrong, cruelty and kindness, loyalty and manipulation. A remarkable bonobo named Kuni, to recount one example, saw a starling hit a glass wall and plummet to the ground. Kuni carefully picked up the stunned bird, set it on its feet, and waited with apparent concern for it to fly. When it didn't fly off on its own, Kuni picked up the bird and carried it carefully to the top of a large tree. Wrapping her legs around the tree to free both hands, Kuni spread the wings of the bird and released it, only to watch it flutter to the ground. Kuni then stood watch over the bird for a good portion of the day until it finally recovered and flew off on its own.[6] This story is close enough to that of the good Samaritan to make it hard to treat morality as a purely human attribute. And we have records of countless other examples of similar animal behaviours.

Primates have learned enough language to communicate with over a hundred symbols. They can do simple maths, punching a key for "3" when they see three candies in a bowl. Primate "societies" are home to such typically human behaviours as male competition, the bullying of nerds, and female solidarity. Researchers find traits such as loyalty, jealousy, and generosity among primates and other species as well. Anthropologists have even observed what look like collective spiritual gatherings of primates, in which a group of chimpanzees will gather to watch, in silence, a beautiful sunset, dispersing after the event when a leader signals it is time to go. The large number of human traits that appear in primate societies is intriguing and sobering, especially as we contemplate the ongoing threat that our activities pose to them.

Does the "acid" of our evolutionary kinship with the primates dissolve anything of importance to Christian theology? I am not persuaded that it does, even though I have found a few

---

[6] Frans de Waal, *Our Inner Ape*, New York: Riverhead, 2005, p. 2.

colleagues who are comfortable with the idea that God's saving power might extend beyond *Homo sapiens*.

The tricky issue for Christianity is teasing out which biblical and theological claims derive from a mistaken picture of science and which are central to the ongoing vitality of the faith. Until recently just about everyone in all cultures perceived an unbridgeable distinction between humans and the higher primates. Certainly the biblical writers and the formative thinkers of the Christian tradition could not have anticipated what we have learned from primate studies in the past few decades. Perhaps they would frame their understanding of Christianity in exclusively human terms, just as centuries earlier they framed Christian cosmology with the earth at the centre of the universe.

Speculations such as these are above my pay grade, of course, and best left to theologians. Still, I find no compelling reason to think that the central message of Christianity is incompatible with humanity's kinship with the rest of the animal world. In fact, this continuity with the animal world may place increasing theological significance on the welfare of animals and ecological responsibility.

Conclusion

Four decades have passed since I first began to wrestle with Darwin's dangerous idea. When I first started to think seriously about evolution – after my physics PhD was out of the way in the mid-1980s – I was optimistic that an equally compelling alternative to scientific creationism could be found. I accepted the label "theistic evolutionist" and confidently asserted, in writing, class lectures, and from pulpits that "evolution was simply God's way of creating", believing I had found a plateau on the slippery slope. I was initially attracted to Intelligent Design when it first appeared, but soon became disenchanted when I discovered that it had no content beyond some assertions that "evolution couldn't do this with help from outside".

I am no longer confident that a viable "theistic" evolution will be developed, although evangelicals are diligently searching for it and some are claiming they have it in hand. For me the label has come to mean simply that I accept what the biologists are telling us about origins and believe by faith that somehow God is working in and through the process. I am uneasy about confident assertions I used to make that evolution and Christian faith were in "harmony". Maybe they are, but it doesn't look that way to me, which is why I retain some sympathy for those who reject evolution.

Christians are now beginning to discuss what evolution means, rather than whether it is true.[7] I suspect that Darwin's dangerous idea may turn out to be like the perennial and unresolved problem of evil – a contradiction to rational belief that we must simply hope does not mean that our faith in Christ is in vain. I hope to be proved wrong.

In the meantime I will gather each Sunday with my fellow Christians at the altar of St Chrysostom's Episcopal Church in Quincy, Massachusetts to celebrate the Eucharist. And I will continue to tell my college students that they can be Christians and believe in evolution.

---

[7] For example, Denis Edwards, *The God of Evolution*, Mahwah, NJ: Paulist Press, 1999; Michael Northcott and R. J. Berry (eds), *Theology After Darwin*, Milton Keynes: Paternoster, 2009; R. J. Berry and Thomas A. Noble (eds), *Darwin, Creation and the Fall*, Nottingham: IVP, 2009; Stephen Barton and David Wilkinson (eds), *Reading Genesis After Darwin*, Oxford: Oxford University Press, 2009; John Haught, *Making Sense of Evolution*, Louisville, KY: Westminster John Knox Press, 2010.

CHAPTER 10

Deluged

Philip Pattemore is Associate Professor of Paediatrics in the University of Otago, in Christchurch, New Zealand. He was born to missionary parents in India, but has spent almost all his life in New Zealand, qualifying in medicine from the University of Auckland. His main research interest is in childhood asthma.

First contact

The first I remember hearing anything about creationism was when I was about eleven or twelve years old, in a slide presentation given in 1968 by the father of a school friend. We were boarders at a school for missionary kids in Ooty[1] in the Nilgiri Hills of South India. I don't remember much about the talk except that the man seemed quite vehement about the six days of creation and Noah's flood, and cast slurs of one sort or another about dinosaur fossils. It all seemed pretty convincing to me, but not particularly surprising – many of these things had been unspokenly assumed as I grew up. What was unfamiliar to me was the forcefulness and fervour with which he presented the subject, suggesting that he was doing battle with someone for these beliefs.

We may have regarded this man as a bit eccentric. I recall difficulty in identifying with his message; even though I was not

---

[1] This has officially reverted to its native name of Udhagamandalum but is still referred to by many South Indians as Ooty – more properly Ootacamund.

qualified to disagree, his unusual forcefulness on the topic meant that I couldn't easily put it into context with what my family and other Christian adults with whom I was familiar believed. His talk just seemed to be a fervent oddity which I had nowhere to hang in my developing framework of beliefs. I didn't even know whether my parents (missionaries in the Pune area of Western India) were creationists – I had never heard them hold forth on the topics this man covered.

I had already become a committed believer by the age of nine and was active in my school dorm in Bible studies and prayer meetings. When I was thirteen years old, my family moved to New Zealand. I was pretty conservative. As a teenager I read many Christian books, most of which were evangelistic or missionary in background, and some of which included books about the rapture, a belief common among conservative Christians. My older brother, however, whose expression of faith developed strongly during university, was always quite dismissive of such speculative writings.

Swept away by the flood

In my last year or two of school I came across *The Genesis Flood*, published in 1961 by Henry Morris and John Whitcomb. I had by then read some superficial creationist material, probably tracts of one sort or another. But *The Genesis Flood* had me enthralled. Morris was an accomplished scientist, a hydrologist; Whitcomb was a theologian. Here they were discussing the creation and Noah's flood in apparently detailed and referenced scientific writing. *The Genesis Flood* caused a deluge of its own – a reaction against evolution. Suddenly many evangelicals, who as a whole had been largely indifferent to the issue, became fervent creationists fighting evolutionary atheism and atheistic evolution, particularly in the USA.

The book details the authors' claim that God created the universe, the earth, and every creature in six 24-hour days. Initially the earth was a greenhouse, cloaked in a thick blanket of water vapour ("the waters which were above the firmament" of Genesis 1:7, KJV). The vapour super-nourished all life, allowing gigantic creatures to live, and shielding Adam and Eve and their descendants from cosmic and UV radiation, allowing them to live for hundreds of years. This meant that the genealogies in Genesis were accurate and the earth was only 10,000 years old at most. But God saw how great was the wickedness of human beings on earth (Genesis 6:5) and He punished humankind by releasing the water from the atmosphere and from under the earth, causing Noah's global flood, the extinction of the dinosaurs and other creatures, and resulting in the geological layers; and the starting again of biological diversity from each pair of creatures saved on Noah's ark. The authors attacked the underpinnings of evolutionary biology, from the evolutionists themselves to the geological column, carbon dating, the fossil record, and (as they saw it) the imaginative creations and frauds of the palaeontologists. As evidence of the recentness of dinosaurs, they included a photo of a fossil human footprint alongside a T-rex footprint (this photo was later admitted to be a falsified construction).

This book got me really excited, despite the scepticism of my brother. I attributed his attitude to two things. Firstly, I had the distinct perception that it was the older brother's solemn duty to cast scorn on ideas the younger brother put forth. But secondly he clearly hadn't read (and wouldn't read) the book, or he might have caught the flame too. The book was not just a book against evolution; in my mind it was a scientific proof of the accuracy of the Bible and the Christian faith. In addition, it was clear that the Christian faith was dependent on such an analysis of Genesis because evolution could not account for Adam, whose sin was passed to the rest of us and was the reason Christ came to die.

In my obsessional zeal I started typing out and classifying the various quotations in the book: famous scientists such as Louis Agassiz who cast doubt on evolutionary theory; evolutionists such as Ernst Mayr who criticized other evolutionists' ideas; others who said something seemingly inconsistent with their cause. I was still at school and did not have insight at this stage into the progression of the science of evolutionary biology over the previous 100 years (Morris and Whitcomb largely addressed evolution as a static idea). I did not appreciate that many of the quotes I was collecting were from the nineteenth century and not particularly relevant to current science, whereas others were taken quite out of context.

Zoology for medics

I continued as a zealous Christian in my final years of school, endeavouring to be an example and a witness to my faith. In 1974 I entered the University of Auckland medical school. The medical curriculum was mapped out in detail from years one to six. Year 1 was basic science – medically relevant physics, chemistry, zoology, and behavioural science, with a few other bits and pieces such as sociology and computer science thrown in. We started lectures at 8 a.m. and had lectures, labs, and tutorials until 4 or 5 p.m. every day. The zoology teaching was a crammed biology course for medical students. We had some brilliant lecturers, led by the memorable Professor Morton, whose vivid full-colour drawings of frogs and other creatures were carefully prepared on the chalkboard beforehand, and persisted for weeks afterwards, despite the janitor's efforts to remove them (I think Morton must have used wax crayons). He would act out the brachiating of a gibbon, and stand on the table at the front of the lecture theatre and flap his academic gown to demonstrate the flight of a pterodactyl. More importantly he was one of New Zealand's greatest marine zoologists. He had also written a book called *Man, Science and God*, a reflection on his beliefs in the harmony of science (including evolution) and Christianity, for which he was respected, but which I never read.[2]

Marching as to war

During this first year, I was interested in getting other Christians together to meet, study the Bible, and pray regularly. It wasn't stunningly successful. My immature conservatism turned off a number of interested people. But I had one good friend whose attitudes on evolution and creation were the same as mine. As our lecturers explained evolutionary theory throughout their lectures on invertebrate and vertebrate biology, we stood up and questioned the science. We used arguments from Morris and Whitcomb. At first it was relatively benign. The class was asked to write an essay on the origins of life. We were given background reading about the experiments of Stanley Miller who passed electric currents through a biological soup and produced amino acids, and an essay by George Gamow on the seeming mathematical certainty of a random event (like life developing from lightning striking a biological soup) happening given

---

[2] John Morton, *Man, Science and God*, London: Collins, 1972.

enough time. I wrote a very ardent essay dismissing these ideas, and rejecting biological evolution (which was not the topic), using many of the quotations I had gathered. Surprisingly I got an A+ for my essay. However, so did another student who had written in support of a God-guided appearance of life and evolutionary development. No one else got an A+. Such generosity and broad-mindedness of marking was a surprise.

However, as our discussions and arguments with our tutors over the subject continued, some in the zoology department became uneasy. The head of zoology came and talked to us about population biology as an argument to denounce the Bible. He showed us the impossibility of the accounts in Genesis that seventy people went down to Egypt, and that 400 years later (in Exodus) they had 2 million descendants who escaped through the Red Sea. He ignored certain facts in the text, like the Egyptian servants who willingly went with their Israelite families, and the likelihood of marriages outside the descendants of the seventy. However, he preached evolution at us, almost as vehemently as I remember that parent who had preached about creationism at school. After this we felt like we were daily force-fed evolutionary theory until many people were fervently sick of the topic, whether they agreed with it or not.

I don't think I convinced anyone of my ideas during that time, and they hadn't convinced me of theirs. The only person who impressed me and had different views from mine was the other student who got an A+ in that essay. There was a lack of preaching, and a humility about the way she presented her theistic evolutionary views that I respected, even if I didn't agree with her.

All I can remember of zoology after thirty-five years of medicine

My recollections of my thoughts on the subject after that first year are hazy. I suspect that we were sick of the unproductive arguments. Or perhaps the excitement of studying "real" medical subjects – organ-system-based anatomy, physiology, and biochemistry in the second and third year, and learning about real diseases and real patients in the fourth and fifth, and the fully clinical sixth year – eclipsed the controversies about creation and evolution. And yet, what we studied in first-year zoology did not disappear and I am sure it affected my later thoughts.

One of my recollections is Professor Morton's fondness for the amphioxus (or lancelet), a curious creature found (though not uniquely) in certain New Zealand coastal waters. Amphioxus looks a bit like a fish, but it has no backbone. It is therefore an invertebrate, but unlike most invertebrates it has a *notochord*, a rod-like structure that provides support for its spinal cord equivalent along its length. Vertebrates also have a notochord as embryos which develops into part of the backbone during gestation. Amphioxus is a chordate, a group that includes the vertebrates (fish, amphibians, reptiles, mammals, and birds), and only two other groups, tunicates and hagfish. In reality, amphioxus doesn't fit neatly into either invertebrates (it has the forerunner of a vertebral column), or vertebrates (it doesn't have a proper vertebral column). The invertebrate-vertebrate division is (or was) one of the most fundamental in biology, separating creatures with very different form and function, and separating specialists and textbooks – how can a creature sit on the fence between them? Amphioxus ungraciously did not fit neatly into my conception of a "kind" that, according to Morris and Whitcomb, God specially created separately from any other kinds.

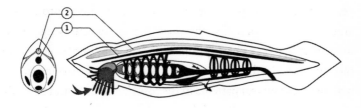

Figure 10.1 Amphioxus or lancelet (Wikimedia Commons). The notochord in the diagram is the dark stripe labelled 1, below the dorsal nerve cord (labelled 2).

Another creature, the axolotl, intrigued me. In its natural state it lives much like a tadpole or amphibian larva all of its life, and it reaches sexual maturity and reproduces in this state. Yet, a stunning thing happens when a little iodine is added to its water; it loses its gills, develops its legs, and crawls out of the water as a salamander. It is a salamander that has developed the ability to reproduce in an iodine-deficient situation, despite not maturing in other ways. Did God create it as a salamander? If so, how did it develop the ability to reproduce as a larva? Did God create it to be a permanent larva? If so, why did He give it the ability to develop into a salamander with a touch of iodine? Lungfish also intrigued me – fish that can survive on land for a period, breathing like an amphibian. There were many strange species in the world that were difficult to box into Morris and Whitcomb's "kinds", that seemed to lie between categories, and that were very odd for God to have specially created. Nor did the Fall or the flood explain them.

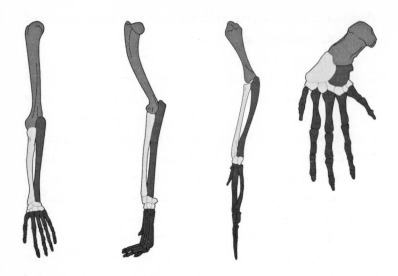

Figure 10.2 Forelimb bones homology. Left to right: human, dog, bird, whale. (Wikimedia Commons)

Among my favourite texts in zoology was Alfred Romer's *The Vertebrate Body* (Saunders, 1978). This cannot have failed to impress me, with its scores of comparisons between different vertebrates of organs and structures. A well-known example is the bones of the forelimbs in amphibians, reptiles, mammals, and birds, which all have the basic structure – one upper arm bone, two lower arm bones, a collection of wrist bones, and five digits, albeit that in animals like the horse, some of the digits are present only in the embryo, or as tiny remnants. Even the limbed fish – coelacanths – have a very similar structure. The book was full of these comparisons – every organ system in the body was considered.

Every zoology student has to dissect creatures, and I found it odd that frogs had a gastrocnemius muscle in their legs, like humans, that we could stimulate to contract with an electric current, and this helped us to understand nerve and muscle activity in humans. In rats, the successive main arteries branched off the aorta in the same order and to the same organs, as in humans. During our pre-clinical years we dissected human bodies, but we also conducted physiology experiments on other animals – in order to learn about human physiology. So structure *and* function in other animals was very similar to that of humans. When we studied biochemistry, the molecular mechanisms of living creatures were even more alike. Insulin, the defining deficiency of diabetes mellitus in humans, was corrected by insulin from pigs, but it is produced by all vertebrates, including fish, and even by amphioxus. In pharmacology we studied not only hormone drugs derived from animals, but also drugs that had been discovered because of their effects on animals, or tested on animals, and then used in humans with the same effects.

It's all very well God sticking to certain patterns, but why did He separately make *each and every one* of the creatures with the same or similar underlying biochemical patterns? Did He not have any more imagination than that?

Although I put the debate aside in my head most of the time, I don't think these uneasy ideas ever left me. Nor did my brother's continuing disdain for creationism diminish; he was, by the end of my pre-clinical years, completing his Master of Physics degree, and was president of the Evangelical Union at Auckland University; there was no sign that belief in evolution had compromised his faith.

The death of Darwinism in South Kensington?

Even by the end of my medical study, however, I remained suspicious of evolutionary biology – I was unwilling to commit to it, even if I was also somewhat uncomfortable with my earlier simplistic faith in creationism. At some stage I came across an article in a science magazine, entitled "Death of Darwinism in South Kensington". It was about a new method being described and used in the Natural History Museum (South Kensington, London) of grouping creatures and fossils (cladistics) using no prior assumptions about evolutionary ancestry, but based simply on the number of shared physical features.[3] Some evolutionary biologists believed Darwin's ideas were being ditched because relationships would be decided without reference to mainstream evolutionary theory. The idea intrigued me. It seemed to be a sensible and unprejudiced method. Would its use damage or confirm belief in evolution?

A child's-eye view

After graduating, and registering, I specialized in paediatrics. I wanted to be prepared to help in the Third World, and I had heard that surgery, obstetrics/gynaecology (O&G), and paediatrics were the most needed specialties in many regions. Although I enjoyed assisting in surgery, it became clear that my eyesight was not good at locating the depth of ligatures that needed cutting deep in an operating field. I was told I had keratoconus – glasses didn't help and contact lenses were not available. O&G did not appeal and required surgical skills too. Paediatrics it was, then. I had already found out how much I enjoyed dealing with children. A common saying around the wards was that physicians (internal medicine specialists) knew everything but cured no one, whereas surgeons knew nothing but cured everyone. The exaggeration reflected

---

[3] Cladistics diagrams (cladograms) have now evolved into a way of displaying the closeness of relationship based on genes or proteins in comparative genetics.

an impression that internal medicine at that stage was more academic than surgery, but involved lots of long-stay patients with chronic incurable diseases such as rheumatoid arthritis, cirrhosis, emphysema, and chronic heart failure. A surgeon would operate and discharge patients quickly. Paediatrics seemed to me to enjoy the best of both worlds – most sick children admitted to hospital get better and go home very quickly, but paediatrics also offered the challenge of a very academic, research-intensive specialty like internal medicine. I started my paediatric training at the end of 1981 and qualified in 1986 (these days it takes another year or two to get through the hoops).

During that time I met my wife, Wendy, who was at that stage training in O&G, and we got married in mid-1984. The busy-ness of our respective training positions during that first six months of marriage caused us to take stock, and in 1985, when I had the opportunity to do elective work, I applied and gained a part-time Medical Research Council Fellowship, taking part in a large survey of asthma in Auckland schoolchildren and comparing their prevalence of asthma with same-aged schoolchildren in NSW, Australia – the first time a cross-country comparison of asthma had been done using the same survey tools. That decision was the major step leading me into the field of respiratory paediatrics. At the same time, Wendy decided that two specialists in one family was going to be too much, and as I was further on with my training than she, she magnanimously gave up her ambitions to be an obstetrician and took a job as a locum general practitioner and continued in that specialty for twenty-five years.

There followed a couple of years as a locum paediatrician and the birth of our first son, and then I did what many New

Zealand people do – got some "OE", or "overseas experience". My wife, our son, and I went to Southampton, England in 1988 for two years of research into asthma.

Virus DNA

My research in Southampton involved identifying viruses during episodes of asthma in children. The MRC Common Cold Research Unit in Salisbury, not far from Southampton, had developed new tests for the otherwise very elusive common cold viruses and wanted a field trial of these tests. Using conventional but laborious viral culture, people had found common cold viruses (especially rhinoviruses) to be significant triggers of asthma, but the numbers were small, and most doctors believed that severe asthma attacks were triggered by allergy. The new technique involved DNA probes for these viruses, and it very quickly evolved with a new-generation technique using PCR (polymerase chain reaction), in which the identifying DNA segments of the viruses that were being sought (if they were present at all) were amplified millions of times, so that the viruses could be traced, even when present in small numbers. Using these techniques, we found that at least 85 per cent of asthma attacks in children were associated with virus infections. More recent studies have not only confirmed this but put the figure above 90 per cent. (The main paper we published has been cited more than 1,400 times by other research articles.) Little did I know then the role that PCR, the technique we had latched onto and found so useful, and related techniques would play in comparative genetics and evolutionary studies, once the human genome project was complete.

While I was in the UK I read a fascinating book by Vernon Blackmore and Andrew Page: *Evolution: The Great Debate.*[4] The book discussed many aspects of evolutionary theory and creationism, including the cladistics affair described above, and showed me that the evolution debate was no simple matter of Christians versus atheists. It also gave me a lot more confidence about the science of evolutionary theory, and a lot less confidence in creationism; the credentials of the latter to speak either for Christianity or about science were severely knocked. I realized that evolutionary biology was not atheistic propaganda, and was not a threat to my faith. In fact, there was more evidence of God's creative power in a system with the potential to develop itself, than in a six-day creative spurt, followed by stasis and then decline.

Very much alive in South Kensington

On our first trip to the Natural History Museum in London, I found myself drawn to and absorbed by an exhibition called "Our Closest Relatives", a display of hominid fossils and palaeontological findings from various parts of the world and lengths of time in the distant past. I found myself face to face with applied cladistics in its home. What impressed me was the lack of preaching evolution – it could not have been more unlike what I remembered of evolutionary biology in my first year at medical school. In each display the viewer was asked: "Which group does this creature most closely resemble? Apes or humans? Apes or Australopithecines? Australopithecines, or *Homo habilis*? *Homo habilis,* or *Homo erectus*? At each point the defining characteristics of the main groups were set out, and the displayed creature often

---

[4] Vernon Blackmore and Andrew Page, *Evolution: The Great Debate,* Oxford: Lion, 1989.

shared characteristics of two groups, or was intermediate between them. Brain size, use of tools, of fire, and respect for the dead, all developed as one moved from creatures that looked more like apes than humans, to creatures that looked more like humans than apes. Moreover, there was a gradual shift of characteristics, not sudden jumps.

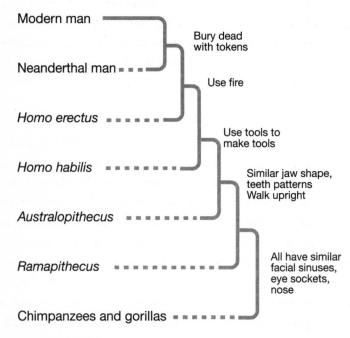

Figure 10.3 Cladistic diagram of hominins, redrawn and adapted, from the display "Our Closest Relatives" in the Natural History Museum, London.

I found myself thinking: "The missing link is not missing at all – there are a myriad of links between apes and humans." It was not the atheistic presentation I expected, but nor did it indicate the "Death of Darwinism".

I cannot place the moment when I started to favour evolutionary biology over creationism, but after seeing this very non-confrontational display there was no doubt in my mind about where I stood.

Did these close similarities, identified by the cladistic tree diagrams, imply shared ancestral relationship, and how would you identify that such relationship was more than just looks? And how did this fit into a solid theological understanding of the origins of humans and the origin of sin? These were questions to which I had no definite answers at this stage.

Meanwhile, back in the Antipodes

In December 1990, we returned to New Zealand, and after a further year as a research fellow in Auckland, I obtained a position in 1992 as Senior Lecturer in Paediatrics in the Christchurch School of Medicine, a clinical school of the University of Otago. Research into asthma was ongoing, but I had to give time to teaching, as course convenor for the Paediatrics module in Christchurch. I was aware since medical school days that I had an ability to digest a complex subject and explain its core features to other people, using familiar analogies. Teaching became a central part of my work. Teaching carried over into church life – I was also asked from time to time to speak on Bible passages or themes at our church. In 2007 I was appointed as Associate Professor in the Paediatrics department, partly on the basis of my teaching experience.

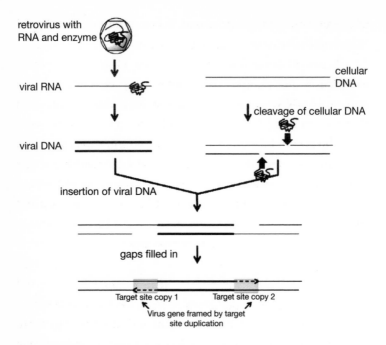

Figure 10.4 Diagram of retroviral DNA insertion (courtesy of Graeme Finlay).

Somewhere around 2002–2003, Graeme Finlay, a friend of my brother, sent me a draft of a booklet he was preparing called *God's Books: Genes and Genesis.*[5] Graeme is a cancer biologist, and studies the genesis of cancers. In the late 1980s and the 1990s, rapid methods of cloning and reading the DNA signature of cells had developed, and it was now clear that alterations of DNA by retroviruses and by jumping genes were common triggers of cells losing control over their growth and reproduction and becoming cancers. What is more, the exact original DNA alteration (e.g. insertion of retrovirus DNA) that caused the cells to grow out of control could be found in every one of the cells of the cancer

[5] It was published as *God's Books: Genetics and Genesis*, Auckland: Telos, 2004.

wherever it grew and metastasized. That unique alteration traced their origins as clones of the original damaged cell.

When Graeme discovered that the DNA signatures of retroviruses and jumping genes were being commonly found in human DNA, and many were not only shared among all humans, but were also found in identical form in the same genes in chimpanzees, he realized that the same thing was going on as in cancers – something equivalent to cloning from a cell that suffered the original event. The events – the retrovirus or jumping gene inserting its DNA into the cell DNA – were haphazard and fairly unscrupulous about which one of the billions of spots in the host DNA they attacked. Like lightning, they were unlikely to strike exactly the same spot twice. Just as in the cancer cells, the retrovirus DNA in our genes demonstrated the ancestral relatedness of all humans. But by the same token it also showed a shared ancestral relationship of humans and chimpanzees. There were many thousands of identical DNA virus or jumping gene insertions in common between humans and chimpanzees and also other apes. Each of these insertions had struck one and only one ancestral cell in the germ-line (a sperm or an egg cell), and had been passed on unchanged to all the descendants of the creature possessing this altered cell. Both humans and chimpanzees were co-heirs of millions of identical, one-off, historical events in their DNA. This was a clear demonstration of their shared history and biological ancestry, but it was entirely independent of Darwin's or anyone else's theory of evolution.

Graeme realized he had a responsibility to tell the church that creationism was on a hiding to nothing. He published the booklet, not only to document these genetic similarities between humans and chimpanzees, but also to document how the description of human origins in Genesis was actually more appropriately orientated to the pre-scientific audience for which it was intended. It was about God and His relationship to humans, which was a concern for all ancient people, not about scientific origins, which are a late development in human thought.

I must confess to not understanding Graeme's ideas very well in his draft, but when I read the printed booklet, it was like a light had turned on. Firstly, there was biological proof of evolutionary relationships. Secondly, there was a much more robust reading of Genesis and the Scriptures as a whole. There was no need for the tenuous swinging of creationist interpretations of Genesis that had to roll and punch with each scientific discovery, furiously reinterpreting, or finding faults in the science, or the scientists, before any Christian was infected with belief in evolution (you can discover this reactionary process still happening in creationist websites).

Graeme showed that Genesis was not a biological design document; rather, it was a polemic against polytheism and paganism (and, by continuing analogy today, with what passes for atheism). Genesis was written to an ancient people to describe their relationship with one God, whereas the other nations worshipped mere objects of God's entire creation – the sun, moon, stars, the sea, and the creatures: "For all the gods of the nations are idols, but the Lord made the heavens" (Psalm 96:5, NIV). This message was the one still relevant today. God is the creator of everything – you don't have to defend God's cause by trying to define which groups were separate kinds, created separately, as though God were a toymaker. The kinds in Genesis were a pre-scientific human method of grouping animals, and had nothing to do with Linnaeus's species, or cladistic diagrams.

Sharing the story of the genes

As Graeme's ideas firmed up in my mind, I wanted to share them with others. Around 2007 some of the young people in our church, about to go to university, were being addressed by a number of people in the church about the significant issues that would face them as thinking and committed Christians. I suggested I talk to them about science, origins, and evolution. I started with my experience in zoology, which I regretted as it was unproductive, confrontational, possibly uncharitable, and not a helpful testimony to the love of God. I then discussed what I had learned, particularly from Graeme's book.

After this talk, I decided I had better discuss with the church what I had been telling their young people. I arranged to give a talk which kept growing, ending up as five talks in all: understanding Genesis, understanding genes (my poor fellow Christians had to do homework to read up about genes and inheritance), understanding common mutations and common ancestry, how we deal with the origin of sin, and how we regard the human soul in an evolutionary context. As I worked through these issues, and read around them, my own ideas further developed. Having survived the end of the series without being stoned, I wondered to whom else I should talk. At that point my older son, Matthew, suggested I write a book. I did – based on the five talks; it is now a self-published book, *Am I My Keeper's Brother? Human origins from a Christian and scientific perspective.*[6]

Insights from the journey

My progression from ardent creationist to what I have called in the book an informed theist (aka theistic evolutionist or evolutionary

[6] Available online at www.amimykeepersbrother.com (accessed 8 July 2014).

creationist) has been a gradual one. As a creationist I was on edge all the time about what beliefs evolutionists might try to force on me or my friends. My faith in God is no longer threatened by evolution or science or, for that matter, creationism. It is settled and steady and sees a much broader and rounder picture of all that God has done and made. In my book I described the difference (for me) between seeing the universe as the creationists describe it, and as science has been discovering it. It is like transforming a black and white image into full colour, a 2-D image into 3-D, a static image into an iMax movie, a mono playback into stereo. It is the difference between an advertisement for a toy universe and the real cosmos.

One of the aspects of creation I continually marvel at, and often remark on to my students, is the development of a human being from a fertilized egg, through embryo, fetus, newborn, infant, toddler, pre-schooler, schoolchild, teenager, and adult. No one questions that this amazing sequence is a path of natural development. Several times in my book I have used this as an analogy of the even more remarkable development of life on this planet from simple beginnings. It helps me to understand how the story of creation can develop naturally, but it makes the tale more wonderful, not less.

As a scientist, I have reviewed many scientific articles and research proposals in my field. I have had to learn to recognize the marks of sound and unsound science and reasoning. As a teacher I have come to recognize the power that teaching has on one's own beliefs – it is easy to "fill-in" gaps in the science in order to explain and give opinion, and then start to believe that the opinion itself is the science. As a doctor I have had to deal with the power of self-styled "experts" who work within a non-scientific, or quasi-scientific framework to treat patients. Distinguishing good science from non-science is not always easy when the latter borrows the language of the former to present its case, but it is a necessary discipline for any who aspire to an honest search after truth – such as I would hope are all scientists and all Christians. The language of so-called scientific creationism today is borrowed from that of scientific researchers, but it appears to me that "research" in this field starts from a theological dogma, and then seeks literature evidence or argument to support its dogma and undermine all other views. Such an approach is not unprecedented among scientists, but I cannot see it as an open-minded search for truth in the spirit of those who joined together to form in London the Royal Society.

I am not talking about the absence of doubt. There are always doubts – whether the source from which you got the information is reliable, whether there is yet another way of looking at things, whether you have missed something crucial. Doubt was there aplenty when I believed in creationism. But doubt is not a threat to faith, but rather a friend. Doubt is there to refine faith, to test it, to rub off the rough corners, to shake what can and should be shaken, to provoke ongoing curiosity, and to prevent the arrogance of believing that I know it all. I certainly do not know the answers to all the theological and scientific mysteries that the universe and the Bible present to us.

My wife and I own a small villa on the beach on the west coast of the South Island of New Zealand, three hours' drive across the Southern Alps from Christchurch where we live. On our regular trips, through the magnificent mountain landscape of snow, ice, rock, shingle, river, and native beech forest, we are in the habit of tuning in to the creative and redemptive work of God by way of listening to tapes of talks by Tom Wright, helping us to a better understanding of the New Testament and the life, death, and resurrection of Jesus, and giving us a renewed interest in the New Testament documents and their robust historical footing. We are on a journey of exploration along with many others, and I hope that along the way we can learn from each other, as well as from the Scriptures with the Holy Spirit's guidance. My goal is God Himself; the snatches that I have already seen of His glory and power in the universe are enough to keep me going along the way.

CHAPTER 11

Evolutionary *Metanoia*

Wilson Poon is Professor of Condensed Matter Physics in the University of Edinburgh, where he researches the properties of colloidal suspensions and the biophysics of bacteria in the School of Physics and Astronomy; he also teaches science and theology in the School of Divinity. He was born in Hong Kong and came to school in Britain in 1979. He was appointed to Edinburgh following an undergraduate degree and a PhD at Cambridge and a brief period as a lecturer at Portsmouth Polytechnic. He has served two terms on the Doctrine Committee of the Scottish Episcopal Church, and currently sits on the SEC's Liturgy Committee. He was elected Fellow of the Royal Society of Edinburgh in 2004, and has been recently awarded a European Research Council Advanced Grant to work on the physics of self-propelled particles.

If you never change your mind, why have one?

Edward de Bono

When I was a child, I spoke like a child, I thought like a child, I reasoned like a child; when I became an adult, I put an end to childish ways.

Paul (1 Corinthians 13:11, NRSV)

Christianity is a religion of "mind changing". Jesus' opening words in Mark's Gospel were, "Repent and believe (*metanoeite kai pisteuete*) the good news!" (Mark 1:15, NIV). Outside the New Testament, the semantic range of *metanoein* and its cognate noun, *metanoia*, encompasses all "changes of mind", whether religious or not. Thus, for example, the words "*metanoeite kai pisteuete*" were used by Josephus the Jewish historian (a younger contemporary of Paul), in his capacity as an agent of the occupying Roman authorities, to persuade a rebel leader to abandon armed resistance and trust in Josephus's way of peaceful coexistence.

In this wider sense, scientific research entails continuous *metanoia*. When J. J. Thomson discovered the electron in 1897, he pictured it as a minuscule billiard ball. Subsequent work, including experiments by his son G. P. Thomson, showed that electrons sometimes behaved as waves. The "father of the electron" had to change his mind about his own discovery quite dramatically. Thomas Kuhn's characterization of such scientific *metanoia* on the grand scale as "paradigm shifts" is well known, but little episodes of mind changing in the laboratory happen daily, triggered by new data and by the continual dialogue between researchers.

This is an autobiographical essay on how one scientist-Christian changed his mind about evolution. It is less a Newmanesque *Apologia* than an Augustinian *Confessions*, less of a justification of why I changed my mind than an introspective reflection of the process of my Christian-cum-scientific *metanoia* about evolution.

Beginnings

I grew up in Hong Kong. Neither of my parents were Christians at that time, but they sent me to an Anglican secondary school because of its academic excellence, and before that, to its feeder primary school and kindergarten. Christianity was a constant but low-key presence throughout. In secondary school, we learned the outline of the biblical narrative (Abraham to Paul) "at face value", without ever discussing whether "it was really so". There were morning assemblies with hymns, prayers, and short homilies. At Easter, there would be an all-school choral service at St John's, the Anglican cathedral. No one, staff or pupil, had to be a Christian. I certainly was not when I began secondary school and started my formal education in science. The curriculum for public examinations was largely "classical": mechanics, heat, light, and electricity (physics), reactions in test tubes (chemistry), and the physiology of the "higher" plants and animals (biology), without any study of evolution.

I can't remember why I decided to get baptized and confirmed during my last year in Hong Kong. I think it was precipitated by my decision to move to America or Britain for further studies. Since both were allegedly Christian countries, I seem to recall wondering (perhaps prompted by someone else) whether I accepted Christianity for myself or not. My precise conclusion is lost in the mist of time. Looking back, I think it was more that Anglican worship had become meaningful to me after prolonged exposure, rather than that I thought Christianity was in some theoretical sense "true"; and, somehow, I realized that if *this* stuff had become meaningful, it required an act of public commitment. I asked my Scripture teacher that year, a practising Christian, what I should do. She pointed me to a baptism and confirmation class at the cathedral, and later became my baptismal sponsor. Her baptismal gift to me, a copy of C. S. Lewis's *The Problem of Pain*, was prescient.

It turned out that a number of my classmates were already Christians, but they practised their faith outside the orbit of "school Anglicanism", which they suspected was mostly nominal. They initially did not quite know how to take the apparent sudden conversion of one of the academically brightest of their peers to the "establishment" version of the faith. Eventually, one of them came to chat to me, and asked me to explain why I sought baptism. After browsing through some of the material I was given to read, I wrote a long essay in reply. It was clearly convincing – I was invited to join their fellowship meetings.

To survive, infants in faith, like biological infants, bond instinctively to those who give them caring attention. While my faith was conceived in the *milieu* of school Anglicanism, it was this group of "non-establishment" Christian classmates who proffered the hand of fellowship at the starting line. I joined them. So from day one, I was introduced to the idea of a "church within the church": among the larger body of professing Christians, only few, an in-group, were the "real McCoy".

From the start, I knew it was *de rigueur* for in-groupers to sign up to having been "born again" (John 3:3), and born-again Christians spoke as if they had direct lines to God: "The Lord guided me to do this." Matters of belief were settled by quoting chapter and verse: "The Bible says so here." Genre, context, plurality of voices, etc. were seldom, if ever, allowed to complicate the literal reading of isolated proof texts. I bought into these "group traits" lock, stock, and barrel, although interestingly, I continued to worship on Sundays at the "establishment" St John's Cathedral.

Some psychologists suggest that the maturing human person passes through a number of predictable "stages". The American theologian James W. Fowler has built on this and constructed a phenomenology of the "stages of faith", most famously in an eponymous 1981 book (from where my quotes are taken).[1] In Fowler's scheme of seven stages (numbered 0–6), the first year of my Christian journey corresponded to stages 0 and 1. Stage 0 is when the (faith) infant instinctively bonds to its primal carers. Of those developing through Stage 1, Fowler says that "[they] can be powerfully and permanently influenced by examples, moods, actions and stories of the visible faith of primally related adults". These were my fellowship group. I have indeed been "powerfully and permanently influenced" by them.

First, I have learned from them that the end of Christian discipleship was to seek and do God's will: "Thy kingdom come, Thy will be done in earth, as it is in heaven" (Matthew 6:10, KJV). Though today I no longer claim that "The Lord has guided me" to do this, that or the other on a day-to-day level, the conviction has grown over the same period that God has called me to a vocation in science. Secondly, I have learned from these friends that Scripture is authoritative. It took a while to understand that "authority" did not absolve me from a responsibility to interpret rightly. Nevertheless, Scripture has remained authoritative for me. Finally, and less helpfully, I was socialized into an in-group mentality, which took many years to shake off.

Toddling into creationism

I left for England in 1979 for two years of pre-university studies at a boarding school. I arrived "ready-biased" against its formal religious apparatus – compulsory chapel run by two Anglican chaplains. So I went looking for an in-group, and found it in the

[1] James W. Fowler, *Stages of Faith: the Psychology of Human Development and the Quest for Meaning*, New York: Harper & Row, 1981.

home of a chemistry teacher, who ran an informal Christian union whose members were also (mostly) "born-again Christians", guided quite directly by God in their daily actions. This kindly teacher introduced me to home-made thick-cut marmalade, the Isle of Mull, and Christian books, of which he had an attic-full. Between the rafters of his house, I discovered that I could actually *think* about my new-found faith, and started devouring Bible commentaries and other theological writings.

At this school, I first encountered vocal opposition to my Christian faith, and was relieved to discover *Evidence That Demands a Verdict* by Josh McDowell[2] in the attic. I was so impressed that I later bought my own copy. Rereading the preface now for the first time in two decades, it is easy to see why I was impressed: "The evidence proving the deity of the Lord Jesus Christ is overwhelmingly conclusive to any honest, objective seeker after truth." Four hundred pages of just such apparently cast-iron evidence follow. I can imagine even now how I must have felt all those years ago as I turned the last page: "game, set, match, Christians".

In the attic, I also discovered books advocating a "biblical science" based on a literal reading of the first eleven chapters of the book of Genesis – creation in six 24-hour days and a subsequent global deluge. These books sent me to Genesis 1–11, which up until then I might never have read – my Scripture education in Hong Kong had started with Genesis 12 (Abraham). Now, a problem and a solution presented themselves simultaneously. Problem: six-day creation, which seemed certain to be ridiculed by unbelievers. Solution: creation science! I was instantly captivated, and soon convinced. I don't think my chemistry

---

[2] Josh McDowell, *Evidence That Demands a Verdict*, San Bernadino, CA: Here's Life Publishers, 1972; revised editions 1979, Milton Keynes: Authentic, 1999.

teacher ever made clear his own position, but neither did he dissuade me from my new-found conviction.

Fowler says of those journeying through Stage 2 that their "beliefs are appropriated with literal interpretations" and that they "will insist on demonstration or proof for claims of fact". My fondness for McDowell and the rapidity with which I was won over by "biblical science" fitted the bill perfectly.

The adolescent creationist

Thus it was that I arrived at Cambridge to read natural sciences in 1981 a convinced six-day Young Earth Creationist. I already knew where to find the in-group: the Cambridge Inter-collegiate Christian Union (CICCU, pronounced "kick-you"), of which I immediately became a member, and later, in my final year, its Bible study secretary. As at school, I combined in-group and "establishment", attending regular services at the college chapel.

I learned much from my time with CICCU. In particular, its weekly "Bible readings", where an invited speaker expounded a passage of Scripture for an hour, were of very high quality and theologically mostly mainstream. Nevertheless, CICCU was certainly an in-group. Members and invited speakers had (and have) to sign a "doctrinal basis". The basic substance of its eleven clauses is unexceptional in the context of traditional Christian belief. However, the black-and-white manner in which some of the points are stated and the exclusive tone of some of the claims render it unpalatable to many in mainstream churches. For this present purpose, clause three is worth quoting in full: "The divine inspiration and infallibility of Holy Scripture as originally given, and its supreme authority in all matters of faith and conduct." The precise meaning of "infallibility" caused much internal debate, but as far as I was concerned, a literal interpretation of Genesis 1–11 simplified matters. I was pleased to discover other creationists within CICCU. We formed a sort of "in-group within the in-group" who prided ourselves on taking clause three more seriously than the others.

My creationist reading during these undergraduate years concentrated on the physical implications of interpreting Genesis 1–11 literally. What would be the consequences for paleoclimatology of a "canopy" (or shell) of water (vapour) around the prediluvian earth? This constitutes the "waters … above the firmament" (KJV) of Genesis 1:7, which rained down in the Noahic flood. Would the dead bodies of the animals and plants destroyed in a violent flood separate out as the waters receded to generate something like the observed fossil column? Two 500-page technically worded tomes on such matters survive on my shelves, alongside two slim, popular creationist critiques of biological evolution.

Through such reading, I extended my understanding of the extent of "bible science", collecting more and more phenomena that allegedly could be fitted into a literal reading of Genesis 1–11. I did little to work out for myself whether any of these "fits" actually stood up to proper scrutiny. In any case, I was largely incapable of making such judgments at the time, partly because of a lack of specialist knowledge, but mostly because I had no idea how to go about making such judgments. My ongoing advanced education in physics did not train me to evaluate rival scientific claims, since we were only supposed to be fed the truth, which was our task to assimilate. So I learned creationism mostly by simply trusting what I was told by the PhD-qualified authors of the books I was reading.

Fowler's Stage 3 represents the adolescence of faith. Adolescence is when youths search for and create personal identities, as they begin to form increasingly accurate impressions of how they look in other people's eyes: "I see you seeing me/I see the me I think you see" (Fowler's couplet). Peers who function as such "mirrors" for the formation of self become "chums". Although the adolescent may feel otherwise, the locus of authority at this stage is external, and resides in the "significant others" in whose eyes the teenager sees reflections of himself or herself, or "in the certified incumbents of leadership roles in institutions". Importantly, the adolescent begins to form a "personal myth", or metanarrative – a "master story" of the stories of his or her past – and learns "to project the forming myth of self into future roles and relationships".

After having Stages 0–2 compressed into three short years, my faith started to catch up with my biology at Cambridge. Biologically, I was a late teenager when I arrived. Here, parts of my faith development moved into Fowler's adolescent Stage 3. Most importantly, I was beginning to construct a "story of stories" about my own Christian journey. I had been quite sure from the start that my scientific vocation was God-given. But the question was, "Why?". Science wasn't exactly on the normal menu of "Christian callings" among any of my in-groups, who tended to think of "vocation" in terms of ordination or missionary work, or failing that, medicine. Now an answer began to emerge: God had led me to a top university for professional training so that I could be a creation science champion! The "story so far" fitted neatly into this scheme, which also gave me a strong sense of where I was going.

This "faith self" emerged partly in the mirror of other CICCU creationist "chums". I did not know them well socially, but our "chumship" (Fowler's term) was expressed in public meetings, where we stuck together to argue with speakers (such as the editor of the present volume) who advocated non-literal interpretations of Genesis 1–11. Interestingly, mainstream CICCU members who were not creationists also fulfilled an important "mirror" function for me as I imagined how they saw me. I seem to remember a creationist "chum" putting it like this: "When they see someone as bright as you believing it, it should make them think again." This I saw as the duty and privilege of "witnessing", and sought to convert others to this position. But, as already noted the locus of authority for my creationism at this time remained firmly external.

These aspects of my faith fitted into Fowler's Stage 3; other aspects remained firmly in Fowler's "mythic-literal" Stage 2. For a start, I was a keen member of an organization whose "doctrinal basis" was couched in the kind of black-and-white language that is a Stage 2 trait. Moreover, Fowler suggests that transition from Stage 2 to 3 is often precipitated by facing up to "conflicts between authoritative stories", quoting as an example "Genesis on creation versus evolutionary theory". I certainly perceived this conflict, but did not face up to it, and remained stuck in literalism, another Stage 2 trait. Fondness for literalism is correlated with a third Stage 2 trait, the "[insistence] on demonstration or proof". I needed some clear-cut thing I could point to and say, "There, that's why I believe in God." To my mind, science was the source of definitive proofs. So, if creation science was valid, then I would have found something for which "God" was the only incontrovertible explanation. This was classic McDowell, but only better (because "scientific"). It was "game, set, match, Christians" again.

Not dealing with a perceived conflict such as "creation/ evolution" meant living with painful "cognitive dissonance", which the educationalist John M. Hull has reflected on extensively in his exploration of the question "what prevents Christian adults from learning?" in a book with that title.[3] Four strategies struck a chord with me: separation, ideological compensation, hardening, and evangelism. I counted myself part of an "in-group" who had separated out from mainstream CICCU to keep alive an uncompromising "biblical faith". Such an in-group compensates for the pain of cognitive dissonance by identifying itself as God's elect, comforting themselves that the elect has always been a minority, or "remnant". Under ideological hardening, "more and more ideas are firmly lodged within the authoritative constellation". I record above how my reading continually extended the range of coverage of "bible science". Hull suggests that these strategies "may become the preparatory step toward a more aggressive form of cognitive dissonance reduction, namely, mission and evangelism". Again, as noted already, I had a strong sense of being a "witness" for creationism during this period. Thus, I graduated with a degree in physics and theoretical physics with all four cylinders of cognitive dissonance reduction firing: it was costly being a creationist!

Jonah's gourd

At the end of the book of Jonah, we read about a bush (translated as a "gourd" in the KJV) that miraculously "came up in a night, and perished in a night" (Jonah 4:10, KJV). My creationism was like Jonah's gourd – it started more or less overnight when I found those books in my chemistry teacher's attic, and then it

---

[3] John M. Hull, *What Prevents Christian Adults from Learning?*, London: SCM, 1985.

faded about as fast soon after I started my PhD: I was no longer a creationist by my second year. Why? Looking back, it is clear that I was a creationist not because I was particularly convinced by one or more creationist claims. I swallowed creationism whole when I first encountered it mainly because it made immediate sense in a particular kind of in-group environment. When that environment disappeared, creationism withered.

I had belonged to in-groups from the beginning in Hong Kong until the end of my undergraduate studies. The in-group that nurtured me through Stage 0 of my faith drew me into a literal, context-free hermeneutic – "the Bible says so", and taught me to expect direct divine agency – "the Lord guided me to do this". Fowler suggests that the "pre-images of God" formed at this stage exercise powerful, because largely subconscious, influence on later faith development. I looked for, and found, an in-group at boarding school in England that continued to offer me a practically-identical faith environment to the one in Hong Kong, but also introduced me to an apologetics of "overwhelmingly conclusive evidence". When the seed of creationism was planted in this context, the gourd came up overnight!

CICCU offered basically the same in-group environment again, but also a context in which I and other creationists could feel that we were doing "just a little better" than the wider in-group in upholding scriptural authority. I needed these layers of "ingroupiness" (amazingly, this word *is* in the Oxford English Dictionary!) to feel safe in a faith whose validity was still based largely on external loci of authority and black-and-white proofs. On the other hand, creationism, which exacted a high price in cognitive dissonance, needed ingroupiness to survive.

This symbiotic complex imploded when I stopped belonging to in-groups. CICCU was essentially an undergraduate organization, and I simply dropped out of it after graduation. I could have kept up the ingroupiness if I continued to attend the city-centre church of my undergraduate days, where the majority of term-time worshippers, the curate and the vicar, and many visiting preachers were current or past CICCU members. Soon after the start of my PhD, however, I moved to St Barnabas, another Cambridge church which was attended by a close friend of mine. The congregation "St B's" at that time were mostly "normal townies".

Interestingly, I had always attended non-in-group congregations like St B's – St John's Cathedral in Hong Kong, and chapel at boarding school and college. But in each of these, I also belonged to an in-group that partly defined itself against precisely such "others". Now I kicked the in-group habit for good, and threw myself into the life of a congregation whose members were secure enough in their own faith that they did not need to define themselves against any "others". This is one of the characteristics of Fowler's Stage 4, when "the self ... now claims an identity no longer defined by the composite of one's ... meaning to others".

No longer protected by an in-group where a narrow understanding of divine agency was bolstered by a particular kind of literal biblicism, the gourd of creationism withered overnight. There was no renunciation ceremony at which I embraced evolution. I only learned evolutionary science much later. For now, creationism simply ceased to matter to me, and was quietly dropped, without any immediate replacement. I simply got on with enjoying the new-found freedom of a non-in-group faith existence: no more thought policing, of myself, of others, and by others. The four cylinders of cognitive dissonance reduction could at last stop firing.

The vicar of St B's, Douglas Holt, became my mentor *extraordinaire*. He drew me into philosophy, i.e. thinking about thinking, which started a long road of exploration into the philosophy (and in parallel, the history) of science. Both explicitly and by the example of his preaching, Douglas also insisted that I think about the meaning of "meaning" (i.e. hermeneutics), an exploration that I had started when I was CICCU Bible Study secretary. Most importantly, Douglas helped me formulate a theology of creation, which became the theological replacement of my former creationism. This led to a more adequate theology of scientific vocation. With Douglas's help, I realized that, wonderfully, the Christian gospel promised the redemption of *the whole of creation*. Ephesians 1:10 says this prosaically, while Revelation 21:24 gives a pictorial version. In his vision of the heavenly city, John saw that "the kings of the earth will bring their glory into it" (NRSV). Given clues from the rest of Scripture (especially Isaiah 60–66), I came to understand this as saying that *all* that was good and true and honourable in human culture would be transformed and gathered into the new creation to add to its splendour. For a faithful creator, this must include all good science (together with Schubert's *Impromptus*, thick-cut marmalade, Mull, and a lot more). A vocation in science does not need to mean championing "creation science".

The end of my PhD coincided with a painful and turbulent period in my personal relationships: God felt very distant, even absent all together. I thought and read a lot about "the problem of suffering" (back to the baptismal gift from my Hong Kong Scripture teacher!). The cross took on a new depth of meaning. It assured me of God's presence with me in my pain. It took a decade, until well after I started lecturing in Edinburgh University, for me to realize that these experiences had broader implications. I came to see how hankering after "overwhelmingly conclusive proofs" for God's presence in the world, which was one of the main motivations for my brush with creationism, was wide off the mark. If the Jewish malefactor crucified on a Roman gibbet was the only-begotten Son of the creator and sustainer of the universe, then this God is unlikely to have made a universe in which explicit reference to Godself is needed at every explanatory juncture. Indeed, as Julian of Norwich so movingly portrayed in her fourth vision, the creator giving independent existence to any creature, even a hazelnut, represents an act of divine self-emptying. Thus, we may expect an enterprise such as modern science to succeed, i.e. humans should be able to give naturalistic explanations of the universe *without* constant recourse to divine agency, if the creator is none other than the God and Father of our Lord Jesus Christ. Much later, someone pointed me to the poetry of R. S. Thomas, which poignantly explores this theme in the context of modern science.

The light of evolution and the weight of evidence

It took ten years for a theological replacement for creationism to emerge; it took just as long to start sorting out the science. I was woefully ignorant of biology in general, and of evolution in particular, when I was appointed to a lectureship in 1990. In Edinburgh, I began researching "complex fluids", liquids containing mesoscopic – "middle-sized" – components such as colloidal particles and long-chain molecules (polymers). Life is "complex fluids come alive"; so I got seriously interested in biology for the first time in my professional career.

One of the first biophysical problems I tackled was protein crystallization. Molecular biologists need to crystallize proteins (a very special kind of polymer) to solve their structures using X-ray diffraction. While it had long been known that most proteins crystallize only reluctantly, no one seemed to have asked why. With a colleague in 2004, we realized that proteins had probably evolved to be difficult to crystallize, since the conditions *in vivo* were precisely those that should be quite favourable for crystallization, but crystallization *in vivo* would almost always mean trouble. This was the first time that I had engaged in evolutionary reasoning, and it got me interested in evolution in a big way, so much so that ten years later, I now find myself studying the evolution of bacterial resistance to antimicrobial agents. In this process, I have learned two important things.

First, I now understand Dobzhansky's aphorism, "Nothing in biology makes sense except in the light of evolution."[4] The answer to practically every "Why?" question I have asked myself about biology is "because it has evolved that way by natural selection". Secondly, evolution gives biology a different texture to physics. In physics, a "smoking gun" reading of progress is often plausible. Newton predicts that the sun's gravitational field shifts apparent stellar positions by half of what Einstein predicts. Eddington saw the larger value; *ergo*, Einstein one, Newton nil. Historians of science dispute the details of this simplistic account, but its flavour is recognizable to all physicists – we like smoking

---

[4] Theodosius Dobzhansky, "Nothing in Biology Makes Sense Except in the Light of Evolution", *American Biology Teacher*, 35 (1973), pp. 125–129; see also Chapter 2 by Emily Sturgess.

guns. Making the case for evolution is different, as Darwin's *Origin of Species* amply illustrates. It is more like prosecuting a murder where there was no smoking gun, and perhaps even the body was missing. The case ultimately convinces not because of a single knock-down argument, but because of the weight of accumulated evidence. If my formal scientific education had schooled me in evolutionary reasoning, I would have understood both of these things, and might not have succumbed quite so easily to creationism.

Putting an end to childish ways

I have interpreted my journey in and out of creationism using Fowler's "stages of faith". For Fowler, faith (with a small "f") is the fundamental human quest for meaning, which develops from birth through predictable stages, though the later stages may become delayed or stunted. This framework is most straightforwardly applied to persons born into (say) Christian homes. Towards the end of *Stages of Faith*, Fowler discusses the interesting, and pertinent, complications that arise with conversion, e.g. when someone with no overt religious beliefs is converted later in life to one of the faiths such as Christianity. Now, growth in Faith with a big "F" (my terminology) intrudes into a quest for meaning in a different faith (small "f") system (say, secularism) that has been ongoing since birth.

Fowler describes six conversion scenarios; the sixth applies to me best: "conversional change that blocks or helps one avoid … faith stage changes". When I left Hong Kong at the age of seventeen, I was probably in Stage 3 faith (small "f") in terms of my overall development, and was poised to move into the young adult Stage 4. Beginning my Christian journey the way I did and meeting creationism at the time I did caused regression in some respects to Stage 2. I got stuck straddling Stages 2 and 3 for a decade. I only started moving again after I became a member of St Barnabas, when I was nearly thirty. Creationism, and the ingroupiness that it fed off, led to a serious delay in "[putting] an end to childish ways" (1 Corinthians 13:11, NRSV).

Most of my explorations described in this chapter have been on the religious aspects of my journey; but in so far as science is a system of meaning, it is also a "faith system" in Fowler's sense. A conventional degree education in physics seems to leave the apprentice scientist *qua* scientist somewhere in Stage 2. That was one of the reasons why my *metanoia* about creationism was so late in coming. My observation is that training in biology, which seems to rely less on a black-and-white "one proof per theory" mentality ("smoking gun") does better – many biologists graduate as Stage 3 scientists. Interestingly, much of the polemics launched on behalf of science against Christianity and other religious faiths seem to me to have come from secularists whose faith straddles Stages 2 and 3, with the most vocal rants betraying an infantile rage from even earlier stages.

Our science education system, with its almost complete neglect of the history and philosophy of science, does almost nothing to help scientists make the transition into Stage 4, which involves critical reflection of one's faith system in the light of other systems. Lord May, in his final (2005) anniversary address as President of the Royal Society, named fundamentalism as one of the main "threats to tomorrow's world". Creationism is part of this threat. Educators who want to play a part in dealing with this threat need urgently to attend to the "faith development" of scientists; but that is another story.

CHAPTER 12

Deliver Us – From Literalism

Paul Thomas is a Norwegian of Somali descent. He was born in Saudi Arabia and attended an Anglo-Indian boarding school in India for ten years. He works in the education sector in Oslo, Norway, having achieved a PhD in Education from King's College London.

I converted to Christianity in 1986 from an orthodox Muslim background. I had an "other-worldly" experience whilst asleep. I met Jesus Christ, and found a completely new impression and understanding of Him. I can't really explain this, but my encounter was entirely compatible with the biblical account. It has defined my life ever since. In the culture in which I grew up, a literal hermeneutic textual tradition goes unchallenged. Presumably linked to this, there is very little support for the theory of evolution in most Muslim countries. In countries such as Tunisia, Egypt, Turkey, Pakistan, and Malaysia, only 15 per cent of people surveyed believe Darwin's theory is "true" or "probably true".[1] They even reject the fact that it should be taught as scientific knowledge.

Brought up in such a tradition, one could say I was predisposed towards the sharp literalist tradition that characterizes Christian creationism. Furthermore, the plethora

---

[1] Salman Hameed, *Science*, 322 (2008), pp. 163–164.

of denominations and lack of consensus on important doctrinal issues in Christianity led to me gravitating towards the certitude and charisma exuded by Christian creationists.

During the early 1990s, I attended a Pentecostal church in Oslo, Norway, presided over by an American missionary from Louisiana. At the time I was in thrall to the creationist teachings of the late Dr Henry Morris and the school of creationist thought that he spawned. To be fair, the pastor did say on a number of occasions that the first chapters of Genesis could not be straightjacketed into any one interpretive template. He was open to the notion that "one day could be a thousand years" in God's timeline, but somehow, those words fell on deaf ears. Looking back, I guess an additional reason for my creationist beliefs was that another Pentecostal pastor from Stockholm, Sweden, with whose church we often had joint meetings, had already been effective in persuading us about a literal six-day creation. It was he who gave me and others in the church creationist literature written by Dr Henry Morris, Ken Ham, Kent Hovind and others, propounding a young earth, literal six-day model as the only possible interpretive schema for understanding the book of Genesis. The glossy magazine of the Creation Research Institute peppered with articles written by scientists with impeccable scientific credentials soon won me over.

It was only gradually, as I read more widely, that I realized that even in Islam there was a tradition of hermeneutic elasticity with respect to issues of origin. My reading of the relationship between Islam and science in the last 1,400 years, and particularly in the contours of the evolution-creation debate, showed that many of the celebrated scholars of the "Golden Age" of Islam such as Ibn Sina, Ibn Rushd, and al-Farabi (and Ibn Khaldun who lived much later) held beliefs that seemed crudely to anticipate modern theories of uniformitarianism and evolution. Significantly, their apparent flexibility in engaging with Greek learning indicated some epistemological openness. For example, al-Jahiz in the ninth century AD wrote: "Environmental factors influence organisms to develop new characteristics to ensure survival, thus transforming into new species. Animals that survive to breed can pass on their successful characteristics to their offspring".

Ziauddin Sardar has argued that the classic Islamic conceptualization of knowledge (*ilm*) should be seen as an inclusive or holistic arena where dialogue takes place with scientists, theologians, philosophers, artists, and others.[2] He suggests that colonialism supplanted this Islamic milieu by imposing modern structures and institutions of society on it, with the aim of establishing a Western hegemony. This squeezing of intellectual space led to Muslims revisiting the question of knowledge and its legitimate parameters. It induced a humiliation and subservience which spawned a defensive "enclave mentality" where knowledge (*ilm*) was narrowed down to religious knowledge alone.

Colonialism with its inherent modernism carved up spheres of knowledge and interaction in the Muslim world, leading to dependence, compliance, and subservience to the colonial powers. Islam historically encompassed the notion of consensus (*ijma*) through dialogue. A new and truncated reading of community (*ummah*) raised the status of religious scholars and thus reduced the consensually produced pool of knowledge from various disciplines. It may be that the earlier democratic tradition became gagged by this hegemonic religious discourse,

[2] Ziauddin Sardar, "Beyond the troubled relationship", *Nature*, 448 (2007), pp. 131–132.

promulgated by the ascendant *fiqh* (school of legal jurisprudence) orthodoxy.[3] Reduced to adjudicating on matters of faith and interpretation of religious texts, this led to the stagnation of the openness advocated by Averroes (Ibn Rushd) in the twelfth century. This reductionism meant the cross-pollination of knowledge characterizing the "Golden Age" of Islam gradually sputtered to a halt. Islam now lacked the earlier status it enjoyed as a viable source of knowledge. It could well be the reason why a majority of Muslims today eschew the notion of teaching evolution in schools. In my own PhD research in London, UK (2009–12), twenty-four of the twenty-five Muslim interviewees rejected the theory of evolution.

This "double-reinforcement" of literalism – by both Islamic and Christian indoctrination – skewed my approach to science. In order to understand why I discarded this view, it is relevant to consider the core tenets of the particular brand of creationism I accepted. They are particularly associated with the late hydraulic engineer Henry M. Morris and his assiduous proclamation of an earth no more than 6–10,000 years old and a literal historical flood (Genesis 6) to account for the physiographic formations of the earth's surface ranging from sedimentation patterns, the fossil record, and the Grand Canyon. Morris is widely considered to be the father of the movement that goes under the name of "creation science".[4] Morris's influence is well-illustrated by a paper written by Stephen Layfield, head of science at the

---

[3] Bassam Tibi, *Islam's Predicament with Modernity: Religious Reform and Cultural Change,* London: Routledge, 2009; Hans Küng, *Islam: Past, Present & Future,* London: Oneworld Publications, 2007.

[4] Morris's best-known work is *The Genesis Flood,* written with the Old Testament scholar John Whitcomb, but he is the author of many other books, including *That You Might Believe* (self-published, 1946), *The Bible and Modern Science* Chicago, IL: Moody Press, 1951; he edited *Scientific Creationism,* San Diego, CA: Creation-Life, 1974.

(UK) Christian city academy Emmanuel College, posted on the Christian Institute website and cited with scorn by Richard Dawkins:

> *In view of the current inclusion of Earth Science into the [earth science] component of the National Curriculum, it would seem particularly prudent for all who deliver this aspect of the course to familiarise themselves with the Flood Geology papers of Whitcomb & Morris. These plainly show the superiority of a catastrophe paradigm over and against the still prevailing orthodoxy of uniformitarianism to explain various topological features of the Earth such as fossilisation, sedimentation, lava flows and magnetic reversals, etc.[5]*

Morris's later books are an *ad hoc* cocktail of literalistic readings of the book of Genesis interlaced with a "scientific" approach tailor-made to buttress "creation science". Building on the flood geology of the early nineteenth-century Seventh-day Adventist geologist George McCready Price, Morris elevated Noah's flood as a *sine qua non* event indispensable to understanding our present world. Such a young earth automatically retires the theory of evolution, according to Morris. Morris founded the Institute for Creation Research (ICR) in 1972 to spearhead the attack against evolution. The ICR has successfully collaborated with the Turkish Department of Education in a joint partnership that continues to this day.[6]

Any serious attempt to get to grips with creation science

---

[5] Richard Dawkins, *The God Delusion*, New York: Bantam, 2006, p. 334.

[6] H. Yahya, *The Evolution Deceit: The Scientific Collapse of Darwinism and its Ideological Background*, London: Ta-Ha Publishers, 1999.

needs some familiarity with the idiosyncratic literalism invested into the global flood catastrophe that transpired in the days of Noah: "For yet seven days, and I will cause it to rain upon the earth forty days and forty nights; and every living substance that I have made will I destroy from off the face of the earth" (Genesis 7:4, KJV).

Morris, aware that current atmospheric conditions would not support a deluge that covered the highest mountain in the span of forty days and forty nights, proposed that "a vast thermal blanket of invisible water vapour" produced a greenhouse effect on the antediluvian world.[7] Such imaginative literalism is germane to an understanding of the mindset of modern creationism. Morris justifies such a water canopy by his inflexibly literal reading of Genesis 1:6: "And God said, Let there be a firmament in the midst of the waters, and let it divide the waters from the waters" (KJV). Creationists such as Ken Ham, Duane Gish, Andrew Snelling, Carl Wieland, and Jonathan Sarfati subscribe to this water canopy theory and use it to explain much about current physiographic phenomena. In their view, the canopy rationally explains the long ages of the biblical patriarchs before the flood. They claim Adam could have lived for 930 years (Methuselah holds the record with 969 years) because the canopy reduced the harmful effects of ultraviolet light and cosmic rays. However, the irredeemably sinful and decadent state of the antediluvian world left God with no other course than to cause this water canopy to pour down torrentially, along with water from subterranean fissures, without respite for forty days and nights inundating the earth and devastating every vestige of dry land. The collapse of the water canopy coupled with the "cleaving

---

[7] Henry M. Morris, *The Genesis Record: A Scientific & Devotional Commentary on the Book of Beginnings*, Grand Rapids, MI: Baker Book House, 1976, p. 191.

asunder" of underground water conduits, resulted in shorter life spans, permanent changes in the earth's atmosphere, and fossils preserved through rapid burial and lithification within no more than 150 days.[8]

I remember uncritically using this pseudo-scientific explanation in Bible studies at our church. Few queried whether there was any evidence for such a "water canopy" and whether the Bible clearly attributes the long lives of the pre-deluge era to this imaginary "water canopy". Morris and his associates had to be considered trustworthy; they were Christians with impeccable academic qualifications. I now interpret all this as meaning that here you have certain men claiming to have "exclusive interpretive rights" to the creation account of Genesis; only atheists and pseudo-Christians would challenge their "God-sanctioned" explanations. It would be some time before I would unshackle myself from their unsteady construction which has nothing to do with the Word of God.

Morris's advocacy of a tight chronology in regard to Genesis is problematic, to say the least. He might claim some expertise as a hydrologist in commenting on the Noahic deluge, but he had no formal theological training.[9] The first and most glaring problem facing creationism is its assumption of the age of the earth. In my early days of fanatic zeal, I remember reading in creationist literature that none of the current methods used to gauge the age of the earth were reliable. Worse still, I was told that there was a "conspiracy" hatched by "evil evolutionists" to conceal the truth of a young earth. It was only when I took the bold leap of reading mainstream scientific literature that I realized the extent to which I had been deceived. I say "bold leap" because I had to overcome

---

[8] Morris (1976), *op. cit.*, pp. 191–205.

[9] Morris (1976), *op. cit.*, p. vi.

an aversion towards reading any literature which contradicted what was considered contrary to our denomination's stance. I vividly recall a Canadian pastor maligning universities as bastions of ungodliness; it made me reluctant back then to attend university. I can still remember the pangs of guilt I felt in reading this "ungodly" material.

Creationist literature is replete with references to the fragile health of Darwin, tacitly implying (with some explicitly stating) that this was divine retribution for inventing a lie which undermined God's credentials as creator. Cautiously I began to read the writings of theistic evolutionists, conscious of the fact that these were maligned by creationists as "sell-outs". I was surprisingly impressed by the humility and erudition in the writings of, among others, Alister McGrath (who later was one of my supervisors at King's College London) and Francis Collins. Darwin himself turned out to be a respectable and modest gentleman-scholar, rather than the monster I was conditioned to eschew. The harsh denunciation of Darwin as the ultimate bad scientist did not fit with the fact that Darwin appeared genuinely perplexed at the notion that his theory should offend the religious sensibilities of anyone. Darwin wrote in the *Origin*:

> *A celebrated author and divine has written to me that*
> *he has gradually learnt to see that it is just as noble a*
> *conception of the Deity, to believe that He created a few*
> *original forms capable of self-development into other and*
> *needful forms, as to believe that He required a fresh act of*
> *creation to supply the voices caused by the action of His*
> *laws.[10]*

[10] Darwin was referring to Charles Kingsley, author of *The Water-Babies* and Regius Professor of Modern History at Cambridge University.

Darwin was no rabble-rouser, and one of the reasons for the long gestation period between his original ideas about natural selection and the publication of the *Origin* indicated a reluctance to stir up any commotion.[11]

It began to dawn on me that one cannot rule out mercenary interests driving the creationist enterprise. Space will not allow me to elaborate on this point, but the fact that some, such as Kent Hovind, who was jailed for ten years for tax evasion, chipped away at the "impeccable" credentials of the proponents of creation science. I soon found out that radioactive isotopes decay at their own characteristic rate which can be known precisely by using a radioactive clock, like potassium argon. Newly solidified crystals in igneous rocks would have potassium-40 but no potassium argon. Potassium-40 decays into argon with the emission of a β-particle. After 1.26 billion years, half the potassium-40 has become argon-40. The potassium-argon ratio enables the age of the rock to be calculated. An array of similar radioactive clocks all converge at roughly the same age for the earth. Uranium-238 decays to lead-208 with a half-life of 4.5 billion years, for example. The very existence of these rocks precludes a young earth 6–10,000 years old.

I mentioned that my pastor was a missionary from Louisiana. Although not a literal creationist himself, many of the preachers invited to our church in Norway were literalists from the Bible belt in the USA. They brooked no opposition to creationism. They operated in a black-and-white world where labels such as "antichrist" and "reprobates" were dished out to anyone or any entity that dared challenge or critique their entrenched views. Once while staying in the house of one such pastor in the USA,

---

[11] R. J. Berry in *Darwinism and Natural Theology*, Andrew Robinson (ed),
Newcastle upon Tyne: Cambridge Scholars, 2012, p. 17.

I was informed that his son, who was then thirteen years old, was home-schooled because the public educational system was "hijacked by communists and evolutionists". What happens to someone who is nurtured in such an environment? Well, for someone like me who fervently desired to be pleasing to the Lord Jesus Christ and win the approval of the leadership and church members, kowtowing to the prevalent discourse was vital.

My final disenchantment and renunciation of "Creationism"

The watershed moment for me came sometime in 1997 when I was advised by a fellow creationist to stop using certain creationist arguments because they were no longer valid. One such "argument", which I was particularly fond of, was what was called "The moon-dust argument". It states that there is a steady amount of intergalactic dust that accumulates on the surface of the moon and other celestial bodies. It follows from this that if the universe was millions of years old, then the Apollo astronauts should have literally sunk into the moon's surface. However they did not, providing a "fireproof" argument for a young earth – so says the creationist. Imagine my horror at being told that this argument no longer holds water.[12] Ken Ham, in particular, unabashedly travels the globe preaching the inviolability of creation science. In his reckoning, any deviation from creation science is tantamount to apostasy. What happens, then, when what was propagated as "Gospel Truth" suddenly is abandoned as error? And how many more of these "errors" are creation scientists concealing? In fact, the website Answers in Genesis keeps a list of these errors. I realized that these people, despite

---

[12] http://www.answersingenesis.org/articles/cm/v15/n4/moon-dust-argument (accessed 9 July 2014).

eagerly touting their PhDs and assuring us of their Christian integrity, were actually doing untold damage to the Christian faith. Paradoxically, the very same Scripture that they would often invoke against anti-creationists was being fulfilled in them: "O Timothy, keep that which is committed to thy trust, avoiding profane and vain babblings, and oppositions of science falsely so called: Which some professing have erred concerning the faith" (1 Timothy 6:20–21, KJV).

A fetish-like obsession with reading literally the creation account in Genesis characterizes the US creationist movement. This literalist lens did not emerge in a vacuum but was informed by the theological debates of the preceding centuries. The rise of liberal theology mobilized some Christians to adopt a siege mentality where in-group versus out-group boundaries were sharply defined. Liberal theology piggybacked on modernity and was perceived as a subversive juggernaut seeking to destroy Christianity. Of the influential four Princeton theologians (Archibald Alexander, Benjamin Warfield, and the two Hodges), Charles Hodge (b. 1797) is considered a main begetter of twentieth-century fundamentalism. He vehemently condemned the teachings of Schleiermacher as having an insidious and devastating effect on Christianity. Interestingly, despite the main objective of the fundamentalists being to restore Protestant orthodoxy through insisting on scriptural inerrancy, infallibility, and inspiration, Hodge and his successor, Benjamin Warfield, appeared to be positively disposed towards evolution. Baptist theologian Roger Olson put it:

> *It comes as a surprise to many people that neither*
> *Hodge nor Warfield found Darwin's theory of evolution*
> *particularly threatening to Protestant orthodoxy. In fact,*

Warfield studied biology in his undergraduate education and always considered himself a believer in evolution. Of course, together with all other conservatives they opposed naturalistic evolution and considered evolution true – and if true, a means God used in creation.[13]

Augustine, respected by many even in the Pentecostal camp, struggled with the creation account. He urged caution in interpreting Genesis literally. He did not perceive the creation as a static, one-time event, but saw God active in creation. Regrettably, the views of Augustine or Calvin with regards to the Genesis account of creation were never raised or discussed.

London University psychologist Peter Herriot describes "fundamentalism as by definition a modern phenomenon, because it is reacting against modernity". In his view, it has five distinguishing features, be it Christian, Islamic or Jewish. The first is a *reactive* mindset which perceives that the chief aim of secularism is to undermine religion. The next four are offshoots of this: a *dualist* worldview that tends to dichotomize all phenomena; the centrality accorded a *holy book* that supersedes all authority; a *selective exegesis* of that holy book as a mechanism to engage hostile forces; and a *millennialist* view of world events, often featuring an apocalyptic showdown between the forces of good and evil.[14] Undoubtedly, my literalist views were shaped in an environment where all the above ingredients were strongly active.

Although the large majority of responses in the Muslim world have been dismissive, the twentieth-century philosopher

---

[13] Roger E. Olson, *The Story of Christian Theology: Twenty Centuries of Tradition and Reform*, Downers Grove, IL: IVP Academic, 1999, p. 560.

[14] Peter Herriot, *Religious Fundamentalism: Global, Local and Personal*, London: Routledge, 2009, p. 2.

and national poet of Pakistan, Muhammad Iqbal, was fascinated with Darwin's theory. To him, the prophet Muhammad was the perfect prototype of humanity and the goal of every Muslim is to attain to his stature. Grounding his acceptance of evolution in the Qur'an, he felt it furnished an excellent framework to conceive of humankind's evolution towards perfection. For Ehsan Mahood:

> *There is nothing more alien to the Qur'anic world than the idea that the Universe is a temporal working-out of a pre-conceived plan; an already completed product, which left the hand of its maker ages ago and is now lying stretched in space as a dead mass of matter to which time does nothing.*[15]

These views parallel those of Christian theistic evolutionists who speak of a *creatio continua* to describe the manner in which God's creative power imparts "openness to the future that releases the present from bondage to past causes".[16]

Iqbal, a disciple of the Sufi mystical Qadiri Order and a devotee of Wali Allah, did not shy away from challenging the *status quo*. Rather than extol God for designing a perfect world with man as the pinnacle of creation, Iqbal penned poems petitioning God to perfect His imperfect creation:

> *Design a new pattern*
> *Create a more perfect Adam*
> *This making of playthings of clay*
> *Is not worthy of God, the creator*

---

[15] Ehsan Mahood, *Science & Islam*, London: Icon Books, 2009, p. 184.

[16] Ted Peters and Martinez Hewlett, *Can You Believe in God and Evolution? A Guide for the Perplexed*, Nashville, TN: Abingdon Press, 2006, p. 123.

If the pattern is poor
What does repetition achieve?
How can the cheapness of man
Meet your approval

Implicit in this lament is an acknowledgment of the flawed nature of design as Iqbal understood it.

My journey from blinkered literalism to a more flexible and open approach grounded in science taught me some important lessons. To begin with, we as Christians need to be more aware of and sensitive to the kind of church environment many of our fellow-Christians are moulded in, in order to help them. My faith in the Word of God and participation in church life has only grown and flourished since I discarded the narrow views imbibed in the early 1990s. Sadly, however, I have left behind many who have been indoctrinated to believe that creation science is a cornerstone teaching in the Bible. They equate being a Christian with upholding the tenets of creation science. Anyone who contradicts a young earth paradigm is considered apostate. Faced with such attitudes, I try to practise 1 Peter 3:15, "But sanctify the Lord God in your hearts: and *be* ready always to *give* an answer to every man that asketh you a reason of the hope that is in you with meekness and fear" (KJV, my italics).

In the spirit of true Christian love, we must avoid name-calling and employing some of the other tactics all too common in debates between evolutionists and creationists. I often ask myself how would Jesus deal with this, before I delve into such discussions. It is possible to win the debate but lose the soul. As an adherent of creation science I was told that all evolutionists were avowed atheists. I was not made aware that there were scholars such as John Polkinghorne, Richard Swinburne, Francis Collins, John Lennox, Alister McGrath, and many others, who felt no conflict in believing in a God who was not limited to one possible understanding of His work in creation. Surely, as long as Christians pray for guidance, knowledge, and grace, the Holy Spirit will guide us all.

CHAPTER 13

How an Igneous Geologist Came to Terms with Evolution

Davis A. Young, PhD was educated at Princeton, Pennsylvania State, and Brown Universities. He taught geology at New York University and the University of North Carolina at Wilmington and then at Calvin College for twenty-six years, retiring as professor emeritus in 2004. In 2009, the Geological Society of America presented him with the Mary C. Rabbitt Award for "Fundamental Contributions to the History of Geology". Among other books, he is the author of *Creation and the Flood* (Baker Book House, 1977), *Christianity and the Age of the Earth* (Zondervan, 1982), *The Biblical Flood* (Eerdmans, 1995), *Mind Over Magma* (Princeton University Press, 2003), *The Bible, Rocks and Time* (IVP Academic, 2008), and *Good News for Science* (Malius Press, 2012).

Childhood

I had the great privilege of being born into the family of the eminent Bible scholar Dr Edward J. Young and his wife, Lillian. They were humble, godly, consistent parents who taught me to trust Jesus Christ as my Lord and Saviour and instructed me in the truths of the Christian faith. They modelled the Christian life in an exemplary manner. My father was a professor of Old Testament at Westminster Theological Seminary in Philadelphia from 1936 until his death at the age of sixty in 1968. He was widely regarded as one of the leading conservative Old Testament scholars of his era. He was also an ordained minister of the Orthodox Presbyterian Church, a small conservative denomination born out of the modernist-fundamentalist controversies of the 1920s and 1930s. I grew up under the potent spiritual influence of these two great Christian institutions.

I developed a strong interest in God's creation. I loved stars and birds, and enjoyed the outdoors. When I was twelve years old, a church friend showed me a small mineral collection that had just been given to him. It included beautiful crystals of zeolites, such as stilbite and chabazite, and associated minerals, such as prehnite and apophyllite, that had formed in cavities of the Mesozoic lava flows of northern New Jersey. I was so captivated by the exquisite specimens that I immediately determined to spend my life studying minerals. I began collecting specimens of staurolite, kyanite, almandine garnet, and tourmaline from the Wissahickon Schist, a formation that crops out in the Philadelphia area. En route to San Francisco that summer with my family, I collected rocks from where they were exposed at the roadside and made modest purchases at rock shops.

Arthur Kuschke, the librarian at Westminster Seminary, loved birds, trees, and fossils. He encouraged my growing enjoyment of God's creation. In talks at our church, he advocated an old earth although he resolutely opposed evolutionary theory. He pointed out changes through time in organisms preserved in the fossil record, but insisted that the changes were limited. Thus trilobites lived from the Cambrian through Permian Periods before becoming extinct, yet these organisms remained trilobites

231

despite dramatic changes. During my teen years, Kuschke introduced me to an extended debate, pro and con evolution, in a book by Donald Dewar and H. S. Shelton, *Is Evolution Proved?* (Hollis & Carter, 1947). I predictably accepted Dewar's creation-orientated arguments.

My father's specialty was Old Testament exegesis, especially Isaiah, Daniel, and the early chapters of Genesis, a subject on which he wrote much. He rejected biological evolution in any form as incompatible with Genesis, although he consistently claimed that Genesis 1 does not determine the age of the earth. He was never dogmatic about the length of the six days of creation. Although granting that the days might represent much longer periods of time than twenty-four hours, he still harboured suspicions about the claims by geologists that the earth is millions of years old.

The result of all this was that I believed in the infallibility of the Bible, trusted Jesus Christ for my salvation, did not accept a rigidly literalistic view of Genesis 1, and was comfortable with a very old earth. On the other hand, I rejected biological evolution. I assumed that all evolutionists were either "liberals" or outright enemies of the Christian faith.

Higher education

At Princeton I majored in geological engineering, in a programme that was heavily weighted with chemistry, physics, and mathematics. I was especially enamoured of igneous and metamorphic petrology, mineralogy, and geochemistry. I learned about radiometric dating and readily accepted the evidence that the earth was billions of years old. During my junior and senior years, however, I attended two lectures to the Princeton

Evangelical Fellowship – to which I belonged – by Princeton alumnus John C. Whitcomb, Jr., of Grace Theological Seminary. Whitcomb and civil engineer Henry Morris had just (1961) published their blockbuster book, *The Genesis Flood*. Perhaps because I had not taken a stratigraphy course, I responded sympathetically to their approach to geology and their claim that Noah's flood was a global deluge which had been responsible for depositing most of the world's fossiliferous sedimentary rocks. In retrospect, this was a bizarre conception of earth history I was accepting: a world full of crystalline Precambrian rocks, billions of years old, overlain by strata laid down by a global deluge only a few thousand years ago. Whitcomb and Morris were diehard anti-evolutionists; *The Genesis Flood* did nothing to dissuade me from the same conclusion.

I retained this peculiar view during my early years in graduate school. While working on my master's degree at Pennsylvania State University, I concentrated entirely on mineralogy, geochemistry, and igneous and metamorphic petrology – not to mention the pretty young undergraduate who later became my wife and mother of my three children. There were no pressing reasons to rethink flood geology or evolution.

For a PhD degree in geological sciences, I went on to Brown University in Providence, Rhode Island. Although I concentrated on petrology I began to study the regional geology of the north-eastern United States including the Appalachian Mountain chain. Questions about the Whitcomb-Morris theory began to arise in my mind. The implausibility of the global flood view was forced on me from the drives my new bride and I used to take on the interstate highway connecting Providence with the Philadelphia area. The Connecticut segment of that highway exposes an abundance of Paleozoic metamorphosed sedimentary rocks thousands of feet thick. These rocks are younger than the Precambrian basement and some even contain deformed fossils. On the Whitcomb-Morris global flood theory they would have first been deposited on the Precambrian basement as sand, silt, mud, and calcium carbonate and then later converted into metamorphic rocks at the high temperatures and pressures existing a few miles beneath the surface. It dawned on me that a pile of sediment and sedimentary rock, thousands of feet thick, would not be buried a few miles beneath the surface within a mere few thousand years. To make matters worse for the flood theory, the deeply buried rocks would also have had to undergo radical mineralogical changes and then return to the earth's surface by erosional removal of thousands of feet of overlying rock, another very lengthy process. My enchantment with the flood theory evaporated as my continued graduate school study of the geology of many parts of the globe led me to realize that sedimentary rocks everywhere are full of features incompatible with a global flood. I also realized that the intrusion of great masses of granitic magma in the Sierra Nevada, the Andes, Japan, and elsewhere, into existing stacks of (metamorphosed) sedimentary rocks, well beneath the surface, demolished the young earth and global flood theories, simply because of the amount of time required to cool and crystallize huge volumes of magma at depth prior to uplift and exposure at the surface as igneous rock.

But I still remained a resolute anti-evolutionist, encouraged in this by the fact that I took no palaeontology courses and was not formally exposed to evolutionary theory during my graduate school career. I had no cause to change my views.

Professional career

My professional career began at New York University (1968–73). While there I completed my doctoral dissertation and received my PhD degree from Brown in geological sciences in 1969. Along with a growing family, an increasingly active church life, and professional obligations, I began to think more seriously about the bearing of Christianity on geology, and started working on a book that offered an extended critique of Young Earth Creationism, flood geology and theistic evolution. *Creation and the Flood* was published in 1977.

My rejection of evolution remained unchanged during my five years at New York University followed by five years at the University of North Carolina at Wilmington. Virtually all of my upper-level classes were related to mineralogy, igneous and metamorphic petrology, and geochemistry. My technical reading overwhelmingly concerned those disciplines; my research focused on the igneous and metamorphic rocks of the New Jersey Highlands.

I had long been interested in teaching at a Christian college, and in 1978 I accepted a position to teach and develop a geology programme at Calvin College, a Christian liberal arts college in the Reformed tradition located in Grand Rapids, Michigan. I taught at Calvin for twenty-six years and retired in 2004. My thinking on evolution changed during those years. The intellectual environment exceeded what I had encountered in the secular universities. Calvin strongly challenged its faculty members to develop and teach distinctively Christian approaches to their disciplines. In practice this that meant that the academics needed to be experts in their specialties but also capable of incorporating theological, philosophical, and historical insights. My readings and conversations broadened considerably, and no longer did I think only about mineralogy and petrology.

At Calvin College, historical, biblical, palaeontological, biogeographical, and biological factors converged to draw me towards acceptance of biological evolution. Most of these factors were in play concurrently. No one of them dominated the others in reshaping my thinking. I experienced no saltatory "aha" moment in which evolution suddenly made sense; my intellectual evolution was gradualistic.

Historical inputs

During the 1970s I became intrigued with the history of science, and especially the history of the relationship between Christianity and geology. I began investigating the ways in which Christian scholars related geological history to Scripture and theology. Great Presbyterian academics, such as Princeton theologians Charles Hodge, Benjamin B. Warfield, and J. Gresham Machen were revered in my home, at Westminster, and in the Orthodox Presbyterian Church. I was curious to learn what these Princeton theologians thought about the age of the earth and was gratified to find that none of these impeccably orthodox theologians accepted the literal 24-hour-day view of Genesis 1 or held to a 6,000-year-old earth. What really made my jaw drop was discovering that both Warfield and A. A. Hodge (one of Charles's sons) were open to biological evolution! Warfield, especially, penned several articles and book reviews in which he typically gave favourable press to evolution, provided it was carefully formulated in a way that protected divine providence and guidance. Warfield's article on "Charles Darwin's Religious Life" made a huge impression on me, because the author drew an appreciative and compassionate sketch of the great naturalist's life, even while acknowledging with regret Darwin's inability to commit himself to Christianity. I read with astonishment David Livingstone's book, *Darwin's Forgotten Defenders* (Eerdmans, 1987), and James Moore's book, *The Post-Darwinian Controversies* (Cambridge University Press, 1981), both of which described the fact that several orthodox theologians, including James Orr, James McCosh, and the Princeton men, accepted evolution to varying degrees. I learned that Asa Gray, Darwin's botanist friend and correspondent, was both a devout Calvinistic Congregationalist and an evolutionist. William Berryman Scott, a Princeton palaeontologist and grandson of Charles Hodge who grew up in the great man's house, was also a committed evolutionist. What is more, I found that the great majority of contemporary Christian biologists and palaeontologists accept evolution as a valid scientific theory. It sunk in that there must be a high degree of evidential legitimacy to the theory that is otherwise so despised in modern evangelical circles.

Original sources

My interest in the history of science further led me to read what Darwin actually wrote. I read *On the Origin of Species*, *The Voyage of the Beagle* and *Geological Observations on South America*, and then *The Descent of Man and Selection in Relation to Sex*. I came away from Darwin's works with two impressions. First, I was in awe of Darwin's ability to marshal a huge mass of evidence from so many directions. He came across as a brilliant, thorough scientist whose expertise encompassed geology as well as natural history. Second, a reading of his works dispelled the notion that Darwin was a rabid atheist ideologue. He struck me instead as suffering from a philosophical and theological naïveté that led him to draw unwarranted metaphysical conclusions from his science. Indeed, Darwin explicitly disavowed being an atheist. Recently I read most of Alfred Russel Wallace's exhaustive biogeographical tome on *Island Life* (Prometheus, 1997 [1880]). It pays to read the original sources!

Biblical studies

Another influence came from biblical studies. The last few decades have seen growing awareness among evangelicals of the relevance of the ancient Near Eastern setting for the composition and interpretation of the Old Testament. We have learned that ancient Israel shared many beliefs about the constitution of the world with their neighbours. It has become clear that Genesis was written in a culture that did not have the same conceptions about the physical world that we do. Bluntly, Genesis 1 was not written to address the issues that are of such great interest to modern science. We are barking up the wrong tree in attempts to extract scientific information from the biblical text; that was not its purpose or intent. Every attempt to do so has failed. The primary intentions of Genesis 1 are to underscore the sole creative activity of Yahweh in contrast to the cosmogonies and beliefs of the heathen nations that surrounded Israel, to emphasize the divine satisfaction with and goodness of creation, and to highlight the image-bearing status of the human race. Understood in this way, Genesis 1 neither addresses nor answers questions about biological evolution, although Scripture emphatically excludes any atheistic, deistic, or pantheistic framework in support of it.

The fossil record

The primary factor in my intellectual transition has probably been increased by acquaintance with fundamental data consistent with evolution in three general areas: palaeontology, biogeography, and molecular biology. As I became more familiar with the fossil record, I began to appreciate the force of the palaeontological evidence for evolution, including transitions within mammalian lineages such as rhinoceroses, horses, and titanotheres, and transitions from fishes to amphibians and reptiles to mammals.

One example that powerfully influenced me concerned modern and fossil Cetaceans. During my student days, the evolutionary history of whales was an enigma, owing to lack of direct fossil evidence. Later on, DNA studies lent credence to the idea that whales are distantly related to hippopotamuses. From my Calvin College colleague, palaeontologist Ralph Stearley, I learned of a wealth of relatively recent finds of various primitive Cetaceans from Tertiary deposits in Pakistan and Egypt. The various fossil remains indicate a remarkable progression from a land-based tetrapod. I learned that modern-day whales possess tiny vestigial hind leg bones that are no longer attached to the pelvis. The fossils show a progressive "migration" of the nostrils from the front of the skull in primitive Cetaceans to their position as "blowholes" on top of the skulls of modern whales. But there was more: University of Michigan palaeontologists have been active participants in field expeditions to search for primitive fossil Cetaceans. With a PhD degree in vertebrate palaeontology from the University of Michigan, Stearley knows the palaeontology staff and arranged some visits for our students to the university's palaeontology museum. There they were, on display – mounted skeletons of primitive Cetacean fossils, showing longer hind limbs and nostrils more forward on the upper part of the face! The museum visit included a special tour of the fossil preparation laboratory where we witnessed the painstaking procedures involved in extracting and preserving ancient Cetacean remains. I could not have asked for more impressive evidence of the transformation of a quadruped adapted to land into modern whales.

The discovery of *Tiktaalik* in the Devonian strata of Ellesmere Island in 2004 ranks as one of the most significant fossil discoveries of all time. The first known fossils of *Tiktaalik* were discovered as a result of a deliberate search for rocks of the precise age in which a transitional form between fish and amphibians would most likely be found. The search team discovered partial and nearly complete skeletons of a creature that had a fishlike body with scales coupled with an amphibian flat head with a movable neck. The webbed lobefins contained primitive upper arm, forearm, and wrist bones. In short, *Tiktaalik* possessed both fish and amphibian characteristics. It was a clear example of an intermediate form of the sort predicted on the basis of evolutionary theory.

Knowledge of the fossil record of birds has benefited from several excellent finds in recent years. Unlike modern birds, the earliest birds, such as *Archaeopteryx*, possessed long tailbones, small sternums, and teeth. The fossil record shows that the avian tailbone diminished in size over time in fits and starts until we arrive at the modern birds that lack tailbones. Likewise birds lost their teeth over time. The astounding discoveries of several species of small *feathered* dinosaurs in north-eastern China during the last two decades strongly corroborate the view that *Archaeopteryx* shared common ancestry with theropod dinosaurs. These Cretaceous fossils indicate that the development of feathers was already established among the dinosaurs. Indeed, dinosaur fossils have been found with several stages of feather development.

Finally, I would mention that recent finds have revealed invertebrate forms from the so-called "Cambrian explosion" (which was several million years long) that demonstrate transitional characters between the modern-day phyla, suggesting that the phyla of today are descended from common ancestors.

Biogeography

As an avid birder, I also began pondering the significance of the geographical distribution of birds and other animals during two visits to the Hawaiian Islands. The endemic Hawaiian birds are primarily honeycreepers (Drepanids), most of which are specific to particular islands or even to restricted portions of single islands. The great majority of honeycreepers, such as the three species of amakihi (common, Oahu, Kauai), anianiau, akekee, akiapolaau, alauahio, and Hawaii creeper, are remarkably similar tiny yellow birds. It struck me as odd that God did not create greater avian variety in the Hawaiian Islands had he in fact created these birds directly. Moreover, the only endemic mammal species on any of the Hawaiian Islands is the Hawaiian hoary bat; there are no endemic land mammals. All the mammals present today (mongoose, cat, rat, pig, etc.) were introduced by humans. Why did God not directly create any mammals in the islands? The introduced ones seem to be doing fine. Why are there no endemic snakes or amphibians in the islands?

The problem of geographical distribution is, of course, global. Why are marsupials (and fossil marsupials) largely confined to Australia? And why does Australia have extremely few placental mammals? Why are hummingbirds and tanagers restricted to the Americas and conversely, why aren't we privileged to see rollers, bee eaters, and hoopoes in the Americas? Such dabbling in biogeography, especially in light of tectonic plate movement throughout geologic time, led me to see that animal distribution is explained more effectively by such factors as dispersion, isolation, and speciation by natural selection than by direct divine creation. Such matters, of course, were addressed with great insight long ago by A. R. Wallace. I have found his book on *Island Life* and Ian Newton's much more recent (2003) tome on *The Speciation and Biogeography of Birds* (Academic Press) to be very illuminating and full of evidence that makes sense in light of evolutionary development.

Molecular biology

Although paleontological and biogeographical evidence was more than sufficient for me to come to grips with evolutionary theory, the striking evidence from molecular biology has been a clincher. Complete or partial genomes of a wide range of organisms have made it possible to piece together ancestries and relationships and genealogical trees that are generally consistent with the paleontological evidence. I am eagerly looking forward to learning more about the world of DNA!

What about *Homo sapiens*?

Finally, it seems to me that hominid fossils, cultural artefacts, and the genomes of great apes and humans are all consistent with an evolutionary origin for the human body. Should growing evidence reinforce the evolutionary explanation of human origins, ongoing discussion about the status of Adam and Eve and of original sin will become ever more urgent. Many evangelicals who have accepted an evolutionary origin for humans seem to be prematurely eager to discard the traditional orthodox view of original sin, and in its place leave us with a very weakened concept of sin. If our sinful nature cannot be traced back to a founder who represented the human race, then how do we account for sin? Many writers seem content to maintain that even without Adam, we are all sinners anyway who need to be and can be cleansed of our sin by faith in Christ. But we are not given a satisfactory alternative explanation for why we are all sinners. We are often left with either a hint or explicit assertion that our sinful nature is due to our evolutionary past. But if that is the case, and if we consider that God created plants, animals, and humans through evolutionary pathways, then we are perilously close to asserting that the creator is the author of sin. He created us in such a way that we would inevitably sin because we had no real choice. We must not go there.

We should be very cautious in trying to reconcile human evolution with the doctrine of original sin. For now I think it best to hold these two beliefs in tension without forcing a "reconciliation" at the expense of Christian orthodoxy. Quantum theory and the theory of relativity are in tension, but neither has been abandoned. Divine sovereignty and human freedom are also in tension, but hopefully most Christians don't abandon either doctrine.

Much remains to be learned about evolution. After all, the field of molecular biology is yet in its infancy. Given that evolution is a grand sweeping theory for the existence, characteristics and behaviour of millions of modern and extinct species of organisms, there are bound to be glaring lacunae in our knowledge. That said, it is clear to me that God has seen fit to employ evolutionary processes to bring His creatures into being. Now that I have a better grasp of the theory of evolution and its supporting evidence than I did fifty years ago, I stand in greater awe of our creator God, who, it would seem, has devised a stunningly ingenious, imaginative process for creating the millions of diverse organisms that make our world a source of endless delight and fascination.

CHAPTER 14

What Does Christ Have to Do with Chemistry?[1]

David A. Vosburg is an Associate Professor of Chemistry at Harvey Mudd College (HMC) in Claremont, California; a Henry Dreyfus Teacher-Scholar; and a Fellow of the American Scientific Affiliation. He earned a BA in chemistry from Williams College and a PhD in organic chemistry from The Scripps Research Institute. He joined the faculty at HMC in 2005 following a postdoctoral fellowship at Harvard Medical School. His research focuses on synthetic organic chemistry, medicinal natural products, green chemistry, and the relationship of science and Christianity.

My college pastor once asked me, "What does Christ have to do with chemistry?" He was encouraging me to see how my faith might inform my intention to pursue a PhD in chemistry, and also how my understanding of chemistry might enrich my faith. I did not have an answer for him, but the question lingered in my thoughts for several years.

---

[1] A shorter form of this essay first appeared as "The Personal Journey of a Faith-filled Scientist" in the Fall 2013 issue of *The Claremont Ekklesia* (http://claremontekklesia.wordpress.com/, accessed 15 July 2014).

Avoidance

I grew up in a Christian family in the US, and when I was seventeen I decided I wanted more than just going to church and keeping a good moral code. By that point, I had read through the entire Bible and adopted an attitude that the universe and earth were both very old, but that the Bible was otherwise to be read in a fairly straightforward, historical sense. I could be considered a passive Old Earth Creationist. I say passive because neither creationism nor evolution came up in my church, and I do not recall any teaching at all on evolution in my schools in Tennessee and Texas. Indeed, the dissections of frogs and cats in my high school biology class (combined with a very unpleasant memory of dissecting grasshoppers as a child) were enough to dissuade me from taking an advanced biology class, or even any biology courses as an undergraduate. I avoided biochemistry because my friends said it relied mainly on memorization, never mind having a prerequisite of introductory biology. My distaste for biology heightened in college with my chemistry professors' assertion that biology was soft, weak, and non-quantitative. I actively participated in the chemistry department's volleyball and basketball games against the biology department, and I internalized this seemingly fundamental disciplinary rivalry. For me, it was not chemistry *and* biology, it was chemistry *or* biology.[2]

As an undergraduate at Williams College in the mid-1990s, I kept my science and my faith separate – not because it had to be that way, but because I did not know how to integrate them. I had not read deeply into issues at the intersection of science and faith, but I was uncomfortable with the perspectives that I

[2] Of course, I had several Christian friends who were biologists, but if they were wrestling with the integration of biology and faith, they did not draw me into those conversations.

had heard – which tended to be either suspicious of science or dismissive of biblical faith. Neither resonated with me, so I tried to ignore both perspectives. As I had only recently claimed Jesus as my own Saviour, I was protective of my faith and sought to avoid areas of potential conflict.

Such evasion could easily have led me to give up my love for science or to abandon my faith. Indeed, if I had been by myself, I might well have followed one of those paths, at least for a time. But I had a group of close friends in the Christian Union[3] (some of whom were scientists) with whom I felt a common identity and purpose. We talked, played, and prayed together. They rejoiced with me, consoled me, and forgave me. Through them I felt God's wonderful love and grace, which sustained me. I thank God for that.

Perhaps I benefited from being a chemist, rather than a biologist, geologist, or physicist – those fields seemed to have more direct points of conflict with traditional Christian faith. Evolution, the fossil record, and an unimaginably old earth and universe were all issues of vigorous contention in some Christian circles. Were all Christians who embraced these scientific ideas untrustworthy? I was not ready to answer that yet, and avoided such controversial topics in my day-to-day life.

A growing openness

My first significant step towards reconciling science with a biblical creation account came from a Sunday school series at my college church on the first chapters of Genesis. My pastor argued convincingly that Genesis 1, in particular, is written from a phenomenological perspective. That is, it is inspired by God,

---

[3] InterVarsity Christian Fellowship

but written from a human perspective and accommodating to an ancient Hebrew understanding of the world. This helped me relax somewhat about scientific or historical interpretations of Genesis, though I still maintained an overall concordist attitude towards the text.

In 1997, I moved from Massachusetts to San Diego to begin my PhD studies at The Scripps Research Institute in organic chemistry. Since I did not pursue biological topics (other than the obligatory bioorganic coursework) nor even prebiotic chemistry (towards understanding the origins of life), I did not encounter any science-faith controversy in my own work. And I was busy enough with my own research and my regular church commitments to have little time for pleasure reading. But I did occasionally venture over to the University of California San Diego bookstore, and on one of these visits, I purchased Michael Behe's *Darwin's Black Box: The Biochemical Challenge to Evolution*.[4] I was captivated by his arguments for Intelligent Design, particularly the descriptions of blood clotting and the bacterial flagellum. In retrospect, this sparked my first real interest in biology. It seemed exhilarating to consider how a scientist might uncover evidence for God's handiwork in creation. I was already familiar with arguments for design in physics, but had no idea that biologists could do the same! My head was spinning as I tried to think of what I, as an organic chemist, could contribute to evidence for Intelligent Design.

But my infatuation with Intelligent Design was not long-lived. On another visit to the bookstore, I bought Ken Miller's *Finding Darwin's God: A Scientist's Search for Common Ground Between*

---

[4] Michael Behe, *Darwin's Black Box*, New York: Simon & Schuster, 1996.

God and Evolution.[5] While not as dazzling rhetorically as *Darwin's Black Box*, I appreciated Miller's evidence-based approach and his openness about his own faith. This was my first encounter with a serious Christian who was not afraid of evolution. In fact, he embraced evolution, and his faith seemed enriched by it. I was not immediately converted to accepting evolution, but I grew more confident that Christianity and science were compatible.

Becoming a biologist?

My deeper engagement with evolution began after I went on to postdoctoral research in chemical biology. This may seem a strange choice of research direction, given my dislike for biology. But this dislike had been based on fairly superficial and immature reasons. Indeed, as I learned more about organic chemistry, I grew increasingly curious about its relation to biochemistry.

As an undergraduate and graduate student in chemistry, I had been constructing complex molecules. My target molecules were typically natural products made by plants, fungi, or bacteria. Often these compounds had interesting biological properties: to react with a protein or kill cancerous cells. Yet what I found most compelling was the intricate chemical structure of these molecules. It often took me and my colleagues years to devise an effective strategy to make our target molecules. How then did the bacteria (or other synthesizing organisms) make the natural products so rapidly and seemingly effortlessly? I became fascinated with biosynthetic mechanisms.

Those biosynthetic mechanisms involve proteins, and this led me to ask questions about the evolutionary relationships between the proteins and their ancestors. How did these proteins

[5] Kenneth R. Miller, *Finding Darwin's God: A Scientist's Search for Common Ground Between God and Evolution*, New York: HarperCollins, 1999.

come to be? Why do they make the natural products? I was going to need to learn about evolution. Furthermore, I would be working with biologists in my postdoctoral laboratory, and I absolutely wanted to have intellectual credibility with my co-workers. Yet my faith was central to my identity. It seemed that I could no longer hide in the safe haven of organic chemistry. As I moved into chemical biology, I would have to confront some of the controversial issues around evolution and the Bible.

The Bible and evidence

Why was I so afraid of doing this? Does the Bible really discourage the honest pursuit of truth? Is it in any way laudable to dismiss uncomfortable evidence? Actually, no. Some passages that came to mind were:

> *You shall love the Lord your God with all your heart and*
> *with all your soul and with all your mind.*
> *(Matthew 22:37)[6]*

> *Great are the works of the Lord, studied by all who delight*
> *in them. (Psalm 111:2)[7]*

> *These Jews were more noble than those in Thessalonica;*
> *they received the word with all eagerness, examining the*
> *Scriptures daily to see if these things were so.*
> *(Acts 17:11)*

---

[6] All my scriptural quotations are taken from the English Standard Version of the Bible.

[7] Psalm 111:2 is famously inscribed at the entrance of both the old site (in Latin) and new site (in English) of the Cavendish Laboratory, home of the Department of Physics at the University of Cambridge.

I believed that God created the universe and that He inspired the writers of the Bible. And if both creation and Scripture were from God, I should be able to trust both. Science and Christianity ought to be compatible, since both sought truth – even if it meant taking evolution seriously.

A role model and new resources

After starting my postdoctoral research at Harvard Medical School in Boston, I attended three William Belden Noble Lectures given there by Francis Collins in February 2003. The titles were, "From Atheist to Believer: A Personal Voyage", "Can a Geneticist Be a Believer? Evolution and Other Challenges", and "Genetics, Ethics, and Faith". I found his personal testimony and arguments in favour of both faith and evolution extremely persuasive, bolstered by his credentials as a world-famous geneticist and former atheist. Indeed, he was the director of the enormously successful Human Genome Project and later wrote the best-selling book *The Language of God: A Scientist Presents Evidence for Belief*.[8] Seeing him in person over several days and observing his enthusiasm for his faith and for science were great motivators for me. Here at last was a role model for me as I tried to reconcile evolution and a robust Christian faith.

In 2005, the year before Collins's *The Language of God* was released, I was delighted to find two other very helpful books that sought to reconcile biblical and scientific perspectives on origins. The first was Darrel Falk's *Coming to Peace with Science: Bridging the Worlds Between Faith and Biology*, in which Falk clearly expresses his strong evangelical faith as well as evidence

---

[8] Francis Collins, *The Language of God: A Scientist Presents Evidence for Belief*, New York: Free Press, 2006.

in support of biological evolution.[9] Less than two months after that, I read Stephen Godfrey and Chris Smith's book *Paradigms on Pilgrimage: Creationism, Paleontology, and Biblical Interpretation*.[10] What I appreciated most about this book was the solid approach to Genesis. Chris had been my college pastor in Williamstown (mentioned earlier in the Sunday school class) and had officiated at my wedding in 1999. I trusted Chris's approach to Genesis just as I trusted Francis Collins's explanation of evolution. I wished I'd encountered these books years earlier, as they might have significantly reduced the emotional toll I was experiencing as I wrestled with these ideas alone.[11]

For me, grappling with the ideas presented in these talks and books was slow and emotionally challenging. I faced many hard questions. What was I resisting, and why? Did I fear a spiritually precarious compromise with secular ideas? Where did I get the idea that science is secular, anyway? How do the most respected scientist-Christians and theologians reconcile faith and science? How might my views of Scripture and of God change? What would other Christians think about me?

In retrospect, I wish that I had talked with my friends about these questions. But the risks seemed too high. Resistance to evolution may be more psychological, sociological, or political than rational or truly theological. But whatever its cause, evolution was a very divisive issue, and I did not want to damage friendships or fellowship. In my case, my identity as a solid,

---

[9] Darrel Falk, *Coming to Peace with Science: Bridging the Worlds Between Faith and Biology,* Downers Grove, IL: IVP, 2004. See Chapter 4.

[10] Stephen Godfrey and Christopher Smith, *Paradigms on Pilgrimage*, Toronto: Clements Publishing, 2005. See Chapter 5.

[11] A newer book that I would also recommend is: Deborah B. Haarsma and Loren D. Haarsma, *Origins: Christian Perspectives on Creation, Evolution, and Intelligent Design*, 2nd edn, Grand Rapids, MI: Faith Alive, 2011.

Bible-believing Christian felt at stake. Ironically, I would not have needed to risk such alienation if I had tackled science and faith questions in community.

Unlike years ago, there are now some good science-faith resources that are well-suited for engaging groups in stimulating conversations. Three films I recommend are *Test of Faith: Does Science Threaten Belief in God?* from The Faraday Institute for Science and Religion; *From the Dust: Conversations in Creation* from BioLogos and Highway Media; and *Origins Today: Genesis Through Ancient Eyes* from John Walton at Wheaton College.[12] My own favourite is *From the Dust* – in part because I wrote a discussion guide for it,[13] and also because it most closely fits what I wish I had seen when I was an undergraduate. *Test of Faith* has less of a theological emphasis and can be used in secular settings. (I helped arrange a screening at Caltech, for example.) I hope more and more group-orientated science-faith resources become available in the future, as I feel strongly that community is a very important factor in achieving compatibility.

Augustine and Galileo

While I did not recruit my friends to help me consider the compatibility of evolution and the Bible, I did find support in a more distant community: Christian scholars of long ago. I have great respect for the deep history of Christian thought, and I was both surprised and encouraged by what Augustine and Galileo had written in the fifth and seventeenth centuries,

---

[12] *Test of Faith: Does Science Threaten Belief in God?*, Dir. Mark Brickman, Faraday, 2009, DVD; *From the Dust: Conversations in Creation*, Dir. Ryan Pettey, Highway Media and BioLogos, 2012, DVD; *Origins Today: Genesis Through Ancient Eyes*, Dir. John Walton, Wheaton College, 2013, DVD.

[13] http://fromthedustmovie.org/wp-content/uploads/2012/08/From-the-Dust-Study-Guide.pdf (accessed 11 November 2013).

respectively. Both cautioned against holding too rigidly to particular biblical interpretations in the face of apparently contradictory evidence.

In *The Literal Meaning of Genesis* (c. 415), Augustine of Hippo writes:

> *In matters that are obscure and far beyond our vision, even in such as we may find treated in Holy Scripture, different interpretations are sometimes possible without prejudice to the faith we have received. In such a case, we should not rush in headlong and so firmly take our stand on one side that, if further progress in the search of truth justly undermines this position, we too fall with it.*[14]

Galileo Galilei echoes this thought in his *Letter to the Grand Duchess Christina* (1615):

> *In St. Augustine we read: "If anyone shall set the authority of [the Bible] against clear and manifest reason, he who does this knows not what he has undertaken; for he opposes to the truth not the meaning of the Bible, which is beyond his comprehension, but rather his own interpretation; not what is in the Bible, but what he has found in himself and imagines to be there." This granted, and it being true that two truths cannot contradict one another, it is the function of wise expositors to seek out the true senses of scriptural texts. These will unquestionably accord with the physical conclusions which manifest sense*

---

[14] Augustine, *The Literal Meaning of Genesis*, 1.18, trans. J. H. Taylor, New York: Newman Press (1982), p. 41.

> *and necessary demonstrations have previously made*
> *certain to us.*[15]

Augustine and Galileo showed me that there was a great precedent in trying to reconcile Christian faith with reason and scientific exploration. To hear this from such prominent historic voices in theology and science was immensely reassuring to me as I re-examined the creation accounts in Genesis.

Interpreting the Bible

The more that I read Genesis 1–3, the more I became convinced that those chapters are actually more concerned with *who* created and *why* we were created than a precise description of *when* the universe began and *how* living things appeared. I came to realize that Genesis was not written primarily to those of us living in the twenty-first century, but to the ancient Hebrews, and through them to the rest of the world. So as a truth-seeking Bible-reader, I needed to consider the original language and genre of the text, and the intentions of the author as interpreted through the conceptual framework of the culture of that time.[16] I also found it helpful to consider other biblical passages describing creation, such as Job 38, Psalm 104, and Isaiah 40.

I now believe the apparent conflict is not inevitable; it arises from flawed interpretations of scientific data and from misunderstandings of Scripture. For example, some people claim that evolution proves there is no God, even though the existence of God is not a scientific question. Others regard Genesis 1

---

[15] Galileo Galilei, *Discoveries and Opinions of Galileo*, trans. Stillman Drake, New York: Anchor Books, 1957, p. 186.

[16] John Walton, *The Lost World of Genesis One*, Downer's Grove, IL: NP, 2009. See also Godfrey and Smith's *Paradigms on Pilgrimage* (see note 10, also Chapter 5).

and 2 as modern scientific or journalistic accounts, despite the fact that Genesis far predates our modern ideas of historical or scientific writing. The conflict does not come from God or nature – we have created the conflict ourselves. Intentionally or not, we often extend science past its natural bounds and use the Bible for questions it does not intend to answer.

But if there seems to be a satisfactory scientific explanation for something, does that mean that God is not involved in it? Absolutely not! The spiritual reality of prayer is not diminished by our observation of electrochemical processes in the brain, just as a kiss is not fully explained by being described as a puckering of the lips, a transfer of saliva, carbon dioxide, and some bacteria. If you've ever given or received a kiss before, that's probably not what you were thinking of when it happened. When I kiss my wife, there is definitely more going on there than a puckering of the lips, a transfer of saliva, carbon dioxide, and some bacteria. If there weren't, she wouldn't let me kiss her, nor would she kiss me back!

So I believe we can be freed from the myth of intrinsic conflict. We can embrace both faith and science.

Christ and chemistry

I can now answer my college pastor's question: "What does Christ have to do with chemistry?" Jesus has everything to do with chemistry, since "all things were created through him and for him" and "in him all things hold together" (Colossians 1:16–17).[17] My response is to love God and to embrace science as a joyful form of worship, discovery, and awe, delightfully learning about God's thoughts and designs at a molecular level.

---

[17] See also Hebrews 1:2–3 and John 1:1–3.

As a synthetic chemist or molecule maker, I especially resonate with J. R .R. Tolkien's concept of sub-creation: human creation that reflects God's image as creator.[18] Sub-creation is illustrated in Tolkien's creation story of Middle-earth:

> *Yet the making of things is in my heart from my own making*
> *by thee; and the child of little understanding that makes a*
> *play of the deeds of his father may do so without any thought*
> *of mockery, but because he is the son of his father.*[19]

My ability to create comes from God's own creativity. Tolkien's concept of rejoicing in this gift of creativity reflects the joy and inspiration I experience as a synthetic chemist.

Molecules are beautiful. Making new ones is a privilege and a cause for joy and worship of God. I delight in molecules, and I believe God does, too. He is the first and greatest chemist, and he has entrusted me with one small corner of his laboratory.

A traditional way to express joy and worship in the Judeo-Christian tradition is in song. Inspired by Psalm 148, I wrote this chemistry-themed psalm:

> *Praise the Lord.*

> *Praise the Lord from the classroom,*
> *Praise Him in the laboratory, too.*

> *Praise Him, all his molecules,*
> *Praise Him, all his proteins and nucleic acids.*

---

[18] J. R. R. Tolkien, "On Fairy-Stories", in *Tree and Leaf*, London: George Allen & Unwin, 1964.

[19] J. R. R. Tolkien, *The Silmarillion*, Boston, MA: Houghton Mifflin, 1977, p. 43.

Praise Him, all alkaloids and steroids,
Praise Him, all you sweet carbohydrates.

Praise Him, you manifold terpenoids
and you polyketides and peptides.

Let them praise the name of the Lord,
for He commanded and they were created.

He formed them from the elements;
He decreed how they should bond.

Praise the Lord from the NMR,
all you chemists in industry and academia,
whether you be famous or not,

carbon and oxygen, sulphur and nitrogen,
electrons that do all His bonding,

you fluorine and chlorine,
light hydrogen and heavy iodine,

all alkanes and alkenes,
every alkyne and aromatic ring,

all amines and aldehydes,
ketones and carboxylic acids,

esters, amides, and anhydrides,
alcohols and ethers.

What Does Christ Have to Do with Chemistry?

Let them praise the name of the Lord,
for His name alone is exalted;
his splendour is revealed in our every molecule.

He has raised up for His people the Christ,
the praise of all His saints,
of the church, the people close to His heart.

Praise the Lord.

CHAPTER 15

Discovering Unexpected
Dimensions of the Divine Plan

David Watts, DSc, is Professor of Biomaterials Science at the School of Dentistry and the Photon Science Institute of the University of Manchester. He is a Fellow of the Institute of Physics, the Royal Society of Chemistry, and the Society of Biology. He received the Research Prize of the Alexander von Humboldt Foundation in 2010 and is a visiting professor at the universities of Jena and Munich (Germany), Padova (Italy), and Oregon Health and Science University (USA). He has personally supervised more than sixty PhD candidates from twenty nations.

It is the glory of God to conceal a matter;
  to search out a matter is the glory of kings.

Proverbs 25:2, NIV

Subtle is the Lord, but malicious He is not.

Albert Einstein

Does God keep screws?

Does God keep screws? This was my first recorded theological question. I am still fascinated by screws: whether pondering the biomechanics of titanium implants screwed into human bone, clipping into an ice-screw high on an alpine peak or engaging in home DIY. Ordinary screws are one of the most common artefacts of Intelligent Design. They could not have made themselves: one "moment" they were a section of metal wire; next they passed through a series of metal-forming dies and emerged with their new screw identity. So the explanation of their origin moves one step back to the creation of the metal-dies.

I remain even more fascinated by God. This is not unusual as, despite the curious inversion of the modern European mindset, theism is probably the default human setting. But fascination is often replaced by fear and aversion. The fact that in my life, God's perfect love has dispelled fear is wholly attributable to His unfathomable grace towards me, through Jesus Christ. This fascination with the divine Being is the mainspring of my life and my participation in the scientific enterprise.

My understanding of God is that of historic Christian Theism, or Christian Trinitarian Theism. That is, I hold convictions about the reality of God as a transcendent personal Being, the God and Father of Jesus Christ, who is as potentially knowable in the same moment and to the same extent as we are each self-aware of our own existence. This means that this God is not an abstract theory, but supremely alive. In a general way, we can say that the physical universe is somehow *embedded* in a personal and spiritual universe. Certainly, without human consciousness, we could know nothing of this.

During my late childhood and youth I was befriended and mentored by two professional scientists: Euan Squires and Alfred Clark who both taught at the Baptist church I attended with my parents and brother. Euan Squires was a theoretical physicist at the University of Manchester who went on to be one the youngest professors in the UK when he was appointed to the chair of Applied Mathematics at Durham and founded a world-class particle physics theory group. Alfred Clark was an industrial chemist who, at no cost to my parents, tutored me through O-level chemistry and introduced me to key issues in science and Christianity, including stimulating books by R. E. D. Clark and Bernard Ramm. Long before I went to university, I was convinced that an underlying harmony between God and science was discoverable.

Absolute and mediate creation

During my time as an undergraduate I read *A Summary of Christian Doctrine* by a Dutch-American, Louis Berkhof, produced by the conservative Banner of Truth publishers. Its cover was a stunning NASA photo of a remote galaxy. I was deeply impressed that the God I worshipped on Sunday was the author and upholder of the vast universe and all within. However, Dr Berkhof's formulation of the "doctrines" of creation and providence was not as theologically nuanced as it might have been. Unlike the earlier and more scholarly *Systematic Theology* by the American Charles Hodge,[1] he failed to make the crucial distinction between *absolute* and *mediate* creation and thereby fertilized the seeds of confusion and needless polarization.

Absolute (or primary) creation may be defined as the act of bringing the entire universe into existence, *ex nihilo*, and thus without the aid of pre-existing materials, as affirmed in Hebrews 11:3. This is virtually foundational to all theistic beliefs, and is articulated by mainstream Christian thinkers such as Augustine

---

[1] Charles Hodge, *Systematic Theology*, New York: Charles Scribner, 1872, volume I, p. 566 ff.

and Thomas Aquinas. We might express this in modern terms by saying that all aspects of physical reality – matter and radiation, space and time, dark matter and dark energy – were/are created *ex nihilo* and thus owe their existence to the will of the transcendent creator. Even cosmic evolution cannot supplant or share in the reality of *absolute* creation, because evolution is a *process* – not an act – and requires some pre-existing material environment for its sphere of operation.

By contrast, the words "create"/ "creation" are also widely used in Scripture texts in a secondary sense of *mediate* creation where pre-existing materials (products ultimately of absolute creation) are used – and are essential – for the outworking of creation. This is apparent in the Genesis 2 narrative of the origins of Adam – whether we interpret the text literally or metaphorically. Adam was *created* from the dust of the ground – via the immanent life-imparting "kiss" from the transcendent Spirit of God. Thus not all creative events directly denote *ex nihilo* creation, although the latter underpins all created existence. This is a vital distinction.

As regards absolute creation, Christian theologians affirm both that this establishes a non-reciprocal relationship of intimate dependence of the creation upon God and also that the creation has a real existence distinct from God. In consequence, God (the prime Cause) has endowed and upholds the universe with secondary causes embedded within physical, material, biological, behavioural, and social existence. In Christian understanding, it is these secondary causes and the specific entities upon which they operate that are the proper and necessary domain of scientific enquiry. The reliability of God underpins the existence, reliability, and discoverability of scientific laws, which have sometimes been transcended in miraculous events, such as the resurrection of Jesus Christ from the dead.

Unfortunately, many before and after Louis Berkhof have confused and conflated these distinct meanings into a dogmatically single creation concept. They invest what is actually *mediate* creation with the qualities of *absolute* creation, so that even the earthly aspects of Adam's origins have been mistakenly treated as "absolute" and thus requiring some kind of *ex nihilo* beginning.

We must do justice to the special – indeed central – place of humankind in God's purposes. But it is not warranted to assert the impossibility of human biological connectivity with the rest of the created order via remote common genetic ancestry, in the light of our biochemical and physiological commonality with the animal kingdoms. I had to recognize the biblical distinction between absolute (*ex nihilo*) and mediate creation if I was ever to formulate an integrated Christian worldview which incorporated the fruits of the scientific enterprise. It took me a long time to recognize this point and its implications. For many years I maintained that creation and evolution, both viewed univocally, were conceptually opposed. This led me to serve as chair of the Biblical Creation Society, although I resigned my membership of the society when it became exclusively focused upon Young Earth Creationism.

Another major influence in my undergraduate days was Francis Schaeffer, with whom I corresponded briefly and met on a number of occasions. His holistic approach to contemporary art, philosophy, and culture and his commitment to Christian re-imagining of the whole of life were marvellously refreshing. He was patient in listening to the questions being raised in our culture, but prophetic in communicating both the inevitability of divine judgment and the good news of God's gracious purposes through Jesus Christ. As respects questions of origins, Schaeffer was wise in laying out a spectrum of options in the possible correlation of biblical teaching and scientific models.

Creation *with* time

Recognition of the metaphysical, non-temporal nature of absolute creation enables us to see that the universe has been created *with* time, rather than *in* time. That time is an aspect of the created universe – on a comparable level to space – was an explicit insight of the great fourth/fifth-century theologian Augustine of Hippo, centuries before Albert Einstein's gravitational theories placed space and time on a similar footing. From this, it follows that the entire unfolding of cosmic and human history in space and time, in whatever form it takes or has taken, can be seen as divine providence. Christian theology cannot specify in advance the precise form of cosmic historical unfolding, since the universe is a "contingent" place – it might have been otherwise from what, little by little, we are finding it to be. The experimental sciences are necessary to examine and explore the world in its complexity and to discover the underlying laws and patterns of behaviour, and rather incidentally, to reveal the "fine-tuning" of physical constants that is necessary for organic life.

Hard and soft sciences

I am grateful for my early education in the physico-chemical sciences and mathematics, leading to qualifications in both physics and chemistry. Pioneers of an earlier generation, such as Michael Faraday and James Clerk Maxwell, both committed Christians, were superb role models for me. My university mentors, including Professor Graham Williams, Sir John Meurig Thomas, and Sir Geoffrey Allen, continued the Faraday tradition of working at the physics/chemistry interface. I confess to a degree of pride in the rigorous nature of these sciences and love to wind up my biological colleagues by quoting Lord Rutherford's dictum: "There are two kinds of science: physics and stamp collecting." It is impossible to hold to this nowadays: life sciences, not least my own field of biomaterials science, incorporate precise physicalist methodologies that go far beyond "stamp collecting". The disdain I used to entertain towards the standards of proof required in biology – particularly evolutionary biology – no longer has any justification. I once accepted an over-neat distinction between normative sciences and historical sciences. The former embody fully repeatable experiments, whereas the latter involve historical reconstructions of past events – such as in the forensic sciences and palaeontology – but I can no longer sustain this distinction.

From my earliest PhD researches, I have focused on time-dependent molecular and material behaviour, including the co-discovery of a precise mathematical function to describe a ubiquitous pattern of behaviour in the time and frequency domains.[2] That itself is the dynamic antithesis to a static perspective on scientific subject matter. My more recent exposure to and research into biological questions, particularly the interactions between biomaterials, cells and organs, has deepened this appreciation for change, time-dependence, and historical reconstruction. So, incorporating "evolutionary" perspectives in science is no longer anathema to me. Even when I was most

---

[2] The Kohlrausch-Williams-Watts (KWW) stretched exponential function, for molecular relaxation processes in the time-domain, and its transforms to the frequency-domain.

opposed to "evolution", my real problem was with "evolutionism" – the gratuitous extrapolation of evolutionary science beyond its proper domain – together with the materialism that often accompanies evolutionism. These are both philosophical parasites on natural sciences *per se*.

I should add that I have always understood the actual practice of scientific research to be "faith neutral". That is, the scientific enterprise is a shared international endeavour by people nominally of any religious faith or none. So, although modern science was nurtured in a Christian culture, I cannot accept attempts to formulate any so-called "Creation Science". Notwithstanding, Christianity does profoundly enrich the scientific enterprise by supplying a matrix within which the enterprise itself becomes both comprehensible and meaningful for our total human experience. Part of this can be expressed in Johannes Kepler's words as the endeavour "… to think God's thoughts after him", if not particularly in Stephen Hawking's phrase: "… to know the mind of God". As Proverbs 25:2 expresses it: "It is the glory of God to conceal a matter; to search out a matter is the glory of kings" (NIV). I find it highly motivating to contemplate the divine Being as having hidden cosmic "secrets", like buried treasure, awaiting the diligent enquiries of His scientist image-bearers.

Can science explain everything?

In principle, the secondary causal network is complete without the regular need to invoke additional divine action or localized "Intelligent Design" to plug critical gaps. So we reject a "God of the gaps". *In practice*, there are manifold details still to be discovered, explained, and understood in scientific terms.

Some key processes within the created order we properly label random or chance, but that is more a measure of their complexity coupled with our relative ignorance. The rich hierarchy of levels of reality (e.g. physiological/cellular/molecular/atomic/ nuclear/ etc.) often requires multiple, *complementary* levels of scientific explanation. Even within a single discipline, such as chemistry, it is frequently appropriate to explain phenomena in terms of both overall energetics (thermodynamics) and reaction (kinetic) mechanisms. Experienced scientists do not reject complementary explanations as superfluous. More importantly, there are many central domains of human life and rational conviction where scientific explanation or justification are neither feasible nor necessary. Physics, for example, is causally incomplete because it doesn't encompass human thoughts and intention. We regularly and correctly make metaphysical assumptions, such as the existence of other minds and the reality of the external world, which cannot "scientifically" be proven. Similarly we make aesthetic and ethical value judgments. Even science itself presupposes logical and mathematical truths. The key to solving many controversies is acknowledgment of the propriety and necessity of descriptions of the same phenomena on different levels of reality. For example, a book can be explained both as paper/ink and as the author's message.

Biological evolution and the origin of life

Biological evolution per se is, of course, inseparable for Christians from the *Origin of Species*. This is the specific area where I have changed my mind and am now persuaded by the scientific evidence for: (i) the evolution of species over time, (ii) the "tree of (biological) life" and thus (iii) the biological connectivity of all living creatures, including human beings. This does not amount to a necessary commitment to either Darwinian or neo-Darwinian evolutionary mechanisms as a total explanation for biological species diversity. However, I have no difficulty in accepting a substantial role for natural selection in this process.

As respects human beings, biological evolution assumes a distant common ancestor between humans and a non-human species. I find the extensive evidence from comparative human DNA sequence analyses much more persuasive than the morphological comparisons of fossils which used to be quoted as the basis of the relationship. The fossil material is still somewhat fragmentary and inferences from it can only be tentative.

Acknowledgment of these implications, drawn from the fairly recent human genome analyses, is a surprising new perspective for me. It amounts to recognition or discovery of an unexpected dimension of the Divine Plan for cosmic and human history. If, like countless men and women before me, I have speculated about divine purposes, I might not have anticipated the extent of either the cosmic or the biological transformations that led to a habitable planet and the development of life up to the genesis of the first human beings. But awareness of these extensive changes – which I interpret teleologically as preparations – gives me an enhanced sense of wonder and awe at the power and wisdom of almighty God.

The origin of life and of the living cell and its constituent organelles are often set within the perspective of cosmic change, rather than the narrower concept of biological evolution. The problem of chemical evolution is a topic for which I am equipped to study via the primary scientific literature. As a research student and then as a postdoc I did in fact dig into this literature and explore these fascinating subjects. Early in my research career I was inclined – mistakenly, I now concede – to infer an unreliable status for biological evolution overall from the rather uncertain scientific status of "chemical evolution". I now unequivocally retract any such extrapolation! Periodically I have re-visited the primary literature, including recent developments such as supramolecular chemistry and self-assembly. There are many hypotheses but as yet no scientific consensus about chemical evolution. As both a scientist and as a Christian, however, I believe it is right to avoid drawing hasty conclusions. We should remain open to the possibility that a convincing and experimentally repeatable total mechanism may be discovered eventually for *abiogenesis*, probably involving surface catalytic templates. But emphatically such a complete jigsaw has not yet been found – or at best, perhaps only a few possible pieces.

The great challenges to formulating and verifying mechanisms for chemical evolution have led many independent thinkers to contend that the quest is futile because the problem is insoluble. A second step is to argue that bridging this massive mechanistic "gap" demands "Intelligent Design". Some advocates do not specify what they mean by such design, but those among them who are theistic apologists usually infer that we should acknowledge *special* divine action in this context. What can we make of this situation? A good dictum is: "Absence of proof is not proof of absence."

At the other extreme, I do find it surprising and very disappointing that some believing scientists and theologians gloss over the real difficulties attending chemical evolution and the origin of the living cell. In several prominent instances the scientists in question are theoretical physicists with probably scant personal acquaintance with the experimental challenges of chemical synthesis, molecular behaviour, and polymerization reactions. It is tempting for them to suggest that these problems are already solved. Unfortunately this is counterproductive for experimental science. It is a real disservice to young investigators to claim that science has all the answers. Rather, we should highlight all the major open scientific questions to stimulate and motivate their enquiries.

Scientific interpretation of the book that interprets us!

Every thoughtful Christian has to recognize that the text of the Bible requires interpretation. While strongly affirming the ultimate divine origin of sacred Scripture, we must also recognize that God has used the writings, personalities, languages, and historical contexts of the human authors of the Old and New Testaments. It is also necessary to be clear about the purpose of scriptural references to the natural world. As Galileo Galilei expressed it in a letter to Christine of Lorraine, Grand Duchess of Tuscany (1615): "It is clear ... that the Holy Spirit's intention is to teach us how to go to Heaven, not how the heavens go." On the other hand, when the biblical narrative moves towards climactic events, such as the resurrection of Jesus from the dead, it is clear that something entirely novel and unprecedented has come to pass that transcends the ordinary and the familiar – then and now.

In coming to my current and mature understanding of these issues – complicated with mistakes en route – I have been privileged to learn from believing biblical scholars of considerable repute, including Dr Ralph P. Martin, who was minister of my home church when I was an undergraduate.

Later I took numerous courses in biblical languages, literature, and exegesis and every opportunity to learn from Professor F. F. Bruce, together with visiting scholars to Manchester such as Martin Hengel and Wolfhart Pannenberg. Later I became personally acquainted with a younger generation of theologians and biblical scholars, including Don Carson, Nigel Cameron, Gordon McConville, and Vern Poythress.

It has been important to me to gain familiarity with both the world of biblical scholarship and, more recently, with the emerging interdisciplinary literature on science and religion. Together with research and publication in my specialist scientific fields, such study makes heavy demands of time and energy. However, it is a great joy to be convinced that "All truth is God's truth" and that the fullness of divine wisdom is incarnate in Jesus Christ.

Never stop exploring...

The above strapline belongs to The North Face company that manufactures high-quality mountain clothing and equipment. I became an avid mountain climber and alpinist in my mid-teens, and it remains one of my principal recreational delights. Among the awesome beauty of the mountains, and especially in the European Alps, I have experienced a tremendous sense of God's power and presence. To adapt the language used in the movie *Chariots of Fire*, I can say: "When I explore, I feel His pleasure." And this remains the case whether the exploration is among the mountains, in the laboratory or in the library. I am always keen to find out what is round the next corner!

The mountains take one amidst immense rock and glacial scenery, including past and present volcanic territory. This has helped me evaluate the theories of friends and acquaintances who persist in defending the so-called young earth (YE) model in the interests of coherence with extreme literalism in the interpretation of Genesis 1.

In general, my YE friends set up a mental grid to interpret scientific evidence which only admits data consistent with short geological timescales; that is, involving rapid geological processes. Data that will not pass this filter are rejected or explained away by a range of arbitrary tactics and sub-hypotheses. The most favoured timescale of so-called "flood geology" would compress the causation of most global geological events into a twelve-month timespan several thousands of years BC.

A commonly invoked contemporary example is the island of Surtsey, off the south-west coast of Iceland. It was formed in a volcanic eruption that began 130 metres below sea level, and reached the surface on 14 November 1963. The eruption lasted until 5 June 1967, when the island reached its maximum size of 2.7 km^2. Since then, wind and wave erosion have caused the island to steadily diminish in size: as of 2008, its surface area was 1.4 km^2. YE advocates point to these rapid erosive processes and suggest that landscapes elsewhere may have been formed as rapidly. However, they miss the significant point that the rocks of Surtsey are very soft in comparison to hard rocks elsewhere – such as granites and even rocks of intermediate hardness such as limestone, dolomite, and sandstone.

YE advocates also explain away the conventional Geological Column (GC) of successive rock strata as a fiction. Indeed, this is essential to maintain their case. However, I am convinced of the empirical reality of the GC, not least by those parts that I have been able to explore directly in the UK, Europe – including the entire Alpine range from France round to Slovenia – and in the Canadian Rockies. Even if one were to ignore an "absolute" timescale for rock strata, based on radiometric isochrons, the cumulative magnitudes of sedimentary, igneous, and metamorphic rock strata, plus their complex inter-relationships, demand that secondary geological processes must have operated over aeons of time. This is, of course, the conclusion reached by the early nineteenth-century geologists, leading to the recognition of "deep time" as a backdrop to both terrestrial and cosmic physical processes.

Although I am here strongly critical of friends who defend and advocate the young earth position, this does not diminish my esteem for them as persons and fellow Christians. Indeed, a great many are, in other respects, shining examples of Christian commitment, enterprise, and personal integrity. I am rather sad, however, that mostly they do not re-evaluate their positions and consider some wider horizons of the science and theology dialogue. However, some YE zealots act in a sectarian and counterproductive manner by insisting upon YE "orthodoxy" as a test of fellowship. It is reprehensible when entire local churches can be infected with dogmatism on this secondary issue; young students from such backgrounds go to university and soon face a crisis of faith. Christian pastors have great responsibilities to address these issues carefully and cautiously.

The theatre of God's glory

For Christians, understanding science involves marvelling at the extent to which our minds are attuned to discover hidden secrets of our cosmic home. As Einstein wrote, "The most incomprehensible thing about the world is that it is comprehensible." But we have been created in the image of the God who has created the entire universe and all it contains; so it is not surprising to find a world that is at least partly comprehensible to our understanding.

Overall, Christian belief affords a rich, intellectually coherent matrix within which the scientific enterprise can flourish, and where discoveries heighten our appreciation of the power, wisdom, and beauty of God. The Christian faith has necessarily disenchanted pagan and animist misunderstandings of nature, but has supplied spectacles with which to view the world as the theatre of God's glory. This is not to close our eyes to human suffering, natural evil or "the groaning of creation" (see Romans 8:22), but to appreciate more fully the Christian-historical trajectory of creation, Fall, redemption, and consummation. The believing scientist is called to work in hope, knowing that their labour is not futile, since we are not end-products of meaningless processes in an impersonal universe, but made in the image of a personal God and serving Him according to His purposes.

CHAPTER 16

The Skeleton in the Cupboard: Why I Changed My Mind About Evolution

Bob Carling is a freelance editor, editorial consultant, publisher, and writer. After a zoology degree and a PhD in pharmacology, he has spent over thirty years in publishing, particularly in STM (science/technical/medical), working for various prestigious publishing companies, such as Baillière Tindall, Academic Press, Chapman & Hall, and the Royal College of Physicians, plus a range of freelance clients including CRC Press and Wiley-Blackwell, also helping edit journals such as *Nature* and *Philosophical Transactions of the Royal Society*. He is Editor of the magazine *The Marine Scientist*.

Ever since school days, I have been fascinated by the natural world. How do plants and animals, especially insects, interact? How did they come about in the first place? Why are there so many different sorts? How do some of the more exotic species, with their strange adaptations to unusual environments, survive, and how did they develop such strange lifestyles? As I grew up, I became more and more interested in what motivates biologists to spend their lives investigating species. I wanted to be one of them.

I fell in love with biology during one of the first O-level

lessons. My biology teacher, Mr "Digger" Marsh, spoke about water and the characteristics of life. I remember my amazement at learning my own body was just over 50 per cent water – with the rest being 12 per cent carbon, 0.2 per cent phosphorus, 0.2 per cent calcium, etc. It made me think, what is it, then, that constitutes "life"? The acronym I learned for the characteristics of life still stays with me – MERRING: movement, excretion, reproduction, respiration, irritability, nutrition, and growth.

I was hooked. I decided to spend the rest of my life as a biologist. Some years later, after I had gained my zoology degree, I met Digger Marsh in the street and I thanked him personally for fascinating me and pointing me in the direction that I was to follow for the rest of my life.

Partly as a result of my parents' unhappy marriage, we moved around a lot in my early life – including spells in West Africa – so my A-levels were not taught by Mr Marsh; by then I was at a different school.

It was at about this time that I became what I would now call a "naïve creationist". I had an uneasy suspicion that there was necessarily a conflict between my personal belief in a creator God and an evolutionary view of the origins of species in the natural world. In a cupboard in my school there was a human skeleton. Someone, possibly the biology master, had stuck a "Jesus is alive today" sticker on its forehead. Although I thought it was funny, I felt awkward about it; it jarred with my Christian understanding. The skeleton in the cupboard represented those who were anti-Christian. As a creationist, I wrote an essay for my new biology master about evolution. It had all sorts of phrases like "*maybe* this was how it happened" and "although not very convincing, the evidence for evolution is…" etc. He was unimpressed.

But I was in love with biology. I announced proudly to some friends at my church that I was going to study zoology at university. One of them warned me that I needed to be careful in case I compromised my faith. Didn't I realize – she said – that atheism was rife in universities and that evolution was a key theory used by atheists to attack Christians?

I puzzled as to why she was so wary. If I must safeguard my young Christian faith, what then should I do with my passion for biology? By that time I had already read about some scientists who were believers – and apparently they saw no problem with a belief in the Bible *and* a biological explanation about origins. But I had also read about Christians who refused to accept an evolutionary explanation of the origin of species. Darwin was wrong, they said. Interestingly, it tended to be those *outside* the scientific profession who were anti-evolution; those *with* scientific qualifications and a Christian belief didn't seem to see that there was a problem. Whom should I believe? There was obviously a sharp disagreement between Christians about evolution.

As well as this ongoing puzzle, I had a host of other worries about objections to the Christian faith. Why does God allow suffering and pain? Why are wars being fought in the name of religion? And so on. I needed to sort out these things, especially if I were to follow my dream of pursuing a career in biology while retaining my Christian faith.

When I was about sixteen years old, I came across the "Evolution Protest Movement" (EPM), the forerunner in the UK of the Biblical Creation Society (BCS). I wrote to the EPM to explain my dilemma as a Christian about biology. I received a very strange answer – a postcard explaining how evolution is a LIE (they used capital letters like that) and that if I were to pursue the study of biology I must fight against evolution.

My father, an agricultural biochemist who was also a Christian, bought me a book by Donald MacKay, a Christian physicist.[1] I read it with huge relief. Here was someone who knew what he was talking about as a scientist and was a firm Christian believer. The clarity of MacKay's writing challenged me to be sceptical of both ends of the spectrum, i.e. atheists who attacked Christianity with evolution *and* Christians who felt it was their duty to attack evolution in order to defend the faith.

However, despite MacKay's little book, and despite reading other apologists for the Christian faith such as C. S. Lewis and Malcolm Muggeridge, I found it hard to think these things through. Was I the only person in the world struggling with this? I felt I couldn't turn to church folks because I was scared that the person who told me that studying biology would compromise my faith was representative of how all Christians of my acquaintance thought. Then, on the other side, there were atheists such as Richard Dawkins who were unprepared to give me any space at all to think that Christian belief made any sense about the world.

While I was struggling with this intellectual turmoil about what I believed, my parents' marriage was disintegrating. This added to the feeling of not being able to talk to anyone who might be able to understand, least of all fellow Christians in church whom (I felt) were not only anti-evolution/anti-science but also anti-divorce.

What was I to do? I became a "creationist" of sorts, i.e. I believed in some kind of scientific explanation about the origins of the world, but I also believed that if God was the creator of the world then maybe some aspects of the evolutionary explanation of the world must necessarily be flawed. I read about "gaps" in the

---

[1] The book was *The Clockwork Image*. It was originally published by IVP in 1974, reprinted in 1997 as a Christian Classic from IVP (Leicester).

fossil record that supposedly could not be explained by evolution. In particular, I could not believe that evolution applied to the origin of the human species. Were not humans specially created by God and therefore not subject to the same evolutionary forces that had acted on the rest of the (non-human) natural world? I started a notebook about objections to an evolutionary explanation of the origins of human beings.

As time went on – and I still resolved to pursue a biology career – the prospect grew within me that I might have to go it alone, battling against both atheistic biologists *and* against fellow Christians who did not (or would not) agree with science. Although I had by that time developed some heroes (such as MacKay) to emulate, I feared I might have to travel a lonely road.

In fact, all this gave me an extra incentive to become a fully fledged biologist. In order to "fight the good fight" against the evils of atheistic evolutionism, I resolved that I must go to university to understand further the reasoning behind evolution and discover more about the dangers prophesied by my church friend. I felt I was somehow called by God to confront the threats to Christianity head-on by gaining a better understanding of evolutionary science so that I would be able to counter them.

Thus armed with a naïve "creationist" viewpoint, and determined to be an intellectual soldier armed to fight against the evils of an evolutionary worldview, I got the relevant A-level grades to get to university. I was going to read zoology and become a scientist.

So what happened that made me change my mind and become a convinced evolutionist?

During my zoology degree, I learned detailed evolutionary explanations of how species come about. We looked at "ring species". If God had created species distinctly from one another, why did He create them so that their appearance changed gradually between neighbours? Doesn't an evolutionary explanation make more sense than creation of these species one by one?

We covered the origins of flight, where we looked closely at the characteristics of intermediary species in palaeontological history – including the famous Jurassic "bird" *Archaeopteryx* and other pre-avian fossils – and we were told about the Hoatzin, a species living in South America that has remnants of dinosaur characteristics, such as a claw on its wings. I remember pondering over the list of characteristics of fully formed birds and comparing these with the characteristics of *Archaeopteryx* and pre-avian dinosaurs. Even though *Archaeopteryx* had feathers and other bird-like characteristics, it also displayed distinctly *non* bird-like characteristics, such as the possession of teeth, a markedly reduced sternum, some major differences in the skull, and a long "true" tail, i.e. a tail with vertebrae. These are found in dinosaurs but not in modern birds.

Evolutionary explanations for the origins of birds and flight made sense to me. The existence of intermediate species between dinosaurs and true birds (such as *Archaeopteryx* – many more have since been discovered) illustrated transitional characteristics beautifully. They were neither fully bird-like nor fully "dinosaurian" – they were so-called "missing links". The biological explanation of such transitional characteristics were far more convincing to me than the "creationist" objections to the evolutionary story, which tried to maintain that *Archaeopteryx* was in fact a true bird – when clearly it was not.

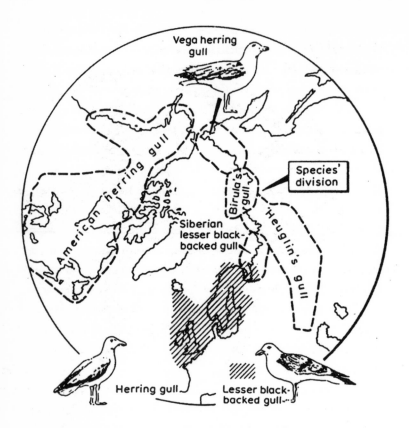

Figure 16.1 A ring species of gulls surrounds the Pole. The change between neighbours is gradual, but in Europe the two ends of the ring are distinct species (adapted from M. Ridley, "Who doubts evolution?", *New Scientist*, **90**, 1981, pp. 830–832).

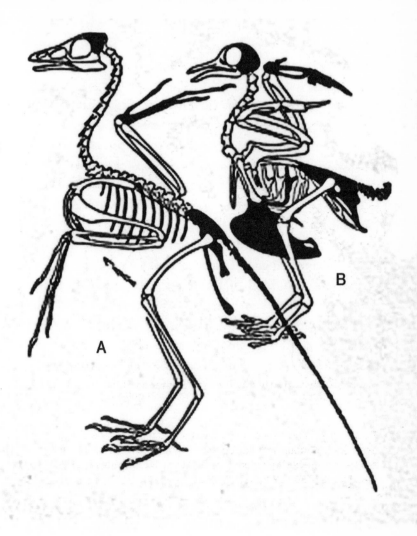

Figure 16.2 The anatomy of *Archaeopteryx* (A) and a pigeon (B).

Looking at the various theories of the origins of flight, such as "arboreal", "pouncing proavis", and "cursorial" theories fascinated me.[2] Such musings about the origins of flight are still subjects for student essays. Despite the fact that it is still not clear *exactly* how avian flight evolved, the possibility that evolutionary change has occurred was far more convincing to me as a young biologist than the idea that God just happened to have created species in a particular way. It seemed to me that "creationists" jumped on any objection, however flimsy, to evolution, even if the evolutionary explanation made sense biologically.

There were also wider problems to face. Why did God, if He is a loving and good creator, use such a cruel and vicious mechanism – survival of the fittest – to create species? I remember studying closely the skull of a blood-feeding bat. The skull had incredibly sharp teeth, superbly adapted to cutting into and feeding on the blood of large mammals. It was difficult to see how a creator God might have created, lovingly, piece by piece, such a superb mechanism for feeding on blood. What about the adaptations of spiders to killing their prey? Why had God invented such superb and efficient killing machines? How could I deal with the thought that God had intentionally devised the dentition and physiology of large cats, perfectly adapted for meat hunting and eating? If God had created them that way, how does this square with the teaching of the Bible? What about the vision of heaven where predators and prey coexist in harmony?

---

[2] Plus the more recent "wing-assisted incline running" theory. For details of these various theories, see John Videler, *Avian Flight*, Oxford: Oxford University Press, 2005.

The wolf shall dwell with the lamb,
and the leopard shall lie down with the young goat,
and the calf and the lion and the fattened calf together;
and a little child shall lead them.

(Isaiah 11:6, ESV)

Reading such biblical material, and seeing how the natural world actually functions, I could not escape the biological question: how will the wolf, the leopard and the lion be in any way recognizable in heaven and resemble anything like wolves, leopards, or lions if their way of life will be so different from how they survive on this earth now? Perhaps passages like these were meant to be read poetically and not literally? But I was hearing a lot of sermons and reading a lot of Christian writers who warned about the dangers of a "slippery slope" – if one agreed with "metaphor" and did not take the Bible literally, where might these thoughts end up?

As part of our course on the ecology of small mammals, we caught some in live traps. I vividly remember a post-mortem examination of one such animal which had a gut full of tapeworms. How on earth did the poor creature survive at all in the wild with such a heavy parasitic load? Yet, clearly it did – and moreover the species *thrived* in that environment. The question arose in another guise: how does a loving God create the natural world in such a way as this? Was this Tennyson's "Nature, red in tooth and claw"[3] writ large in parasites as I squinted down the binocular microscope? On the one hand I was being encouraged to worship God for His amazing creation, and on the other to wonder how He had created it with all its pain and suffering.

---

[3] Alfred Lord Tennyson, (1809–92), "In Memoriam".

To hammer this problem even further home, we learned about parasites in entomology, where tiny wasps lay their eggs near (or even in) the larvae of other insects – and how the parasite larvae, when they hatch, commence to eat the other insect. I found this fascinating and horrifying at the same time. It raised huge theological questions. Some years later, I wrote the following for a conference of Christians in Science in 1993:

> Many still believe that Darwinism has had a devastating, some would say fatal, effect on Christian faith. For example, David Hull:

> What kind of God can one infer from the sort of phenomena epitomized by the species on Darwin's Galápagos Islands? The evolutionary process is rife with happenstance, contingency, incredible waste, death, pain and horror ... to quote Darwin, "I cannot persuade myself that a beneficent and omnipotent God would have designedly created the Ichneumonidae with the express intention of their feeding within the living bodies of caterpillars" ... The God of the Galápagos is careless, wasteful, indifferent, almost diabolical. He is certainly not the sort of God to whom anyone would be inclined to pray.[4]

I also came across the sad descent into madness of the brilliant mathematician George Price, who struggled with the teachings of Christ to be altruistic and squaring them up with the pioneering work of the Oxford theoretical biologist Bill Hamilton.[5]

---

[4] David L. Hull, "The God of the Galápagos" (review of Phillip Johnson's book *Darwin on Trial*), *Nature* **352** (8 August 1991), pp. 485–486.

[5] See Oren Harman, *The Price of Altruism*, London: The Bodley Head, 2010.

Hamilton, Price, and others had been working on a mathematical way of describing how altruism can survive and prosper in a world where evolution apparently dictates that only selfishness can survive. Although rather an extreme case, Price's personal struggle was indicative of the difficulty that many saw between being a Christian and being a biologist.

Fascinated as I was by evolution, being exposed to the teaching that perhaps even altruism can be explained by evolution, and seeing more and more clearly the raw cruelty of nature, did this therefore mean that Christian belief was bogus? I hoped not, but I needed help from expert biologists who were Christians to help me think this conundrum through. I just could not hold with the rather twee "Ah, isn't nature pretty" view, which bore little resemblance to the real biological world that I was increasingly discovering. I could no longer hold with any integrity my naïve creationist point of view.

Did these and other experiences lead me to lose my faith? Absolutely not. Despite worrying that I was completely alone in struggling with this issue – grappling with the skeleton in the cupboard – I found, and was relieved to find, that many others felt just as I did. In parallel to learning more and more evidence for evolutionary explanations for species' change, and thereby becoming increasingly worried that many Christians were wrong in their attacking of evolution, I also began to discover that there were, in fact, many other Christian believers who were *convinced* by evolution. To Donald MacKay was added a large list of other scientists who were believers but who did not attack evolution. Moreover, many of these people found an evolutionary explanation of the natural world's development if anything *encouraged* and *deepened* their faith.

Many of these scientists were members of what used to be called the Research Scientists' Christian Fellowship (RSCF, a specialist group of the Universities and Colleges Christian Fellowship, UCCF). The RSCF was the forerunner of Christians in Science (CiS). Although it took me a while to find out about such people, as soon as I did, I embraced their thinking with great relief.

Membership of the RSCF/CiS (and several years' service on its committee) introduced me to the compatibility of science and faith. I learned about:

- how the origins of science in the sixteenth and seventeenth centuries had deep theistic roots
- how an explanation of something scientifically didn't "explain away" the phenomenon (the fallacy of "nothing buttery", to use MacKay's term)
- how many biologists were, in fact, believers and that the vast majority of these were not anti-evolution, e.g. the Oxford ornithologist David Lack, the ecological geneticist R. J. (Sam) Berry, the botanist Sir Ghillean Prance, and many others
- how a true understanding of the history of science is repeatedly distorted by using the "conflict thesis" to explain what happened in the development of science
- how the "functionary integrity" of creation is a much better way of characterizing the science-faith relationship, as argued for by the American physicist, Howard van Till.[6]

These and other arguments encouraged me to see that rather than a conflict between science and faith, the two areas of belief can, in fact, be reconciled with integrity.

---

[6] Howard Van Till, *The Fourth Day,* Grand Rapids, MI: Eerdmans, 1986.

What, then, of evolution as applied to human beings? It took a little longer to convince me that neo-Darwinian evolution was an adequate and convincing explanation for species change among pre-human species. Here again, as I read Don Johanson's book *Lucy*,[7] and looked at the morphology of such hominid species as *Homo habilis* and *Homo erectus*, and saw how they might have changed through to *Homo sapiens*, I found the evolutionary explanation convincing. My "theology", i.e. my ill thought-out and rather naïve objections to the inclusion of hominids in evolutionary change, would just have to be modified as a result of the overwhelming evidence presented to me by the natural world. The key factor seems to be that only humans are "made in God's image" (Genesis 1:27), and God's image is not an product of evolution.

It was to me – and remains – a puzzle and worry that Christians disagree so strongly about evolution. To illustrate this, some years after I started my career in science publishing, my family and I were planning to move. We visited a church in the town we were contemplating. It just so happened that the Sunday morning service when we visited the church was being led by some students from the local university who were hesitantly – but approvingly – quoting from a scientist called Denis Alexander. It was clear that they didn't know who he was or even whether he was a Christian. The fact that they were nervous illustrated to me that they probably expected some in the congregation to disagree with their quoting Dr Alexander because he (and they) weren't "creationists". I went up to the students afterwards to reassure them that the person they were

---

[7] Don Johanson, *Lucy: The Beginnings of Humankind*, London: Simon & Schuster, 1990.

quoting was a friend of mine and was indeed a believer.[8]

When I served on the RSCF/CiS committee, there were regular discussions as to what might we do about communicating to the church and to the wider community, how can we make it better known that there are many Christians who are scientists and who are firm believers? Moreover, how might we show clearly the problems with the "creationist" viewpoint and that it certainly was *not* the only option for Christian believers? I regularly worried that the committee had made the wrong decision by taking a softly, softly approach, by seeking to influence "creationists" rather than standing up to them publicly.

In 1993 I was rapporteur for a meeting between the RSCF/ CiS and the Biblical Creation Society (BCS). It was inconclusive. However, its influence on those attending was considerable. A number of questions emerged, many of which are still on the agenda for creationists to answer. A letter was sent to the BCS after the meeting – but did not receive an answer:

> *The biologist delights in the marvellous adaptations of animals and plants to their way of life. The teeth, body shape and enormously complex digestive system of the cow is marvellously adapted to eating grass, but so are the teeth, body shape (bones, muscles, ability to spring, claws, eyes, etc.) digestive system and adaptive colouration of the tiger, adapted to being a predator. On your [biblical creationist] view, though the former may have been an act of Creation, the latter was not. It only took place after the Fall when Creation was finished and we may not marvel at these as*

---

[8] Some years later I had the privilege of working with Dr Alexander by editing his publishing tour de force *Rebuilding the Matrix: Science and Faith in the 21st Century*, Oxford: Lion, 2001.

parts of "Creation". But we would not have thought that they were part of Providence either. You have ruled out as not part of Creation at all a very large percentage of the marvellous adaptations to life that every school child is taught to appreciate. Your view seems to prove too much and frankly seems to us to be unbiblical in that the Bible speaks often of God delighting in His creatures including predators (see for instance Job 41 and Psalm 104 verses 21 and 24). May we or may we not admire the spiders web, the chameleon's colour change and the feeding mechanisms of carnivores, from whales to sea anemones as works of creation? If they are not works of creation, what are they biblically?[9]

The continuing lack of convincing answers to such questions illustrates why I remain wedded to evolution.

Since my struggle as a young Christian to come to terms with the challenges of evolution to Christian belief, I have become ever more persuaded that there are many more theological problems inherent in "creationism" than in what is called "theistic evolution".[10] This does not mean that there are

---

[9] From a letter written by the RSCF secretary to the BCS, dated 9 August 1983.

[10] Indeed, if there are problems inherent in the concepts of evolutionary biology, as creationists claim, then present-day biological concepts used, for example, in conservation biology, must be flawed. This could lead to bad biological decisions. If the creationist's view of species is essentially a static one (even if allowing for microevolution within specified taxa), then all of the work on island biogeography by Dan Simberloff, E. O. Wilson and others, which led to concepts routinely used by conservation biologists, could also be erroneous. If this is so, then many of the assumptions of stewardship theology based on conservation biology concepts are erroneous too. Careful scientific biological research must surely trump creationist objections to evolution if we are to make any headway in the conservation of biodiversity.

no problems in theistic evolution but, for me, the overwhelming weight of evidence from our knowledge of the natural world and how it functions points incontrovertibly towards evolution as a fact.

CHAPTER 17

Struggling with Origins: A Personal Story

Denis O. Lamoureux is Associate Professor of Science and Religion at St Joseph's College in the University of Alberta. He trained first as a dentist, and then went on to earn PhD degrees in both theology and biology. He debated with Phillip Johnson in *Darwinism Defeated?* (Regent, 1999), is the author of *Evolutionary Creation* (Wipf and Stock, 2008), and a contributor to *Four Views on the Historical Adam* (Zondervan, 2013).

I struggled with the issue of origins for over twenty years of my adult life. Understanding where we come from influences our beliefs about who we are, how we live with one another, and what we can hope for in the future. So, although in many ways my story is not unique, it is also rather unusual in that I pursued a PhD in theology followed by a PhD in biology in an attempt to make sense of origins. Becoming an evolutionary creationist and believing that the God of the Bible created the universe and life through an ordained, sustained, and design-reflecting evolutionary process involved many challenging moments.

In retrospect, I now recognize that struggle is a vital aspect of our personal relationship with our creator. In fact, the word "Israel" is made up of the Hebrew *śārâ* (to struggle, persist) and *'ēl*

(God). It first appears in Scripture after Jacob had wrestled with God. The Lord then stated, "Your name will no longer be Jacob, but Israel, because you have struggled with God and with men and have overcome" (Genesis 32:28, NIV 1984). Christians are the New Israel and we should expect some trying periods in our walk with the Lord. And I believe that our dealing with the issue of origins will be one of those challenging times.

Entrenched in dichotomies

I was raised in a good French-Canadian Roman Catholic home in Edmonton, Alberta, Canada. There was unconditional love and healthy discipline in my family. Through the 1960s, I was blessed with a fine education by the publicly funded Catholic school system. The issue of origins did not come to my attention until the eleventh grade in a biology class. One of my favourite teachers, Mr Adrien Bouchard, pointed out that evolution does not necessarily force us to reject our Christian faith. He was a man of deep religious conviction, and explained that biological evolution could be seen as God's process for creating all living organisms.

Looking back at this critical period in my life, I would certainly agree. However, simply telling sixteen-year-olds that God could have created life through evolution is not enough to protect them from the challenges of a secular culture, especially if they decide to attend a public university. The full case for evolutionary creation needs to be made to young people.[1] In particular, they require an explanation as to why we should not read the opening chapters of the Bible literally as a historical

---

[1] I prefer the term "evolutionary creation" rather than "theistic evolution" to describe my view of origins. In recent years, the former has been embraced most by evangelical Christians like me.

record. Consequently, when I left high school I was not equipped to protect my faith from the soon-to-follow ravages of university secularism.

In 1972 I entered Collège St Jean, the French faculty of the University of Alberta. The college was the intellectual and cultural centre of the French-Canadian community. At this point in history, French-Canadian Catholicism had just undergone the "Silent Revolution" of the 1960s in which religious issues were gently set aside.[2] Even though the college had deep Roman Catholic roots through the Oblate Fathers, it became largely secularized and steeped in the philosophical thinking of twentieth-century French culture in Europe. Many viewed the existentialist atheists Albert Camus and Jean-Paul Sartre as intellectual heroes. I understood the message of these philosophers to be that life is ultimately meaningless and that our best response is to live so-called "authentically" for the moment. As an impressionable eighteen-year-old, I assumed the intellectual smugness of professors and senior students indicated that scholarship had long ago rejected the existence of God. Clearly no reasonable person could possibly be religious.

Yet, the most powerful force shaping the development of my worldview was science. For me, scientific evidence was more convincing than the arguments of philosophers, because it was tangible. As a science student, I soon embraced a second smug attitude. I assumed that science was the only credible form of thinking. From this perspective, I looked down on those in the humanities because they dealt merely with shifting "opinions" and "subjective" ideas. In contrast, scientists were engaged with hard "facts" and "objective" truth. Presumptuously, I contended

[2] See Michael Gauvreau, *The Catholic Origins of Quebec's Quiet Revolution*, Montreal and Kingston: McGill-Queen's University Press, 2005.

that scientists were the university's "pure" thinkers. After all, there was no need to defend the success of science since everyone enjoyed its fruits every single day. With scientism at its peak in the mid-twentieth century, it was almost inevitable that my generation of students would come to believe that only science could explain reality, and only science could offer solutions to all our problems. Under the influence of the zeitgeist of the public university education in the early 1970s, I was socially conditioned by atheism and scientism, and as a consequence deeply committed to a science versus religion dichotomy.

My very first biology course was on evolution. Just like my high school experience, the professor opened the first lecture by stating that evolution did not necessarily undermine religion. But once again, this had little to no impact on me (though I still remember the moment like it was yesterday). And to repeat my earlier comment, merely telling students that God could have used evolution is simply not enough to fully convince them. A reasonable defence for evolutionary creation must be given by presenting philosophical and scriptural arguments.

The underlying message throughout my evolution course was quite obvious. Life originated only through natural processes with no hint of teleology (i.e. no ultimate plan or purpose). I came to what I thought was a completely logical conclusion: *since evolution is true, then the Bible must be false and so too must Christianity*. I knew that Scripture states the world was created in six days, but I discovered in class that science proves the universe and life evolved. Despite having two instructors in my life telling me that evolution does not necessarily undercut faith, I was nevertheless hopelessly entrenched in the prevalent origins dichotomy. In this mindset, one is either on the scientific side with the evidence for evolution, or on the religious side with the biblical account of creation in six literal days; there really is no credible middle ground. It is important to point out that coming to this conclusion occurred in the very first four months of being at a public university. High school simply had not equipped me to face the onslaught of secularism.

By Christmas 1972, I had rejected the Christian faith of my boyhood and was on my way to an atheistic worldview. Yet there still remained a ray of hope. I recorded in my diary at the end of my first year of university (28 April 1973), "It seems that man is nothing but mere chemical reactions programmed by DNA … But there's more, I'm sure." Though I had dismissed the God of Christianity, there was still a nebulous deity that accounted for life being "more" than just "chemical reactions". In reality, however, I lived as if this God only existed when I desperately needed Him, such as the times when I thought my girlfriend was pregnant. I merely had a God-of-the-emergencies to whom I fervently prayed to save me from the consequences of my foolishness and immorality.

I entered dental school in 1974 and joined the military to pay for my education. A number of my classmates were evangelical Christians. They often shared their faith with me, and I even found their apologetic arguments to be persuasive at times. But more importantly, their consistent and godly lifestyle impacted me more than any rational defence for Christianity. Though I could not articulate it at that time, in many ways, I wanted what they had. I yearned for God and holiness. Of course, the issue of evolution was a stumbling block, since most of these evangelicals were committed anti-evolutionists. Once again, the origins dichotomy reared its head in my life, forcing me to assume that I had only two choices: science and evolution, or religion and creation.

Though the reality of Jesus Christ was being wonderfully displayed in the lives of some of my dental classmates, I was also entrenched in a lifestyle marked by the godless excesses of the 1970s. Moving on from the nebulous deity of the first years of university, I slipped into and out of periods of agnosticism until finally I embraced atheism. In another revealing diary entry, I concluded (20 June 1977), "Love is a protective response characteristic of all animals, except expressed to greater levels in man because of his superior intelligence." I remember writing this entry because at the time I was wickedly cynical. One of my favourite sayings was that "love is a herd response". In other words, humans are merely a herd of animals in heat. It takes little imagination to picture how I treated women. I'm certainly not proud of that. Marriage did not really mean anything to me because it was nothing but a social convention. There wasn't anything sacred about it, because the sacred did not exist. For me, an atheistic view of evolution led to a life with no ultimate moral boundaries.

I graduated from dental school in 1978 and began a four-year commitment to the Canadian Armed Forces. My education had fully persuaded me that happiness was to be found in a self-serving lifestyle. This meant women, rum and coke, and playing as much golf as possible. From the outside, many would say I was having the time of my life. But deep inside of me there was an uneasy feeling. There was an emptiness and a distinct feeling of being "unclean".

A peacekeeper meets the Prince of Peace

In the autumn of 1979 I was posted to the island of Cyprus as a United Nations peacekeeper. There I became a Christian, by the Lord's grace and in answer to my mother's prayers, and as a result of reading the Gospel of John. There were no dramatic signs and wonders, or major crises. I simply yearned for God and holiness. As I read the Bible, I started to have a sense of cleansing. If a conversion point has to be chosen, it was Good Friday. I attended a chapel service and it was there the Lord revealed to me the meaning of the crucifixion – Jesus loves us so much that He died for us (Romans 5:8). I began to weep during the Scripture reading and continued for the rest of the service. In an amazingly mysterious way, an everlasting peace had entered my soul.

The Cyprus tour changed my life for ever. When I arrived there, I was spiritually empty; six months later I returned home to Canada filled with the Holy Spirit and the peace of Jesus. Indeed, I had been born again, a new creation in Christ (John 3:3).

Upon returning home, I was led to an evangelical church with a wonderful pastor. His love for Scripture impacted me deeply, and it continues to shape both my personal walk of faith and professional practice as a theologian. Since this was an evangelical church, the view of origins espoused by most of the members was Young Earth Creationism. They convinced me that evolution was Satan's primary weapon for attacking the faith of young people. This made perfect sense to me because a first-year university course on evolution had destroyed my faith.

Before long, I was steeped in anti-evolutionary literature, including Duane Gish's *Evolution: The Fossils Say No!*, John Whitcomb and Henry Morris's *The Genesis Flood*, and the latter's *Scientific Creationism*. In 1981, I took part in a week-long summer workshop offered by the Institute for Creation Research and there I befriended Canada's leading Young Earth Creationist, Dr Margaret Helder. She held a PhD in botany and was proof there were scientists with real academic qualifications who rejected evolution. During this period I was also introduced to so-called "theistic evolution", but it was quickly dismissed as a view of origins held by liberal Christians because they weren't really committed to Jesus and didn't fully trust the Bible. For me, *true* Christians were Young Earth Creationists.

In the autumn of 1981, I made my views on origins public for the first time. Helder was the co-editor of *Creation Science Dialogue*, and she asked me for a short contribution defending my belief in Young Earth Creationism. The article was entitled "Philosophy vs. Science". In it I enthusiastically promoted my newly found anti-evolutionism. "I challenge anyone who takes pride in their objectivity to entertain seriously scientific creationism. It may very well be the most important study of your life."[3] Obviously, I was still trapped in the origins dichotomy. As the title reveals, evolution was not science, but merely a secular "Philosophy", and real "Science" was in actual fact creation science.

The depth of my commitment to Young Earth Creationism is illustrated by the fact that in 1983 I was studying medicine at the University of Toronto while being paid my full dentist's salary by the Canadian military. After being in the programme for only three days, I left with the intention of becoming a creation scientist in order to attack evolutionists in public universities. I had lost my faith in a first-year course on evolutionary biology and I was committed to defending young Christian men and women at universities from the satanic lie that life evolved. To equip myself for the battle, I planned first to study theology and the opening chapters of the Bible at Regent College in Vancouver,

---

[3] My article can be found at: www.ualberta.ca/~dlamoure/p_yec.jgp

British Columbia. This would be followed by a programme on Young Earth Creationism led by creation scientists Henry Morris and Duane Gish at the Institute of Creation Research in El Cajon, California.

Beyond Young Earth Creationism

During the mid-1980s, Regent College was one of the foremost evangelical graduate schools of theology in the world. Its faculty included leading scholars such as J. I. Packer, Bruce Waltke, Gordon Fee, and Michael Green. Though my intention was to focus on Genesis 1–11, I had a larger agenda. As my diary reveals on the day of registration (30 August 1984): "The Grand Plan: Declare absolute and pure hell on the 'theory' of evolution."

But my plan soon came under attack and I discovered what seminarians before me have experienced – biblical interpretation is much more complicated than what we learn in Sunday school. In a lecture during the first month of the programme, J. I. Packer openly stated that the first chapters of the Bible "were obviously written in picture language". This shook me to the core. Packer was arguably the most important evangelical theologian of the day, and his best-selling book *Knowing God* (IVP, 1973) had brought many people to Christ. I personally knew some of these converts. Packer's claim that Genesis featured "picture language" unsettled most of the students in the class because evangelical Christians are concordists (or better, scientific concordists).[4] In other words, the majority of evangelicals believe that there is an

---

[4] Eighty-seven per cent of American evangelicals read Genesis 1 and Genesis 6–9 as "literally true, meaning it happened that way word-for-word". That is, they believe that the entire world was actually created in six literal days and that there really was a global flood. Survey conducted 6–10 February 2004 by International Communications Research Media, PA at: www.icrsurvey.com/ studies/947a1%20Views%20of%20the%20Bible.pdf

accord or alignment between the Bible and the facts of science, and that Genesis 1–11 offers a literal and historical account of origins.

Challenges to my simplistic literal reading of the opening chapters of Scripture continued in the next semester at Regent. I took a course on the relationship between science and faith taught by the philosopher and literary scholar Dr Loren Wilkinson. I asked him directly what he thought about Young Earth Creationism. He responded bluntly, "It is error." I can still remember how the word "error" rattled my soul. I had previously taken a philosophy course from him in the first semester and had a great respect for his knowledge and integrity. In the final moments of his class, Wilkinson looked at me hard, and then he said, "Denis, I have a serious concern. Should you ever give up your belief in Young Earth Creation, would you also give up your faith in Christ?" That was one question I was not expecting. And that wasn't Wilkinson talking. The Holy Spirit was flowing through his words and casting a light on my understanding of Christianity. I mumbled and stumbled, and never really answered. Deep in my heart of hearts, I knew that my personal relationship with Jesus was much more important than any view of origins. I stepped away from this science and faith class still a Young Earth Creationist, but for the first time as a Christian I asked myself whether or not a literalist reading of Genesis 1–11 was the correct interpretation of God's Word.

For three years, Regent College repeatedly challenged me to rethink how the Holy Spirit inspired the biblical writers. It became quite evident that Scripture had an ancient understanding of the physical world, or if you wish, an "ancient science". As the diagram and verses in Figure 17.1 reveal, the Bible features a three-

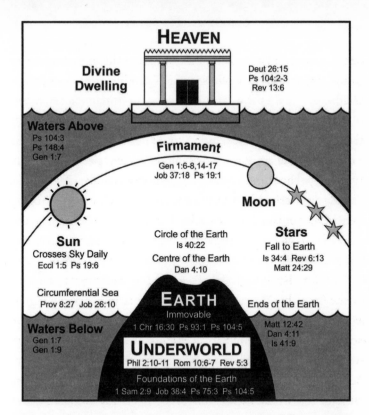

Figure 17.1 The three-tier universe: Regional geography and the horizon led ancient Near Eastern people to believe the earth was surrounded by a circumferential sea. Travel in any direction came to a body of water: Mediterranean Sea is west, Black and Caspian Seas north, Persian Gulf east, and Arabian and Red Seas south. This ancient understanding of the structure of the world sheds light on the meaning of Is 40:22, "God sits enthroned above the circle of the earth, its people are like grasshoppers. He stretches out the heavens like a canopy, and spreads them out like a tent to live in." The "circle of the earth" does not refer to the outline of planet earth, but rather to a circular flat earth viewed from God's perspective overhead. The three-tier universe also assists in the interpretation of Ps 104:2–3, "God stretches out the heavens like a tent and lays the beams of His upper chambers [i.e., divine dwelling] on their waters." In this way, God's heavenly dwelling is set in the "waters above". Note the use of the tent metaphor in both verses to indicate the structure of the universe with a domed heaven overhead and a flat earth below.

tier universe. The presence of this ancient conceptualization of nature is particularly obvious in the Genesis 1 creation account. On the second creation day, God creates the firmament (Hebrew: *rāqîa'*) to separate the waters and create a heavenly sea overhead; He then embeds the sun, moon, and stars in this firmament on day four. From an ancient phenomenological perspective, this is exactly what the structure of the world looks like. The blue of the sky gives the impression that there is a body of water above, upheld by a firm structure, across which heavenly bodies like the sun move daily. In fact, this was the best science-of-the-day in the ancient Near Eastern World.[5]

I also discovered that Genesis 1 is built on an ancient poetic framework, a pair of parallel panels as presented in Figure 17.2. During the first three days of creation, God defines the boundaries of the universe. In the last three days, He fills the world with heavenly bodies and living creatures. Parallels emerge between the panels. On day one, God creates light in alignment with the fourth day's placement of the sun in the firmament. The separation of the waters above from the waters below on the second creation day provides an air space for birds and a sea for marine creatures, both made on the fifth day. Finally on day three God commands land to appear in anticipation of the origin of animals and humans on day six.

---

[5] This ancient conceptualization of the structure of the universe appears in both Egypt and Mesopotamia. See www.ualberta.ca/~dlamoure/h83.pdf (accessed 10 July 2014) and also www.ualberta.ca/~dlamoure/h80.pdf

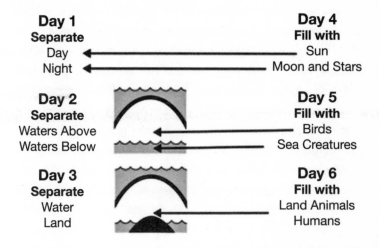

Figure 17.2 The parallel panels in Genesis 1. Recognizing and respecting this ancient poetic (i.e. structured) framework resolves the so-called "contradiction" of the light (day one) being created before the sun (day four). Poetic freedom allowed the inspired author to distinguish the forming of boundaries in the universe (days one to three) from the filling of the world with various creations (days four to six).

It became painfully obvious to me that Genesis 1 could not be a literal and historical account of how the world was made. We do not live in a three-tier universe and history does not unfold in parallel panels. Scientific concordism fails. However, with the many challenges to my Young Earth Creationism, Regent College also provided new approaches to understanding biblical inspiration. George Eldon Ladd's aphorism offered a vital insight: "The Bible is the Word of God written in the words of men in history."[6] It underlines that Scripture indeed contained

---

[6] George Eldon Ladd, *The New Testament and Criticism*, Grand Rapids, MI: Eerdmans, 1967, p. 12.

"the very words of God" (Romans 3:2, NIV), yet these were cast within the context of ancient times. In other words, the Holy Spirit *accommodated* in the revelatory process by coming down to the level of ancient people and using their ancient ideas about nature in order to communicate inerrant, life-changing, spiritual truths. Or, stated another way, the Lord employed an *incidental ancient science* as a vessel to deliver *Messages of Faith*.[7] The inerrant spiritual truth in Genesis 1 was not *how* God created, but more importantly *that* He created. By understanding the ancient historical milieu in which Scripture was inspired by the Holy Spirit, I was freed from the chains of scientific concordism.

Regent College was the most challenging spiritual experience of my life. Ironically, it was the evidence within the Scripture itself that undermined my intention of becoming a creation scientist. After three years of focusing on Genesis 1–11, I came to the shocking conclusion that Young Earth Creationism is unbiblical.

Beyond so-called "Darwinism"

I moved from Regent College to the Toronto School of Theology in the University of Toronto for a PhD in theology specializing in science and religion. My thesis examined the first generation of evangelical scholars encountering Charles Darwin's theory of evolution. I was surprised to discover that many of them did not have a problem with biological evolution because they viewed it as a teleological process. More specifically, evolution was understood to be the Lord's ordained and sustained natural

---

[7] I have termed this interpretative concept as the Message-Incident Principle. For more, see my book chapter entitled "Ancient Science in the Bible" from *I Love Jesus & I Accept Evolution*, Eugene, OR: Wipf and Stock, 2009, or online at: www.ualberta.ca/~dlamoure/ancient_science.pdf (accessed 11 July 2014).

process.[8] These evangelicals embraced the time-honoured Two Divine Books model of the relationship between science and religion. They lived the spiritual messages in the Book of God's Words and they embraced the scientific method in the Book of God's Works. Neither dichotomies nor warfare marked their view of science and religion. These evangelical scholars acknowledged Intelligent Design in nature and even extended it to include evolutionary processes.[9] They saw the reflection of God's mind not only in the details of the world but at an overarching level across the aeons of time.

I was also shocked to find that Darwin himself was not an atheist. Sunday schools had taught me that he was the father of modern atheism. Of course, like most evangelical Christians, I had never read Darwin's *On the Origin of Species* (1859). But I discovered

---

[8] For a fine introduction, see David N. Livingstone, *Darwin's Forgotten Defenders*, Grand Rapids, MI: Eerdmans, 1987.

[9] Regrettably, the term "Intelligent Design" has been co-opted and muddled by the so-called "Intelligent Design Movement." I embrace the traditional definition of intelligent design which asserts that beauty, complexity, and functionality in nature point to a Creative Intelligence. This concept is consistent with the theological notion of natural revelation and the biblical passages Psalm 19:1–4 and Romans 1:18–20. In contrast, ID theorists purport to detect design *scientifically*, entrenching another false dichotomy – biological evolution versus Intelligent Design. ID Theory is a narrow view of design that is connected to miraculous interventions in the origin of life. In other words, it is just another God-of-the-gaps model. For example, parts of the cell such as the flagellum are claimed to be "irreducibly complex". As a result, they could not have evolved through natural processes. With this being the case, ID Theory should be more accurately termed *Interventionistic* Design Theory. See my debate with Phillip E. Johnson, in Phillip E. Johnson and Denis O. Lamoureux, *Darwinism Defeated? The Johnson-Lamoureux Debate on Biological Origins* (Vancouver, BC: Regent College Press, 1999); also see my exchange with Michael Behe, in Denis O. Lamoureux, "A Box or a Black Hole? A Response to Michael J. Behe", *Canadian Catholic Review* 17:3 (July 1999), pp. 67–73.

that in it Darwin declared his belief in a creator who made living organisms through evolution.[10] For example, he argues:

> *To my mind it accords better with what we know of the laws*
> *impressed on matter by the Creator, that the production*
> *and extinction of the past and present inhabitants of the*
> *world should have been due to secondary causes like those*
> *determining the birth and death of the individual.*[11]

I found this passage to be an absolutely amazing insight! Every Christian today believes that we were created in our mother's womb through natural embryological and developmental processes. I have yet to meet a Christian who thinks God intervenes dramatically to attach a leg or an arm to their developing foetus. Rather, we believe that the Lord "knit[s us] together … fearfully and wonderfully made" (Psalm 139:13–14, NIV). So too with biological evolution. It is the Lord's ordained and sustained natural "knitting process" to create all the God-glorifying forms of life on earth.

But the most astonishing discovery made during my Toronto PhD was a letter Darwin had written about his religious beliefs only a few years before his death. Responding to John Fordyce in 1879, he opens, "It seems to me absurd to doubt that a man may be an ardent theist and an evolutionist."[12] In just

---

[10] Darwin refers to a "Creator" seven times and always in a positive way in the *Origin of Species*. See *On the Origin of Species*, Cambridge: Harvard University Press (1859), 1964, pp. 186, 188, 189, 413 (twice), 435, 488.

[11] *Ibid.*, p. 488.

[12] Darwin to Fordyce, 7 May 1879, Darwin Correspondence Project Letter 12041. Online at: http://www.darwinproject.ac.uk/letter/entry-12041 (accessed 11 July 2014). Also in Francis Darwin (ed), *The Life and Letters of Charles Darwin*, 3 vols., London: John Murray, 1887), I, p. 304.

one short sentence, Charles Darwin completely destroys both the science versus religion dichotomy and the creation versus evolution dichotomy. I can't help but ask, "Have atheists like Richard Dawkins ever read the Darwin literature?" To embrace either dichotomy is "absurd"! In addition, Darwin reveals in this letter, "I have never been an Atheist in the sense of denying the existence of a God." So the question must be asked, "Did Darwin actually embrace Darwinism?" No! The so-called "Darwinism" of Dawkins and his atheistic minions is not the Darwin of history, but was created in the image of religious hate-mongering.[13]

The fact of evolution and the overwhelming evidence

Graduate school in theology freed me from scientific concordism and began to offer insights into a Christian approach to evolution. However, I was still a committed anti-evolutionist. In 1991, I entered a PhD programme to study some of the best evolutionary evidence – the evolution of teeth and jaws. My plan was to quietly collect scientific evidence that disproved evolution, and after graduation I would publish my findings and declare war on the scientific establishment.

---

[13] Dawkins seems to believe that insulting Christians is a productive strategy. He claims I am "an intellectual coward" and "a man with an air of desperation". See www.ualberta.ca/~dlamoure/dawkins.html (accessed 11 July 2014). Dawkins also states that "Darwin made it possible to be an intellectually fulfilled atheist". Richard Dawkins, *The Blind Watchmaker,* London: Penguin, 1986, p. 6. For my criticism of his aphorism, see my two-part paper entitled "Darwinian Theological Insights: Toward an Intellectually Fulfilled Christian Theism. Part I: Divine and Intelligent Design", *Perspectives on Science and Christian Faith* 64:2 (Jun 2012), pp. 108–119; "Part II: Evolutionary Theodicy and Evolutionary Psychology" 64:3 (Sept 2012), pp. 166–178. This paper is online at: www.ualberta.ca/~dlamoure/p_darwin_1.pdf and www.ualberta.ca/~dlamoure/p_darwin_2.pdf.

During my study of fossil teeth I started to see a definite pattern through the geological record: (1) the basic materials for teeth first arose as body armour on jawless fish, (2) the jaws of fish then became functional and simple teeth appeared on their margins, (3) with the arrival of land animals, dentitions became specialized and passed through numerous transitional stages, (4) leading to mammals with interlocking teeth and increased chewing proficiency in order to draw more nutrients from prey. In addition, I was seeing all sorts of transitional dentitions and transitional creatures in the fossil record. For many years I was taught by Sunday school teachers brimming with confidence that transitory fossils never existed. However, right before my eyes and even in my hands I saw and held a number of such transitional forms. This was not comfortable, but I could not deny the facts.

This mass of scientific evidence led me in 1992 to ask myself, "Am I headed in an evolutionary direction? I must admit I don't feel so intimidated by evolution as when I was a Young Earth Creationist." At the same time, I had to face my own past honestly. I confessed, "As a Young Earth Creationist, I was hopelessly ignorant." The reality was that seeing the scientific evidence first-hand in the Book of God's Works was a freeing experience. I no longer needed to fear the discoveries that science offered because science was a tool for revealing the glory of God in His marvellous creation (Psalm 19:1).

In the middle of my PhD programme I travelled to England for a science-religion conference sponsored at Cambridge University by the C. S. Lewis Institute. The founding members of the emerging Intelligent Design theory were in attendance – Phillip Johnson, Michael Behe, William Dembski, and Stephen

Meyer. Though I was still an anti-evolutionist, there was something that was starting to nag me. The popular evangelical argument that living organisms were too complex to have evolved gave me an uneasy feeling. Behe had recently coined the term "irreducible complexity" to describe components of the cell he believed could not have evolved. But saying we don't know how cells evolved and therefore God had to create them in one fell swoop wasn't cutting it for me any more.[14] I knew this was a God-of-the-gaps argument.[15] I had used this line of reasoning many times, and now my training in biology was closing many of those gaps. In reality, these were gaps in *knowledge*, not gaps in *nature* indicative of divine intervention. Ironically, the ID theorists were instrumental in pushing me towards evolution.

Alongside my research on tooth evolution, I was studying embryology and developmental biology. An amazing aspect of this science was discovering the incredibly complex concert of finely coordinated biochemical reactions from fertilization to birth. Developmental biology filled my soul with awe and offered reflections of Intelligent Design, and it was this scientific evidence that became the final piece of the evolutionary puzzle for me.

Stated briefly, living organisms go through embryological development using a single basic set of genetic and molecular processes. Striking evidence that animals and humans are evolutionarily related is found in corresponding genes that

---

[14] Behe, *Darwin's Black Box*, p. 39.

[15] For the problem of the God-of-the-gaps, see Denis O. Lamoureux, *Evolutionary Creation: A Christian Approach*, Eugene, OR: Wipf and Stock, 2008, pp. 27–28, 60–62.

determine their underlying body plan (Figure 17.3).[16] In other words, as organisms evolved, they passed down the genetic instructions for a general head-thorax-abdomen pattern – not unlike that in a family in which genes and physical characteristics descend from one generation to the next. Even more significant, experimental studies revealed that manipulating a single developmental gene or molecule can result in dramatic changes in the structure of an organism. This was the key conception that led me to accept evolution. I had seen a *pattern* in the fossil record of teeth and jaws indicative of evolution. Embryology and developmental biology offered a *process* to account for these changes. Let me give an example.

The limbs of fish, amphibians, reptiles, birds, and mammals begin as buds at the side of the developing body. As the limb buds grow, similar developmental genes and molecular processes appear sequentially, but they are expressed in differing combinations and concentrations between different animals. Simple experiments increasing the amount of these developmental molecules in a limb bud can alter the final number of bones in a limb and also change their shapes dramatically (Figure 17.4).[17]

---

[16] Based on F. H. Rundle, J. L. Bartels, K. L. Bentley, C. Kappen, M. T. Murtha and J. W. Pendleton, "Evolution of *Hox* Genes", *Annual Review of Genetics*, 28 (1994), pp. 423–442; G. Panopoulou and A. J. Poustka, "Timing and Mechanism of Ancient Vertebrate Genome Duplications", *Trends in Genetics*, 21 (2005), pp. 559–567.

[17] Drawn by Kenneth Kully, from A. Hornbruch and L. Wolpert, "Positional Signaling by Henson's Node when Grafted to the Chick Limb", *Journal of Experimental Morphology* 94 (1986), p. 261.

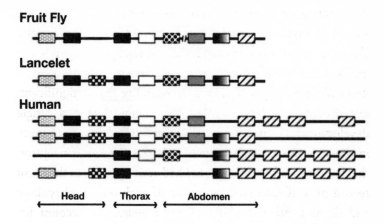

Figure 17.3 Body plan genes. Animals share a series of genes that instruct the development of a basic head-thorax-abdomen pattern. These genes are arranged on chromosomes in a front-to-back order. Organisms early in evolution have only one set of this gene series. This is also the case with simple creatures such as insects. Later and more complex animals have multiple copies. These arise through the duplication of genes and chromosomes, which can occur in organisms. The gene series is split in the fruit fly and appears on separate chromosomes as indicated by the break and slashes. The Lancelet is a primitive worm-like animal with no brain and only a nerve cord. In humans, the gene series is on the four chromosomes and are known as "Hox genes". Missing genes are due to deletion, which is another well-known genetic phenomenon. Hox genes are also found in fish, amphibians, reptiles, birds, and other mammals, indicating that vertebrates descended from a common ancestor with four copies of an original body plan gene series.

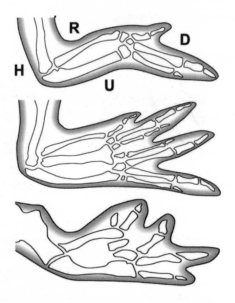

Figure 17.4 Experimental limbs. Placing a developmental molecule on a bead in the developing upper limb of the chick can produce striking differences from normal bone anatomy (top). In one experiment, a limb appeared with seven chick-like digits and a new bone between the humerus and radius (middle). Another experiment produced a limb with five digits similar in number to most land animals today (bottom). (H) humerus (R) radius (U) ulna (D) digits.

Therefore, only a minor genetic modification in the release of a developmental molecule can result in a major change in structure. With these developmental experiments in mind, and looking at the fossil record of the transition between fish and reptiles, it was easy for me to see how fins could have evolved into legs (Figure 17.5).[18]

---

[18] Redrawn by Andrea Dmytrash. Lobe-finned fish from M. I. Coates, J. E. Jeffrey and M. Rut, "Fins to Limbs: What the Fossils Say", *Evolution and Development* (2002), p. 392; fish with fingers from Edward B. Daeschler and Neil Shubin.

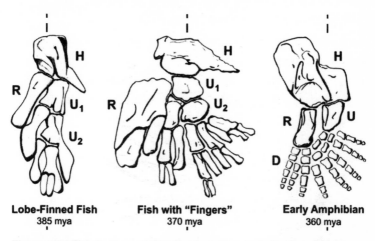

Lobe-Finned Fish
385 mya

Fish with "Fingers"
370 mya

Early Amphibian
360 mya

Figure 17.5 Fish fin-to-amphibian leg transition. Left: *Eusthenopteron*; Middle: *Sauripterus*; Right: *Acanthostega*. mya: millions of years ago

This newly emerging branch of science of the early 1990s, called "evolutionary development biology" or "evo-devo" for short, was the final piece of evidence that convinced me that evolution was a *fact*. After three and a half years of attempting with all my energy to fit the scientific data into an anti-evolutionary theory, I gave up and recognized that the evidence for biological evolution is *overwhelming*. I knew immediately that I would be marginalized within the evangelical community. And indeed this has happened. I have been blocked from teaching at my denominational college and seminary, and evangelical book houses will not publish my books. Nevertheless, I believe we should follow the scientific evidence in God's creation no matter where it leads.

"Fish with Fingers?", *Nature* 391 (1997), p. 133; early amphibian from Robert L. Carroll, *Patterns and Processes of Vertebrate Evolution*, Cambridge: University Press (1998), p. 233.

Final reflections

So that's my story. To be sure, it has been quite a struggle at times. But I want you to know that in being an evolutionary creationist, my love for Jesus and Scripture has not changed one little bit from the time I was a Young Earth Creationist. The Bible is unequivocal: "the word of our God stands forever" (Isaiah 40:8, NASB) and "Jesus Christ is the same yesterday and today and for ever" (Hebrews 13:8, NIV). If anything has changed, my training in theology has made me more focused on the inerrant, life-changing spiritual truths in the Book of God's Words. Similarly, I have a much greater appreciation for the reflection of Intelligent Design in nature after having studied evolutionary biology in the Book of God's Works.

One lesson that I believe is worth taking from my story it is that we need to deal more directly with the pastoral implications of origins. Young men and women today are leaving Christianity in record numbers; science and the issue of evolution are significant factors.[19] As a young person I was told by two instructors that evolution did not necessarily undermine Christian faith. This had little to no effect on me. High school students and university undergraduates need to learn about a healthy relationship between science and religion. In particular, they must be offered the case for evolutionary creation and the many reasons why the opening

---

[19] A Barna Group study published in 2011 reveals that 59 per cent of young people "disconnect permanently or for an extended period of time from church life after age fifteen. One of the reasons for this disturbing exodus is that they perceive "Christianity is anti-science" (25 per cent of respondents), and that they have "been turned off by the creation-versus-evolution debate" (23 per cent). No Author, "Six Reasons Young Christians Leave Church" at www.barna.org/teens-next-gen-articles/528-six-reasons-young-christians-leave-church (assessed 27 August 2014).

chapters of the Bible should not be read as a literal and historical record.

I am quite passionate about this pastoral tragedy happening within our churches. A good part of my academic career has been spent developing materials for young people and I have placed these online free of charge. For high school students, I have a series of High School Web Lectures in audio-slides with handouts that can be found at: www.ualberta.ca/~dlamoure/wlhs.html.

For university undergraduates, my entire introductory course on science and religion is online with 24 hours of audio-slide lectures, 200 pages of class notes, and 100 pages of class handouts. The Class homepage is at: www.ualberta.ca/~dlamoure/350homepage.html.

Acknowledgments

This chapter includes excerpts from my book *Evolutionary Creation: A Christian Approach to Evolution* (2008). Used by permission of Wipf and Stock Publishers (www.wipfandstock.com).

I am grateful to Anna-Lisa S. Ptolemy for her helpful suggestions in the preparation of this manuscript and Margaret Milton for her work during the publication process.

CHAPTER 18

Changing One's Mind Over Evolution

Michael Reiss has a PhD in evolutionary biology. He is Professor of Science Education at the Institute of Education, University of London, a priest in the Church of England and president of the International Society for Science and Religion and of the International Association for Science and Religion in Schools.

Context

I am a science educator. I work on how we can teach science more effectively, both in schools and through such means as museums, the Internet, and so forth. As I have a PhD and undertook postdoctoral research in evolutionary biology and am also an ordained minister, it is hardly surprising that I have an interest in why people for religious reasons do or do not accept the theory of evolution or the notion of a very old earth. For five years in the 1980s I taught science in schools. In that time, I met few students who didn't accept the standard scientific conclusions about evolution and/or the age of the earth. They tended to be very discreet, telling me their views privately rather than in class. I suspect if I had been asked then, I would have predicted that the number of people in the UK who believe in creationism would decrease over time.

And yet this has not happened. While we lack good social science evidence (the same questions have not been asked in successive surveys with sufficiently large numbers of respondents), it seems clear that creationism is not about to wither away either in the UK or elsewhere.[1] Creationism exists, of course, in a number of different versions but something like 50 per cent of adults in Turkey, 40 per cent in the USA and 15 per cent in the UK reject the theory of evolution and believe that the earth came into existence as described by a literal reading of the early parts of the Bible or the Qur'an and that the most that evolution has done is to change species into very similar forms, even if they are new species.[2]

Evolution, creationism and Intelligent Design

Allied to creationism is the notion of Intelligent Design (ID). ID enthusiasts claim that it is a theory that simply critiques evolutionary biology rather than requiring religious faith. Normally no reference is made in ID presentations to the Scriptures or a deity. Rather, it is argued that the intricacy that we see in the natural world, including at the sub-cellular level, provides strong evidence for the existence of an intelligence behind it all.[3] An undirected process, such as natural selection, is held to be inadequate. Notwithstanding, many of those who

[1] Nick Spencer and Denis Alexander, *Rescuing Darwin: God and Evolution in Britain Today*, London: Theos, 2009.

[2] Caroline Lawes, *Faith and Darwin: Harmony, Conflict or Confusion?*, London: Theos, 2009.

[3] William Dembski, *The Design Inference: Eliminating Chance Through Small Probabilities*, Cambridge: Cambridge University Press, 1998; Phillip Johnson, "The wedge: breaking the modernist monopoly on science", *Touchstone*, 12(4) (1999), pp. 18–24.

advocate ID have been involved in the creationist movement (to the extent that the US courts have argued that the country's First Amendment separation of religion and the State precludes its teaching in public schools).[4]

Most of the literature on creationism (and/or ID) puts them in stark opposition with evolutionary theory. Evolution is consistently presented in creationist writing as illogical (e.g. the second law of thermodynamics means that natural selection is unable to create order out of disorder; mutations are always deleterious and so cannot lead to improvements); contradicted by the scientific evidence (e.g. the fossil record shows human footprints alongside animals supposed by evolutionists to be long extinct; the fossil record does not provide evidence for transitional forms); the product of non-scientific reasoning (e.g. the early history of life would require life to arise from inorganic matter – a form of spontaneous generation rejected by science in the nineteenth century; radioactive dating makes assumptions about the constancy of natural processes over aeons of time, whereas we increasingly know of natural processes that affect the rate of radioactive decay); the product of those who ridicule the Word of God; and a cause of a whole range of social evils (from eugenics, Marxism, Nazism, and racism to juvenile delinquency).

It needs to be emphasized that the theory of evolution can be rejected on at least two different grounds. One, which doesn't apply to ID, is where a person believes that a particular way of reading and understanding Scripture (whether the Christian, Hindu, Jewish, Muslim or any other scripture) precludes

---

[4] Randy Moore, "The History of the Creationism/Evolution Controversy and Likely Future Developments", in L. Jones and M. J. Reiss (eds), *Teaching About Scientific Origins: Taking Account of Creationism*, NY/Oxford: Peter Lang, 2007, pp. 11–29.

acceptance of the theory of evolution. The other, which applies to both ID and so-called scientific creationism, is where a person concludes that the weight of objective, scientific (and/or mathematical) evidence is such that the theory of evolution cannot be correct.

By and large, creationism has received short shrift from those who accept the theory of evolution. Over thirty years ago, philosopher of science Philip Kitcher argued that "in attacking the methods of evolutionary biology, Creationists are actually criticizing methods that are used throughout science". He wrote that the flat earth theory, the chemistry of the four elements, and medieval astrology "have just as much claim to rival current scientific views as Creationism does to challenge evolutionary biology".[5]

Many scientists have defended evolutionary biology against creationism[6] and there are an increasing number of agreed statements by scientists on the teaching of evolution.[7] The points frequently made are that evolutionary biology is good science, even if its methods do not involve controlled experiments where the results can be collected within a short period of time; that creationism (including "scientific creationism") isn't really a science in that its ultimate authority is scriptural and theological rather than the evidence obtained from the natural world; and

---

[5] Philip Kitcher, *Abusing Science: The Case Against Creationism*, Milton Keynes: Open University Press, 1983. An even more trenchant attack on creationism was assembled by geologist Ian Plimmer, whose book title *Telling Lies for God: Reason vs Creationism* (Milsons Point, NSW: Random House, 1994) indicates the line he takes.

[6] See, for example, Jones and Reiss (eds), *Teaching about Scientific Origins*.

[7] Such as that from the InterAcademy Panel on International Issues, 2006 and the US National Academy of Sciences (*Science, Evolution, and Creationism*, Washington (DC): National Academy Press, 2008).

that an acceptance of evolution is fully compatible with a religious faith, an assertion most often made in relation to Christianity while more obviously true of many other religions – including Hinduism, Buddhism, and Judaism – although probably rather less true of Islam.

Worldviews and changing one's mind

One way of interpreting a move from creationism to an acceptance of evolutionary theory is to see it as an example of Thomas Kuhn's[8] contention that there are times when existing understandings break down – such as the Ptolemaic model of the structure of the solar system (in which the earth is at the centre) or the Newtonian understanding of motion and gravity – and a completely new *paradigm* takes over. At the time of such a crisis, a scientific revolution happens during which a new paradigm – such as the Copernican model of the structure of the solar system or Einstein's theory of relativity – begins to replace the previously accepted paradigm. Kuhn likens the switch from one paradigm to another to a *gestalt* switch (when we suddenly see something in a new way) or even a religious conversion. It alerts us to the fact that scientific understanding may change for reasons that cannot entirely be reduced to the rational acceptance of new information. How much more is this true for science education and for learning in general! One framework that has proved particularly useful for understanding why people do or do not accept the theory of evolution is that of "worldviews".

There is much unknown about evolution. How did the earliest self-replicating molecules arise? What caused membranes to exist? How key were the earliest physical

[8] Thomas Kuhn, *The Structure of Scientific Revolutions*, 2nd edn, Chicago, IL: University of Chicago Press, 1970.

conditions – temperature, the occurrence of water, and so forth? But the scientific presumption is either that these questions will be answered by science or that they will remain unknown. It reflects a scientific worldview which is materialistic in the sense that it is neither idealistic nor admits of non-physical explanations ("physical" in this sense includes such things as energy and the curvature of space, as well as matter). Although some scientists might (sometimes grudgingly) admit that science cannot disprove supernatural explanations, very few scientists employ such explanations in their work (the tiny handful of seeming exceptions only attest to the strength of the general rule).

The meeting of science and religious interpretation can be illustrated by considering the enormously successful film *March of the Penguins*.[9] Some of the reasons for its success are obvious: the photography is phenomenal; the story of the featured emperor penguins is extraordinary; the adults are elegant; the chicks are irredeemably cute as they look fluffy, feebly wave their little wings and learn to walk; the way in which the birds survive the Antarctic winter is awesome; the plaintive cries of mothers who lose their chicks in snowstorms are heartrending. But an unexpected feature has been the film's popularity among conservative Christians. Entering "march of the penguins Christian" into Google, one finds over a million hits. Number three of these is a review on ChristianAnswers.Net, which describes itself as a "mega-site … providing biblical answers to contemporary questions for all ages and nationalities with over 68-thousand files". After a summary of the subject matter of the film, the reviewer sets out in some detail the

---

[9] Michael Reiss, "Imagining the World: The Significance of Religious Worldviews for Science Education", *Science & Education*, 18 (2009), pp. 783–796.

lessons that the penguins have to teach us about love, perseverance (Proverbs 6:6–8; Philippians 3:14), commitment (1 Peter 3:15), and the existence (Romans 1:20) and character of God (Matthew 6:26).

This understanding implies a seamless integration between science and religion (as opposed to other possibilities – such as conflict, independence or dialogue). It shows a worldview in which it is straightforward to read from penguin behaviour to human behaviour, where the argument is neither entirely anthropomorphic nor one in which the natural world is seen as *the* source of instruction as to how humans should behave. But, significantly, the essential factor is that Scripture has primacy. The natural world is held up not so much as a model for us to imitate but as an illustration of how the natural world can manifest that which God wishes for humanity.

I, with a PhD and postdoc in evolutionary biology, can see the *March of the Penguins* as showing the extraordinary ability of natural selection over millions of years to enable an organism to survive and reproduce in the most inhospitable of environments; to others it is an unequivocal manifestation of Intelligent Design. And, presumably to the chagrin of some of its conservative admirers, the film is also honest about the fact that most emperor penguins are faithful to their partners for only a single breeding season.

Metanoia

In the New Testament, *metanoia* (*μετάνοια*) is usually translated "repentance". Strictly, it simply means "changing one's mind". For the Christian, of course, conversion is the biggest change one can make: "if anyone is in Christ, he is a new creation" (2 Corinthians 5:17, ESV), but its circumstances are different for every individual. It can be difficult. The Bible, of course, has plenty of examples of those who changed, and of those who did not. We see this powerfully in the reactions of those whom Jesus met. While the Scriptures are sometimes read as if religious conversions were spontaneous (a possible reading, for example, of Paul's Damascus Road experience), it is more fruitful to see conversion, even if apparently occurring over a very short period of time, as having both a necessary preparatory phase and a necessary post-conversion phase.

I am not aware of much of a preparatory phase in my own experience. My conversion took place in my second year as an undergraduate during a John Stott mission; it occurred at a time (away from home, the stimulation of new ideas) when anyone might be expected to be receptive to a fundamentally new way of understanding the world. On the other hand, I can certainly testify to the importance of a post-conversion phase and I am grateful to the friends who invited me to the talks and then, with others, continued to support me and made sure that I got straight away into the practices of daily prayer and Bible study and weekly attendance at church and a Bible study group.

Changing from a position where one sees creationism as true to one where one sees the evolutionary understanding of life as valid can, for some people, feel almost comparable. Some of the contributors to this book describe their own experiences. The science educator Lee Meadows is one who has made this journey. He writes about this and his collaboration with David Jackson at the University of Georgia:

> *Our first work together, "Hearts and Minds in the Science Classroom: The Education of a Confirmed Evolutionist"*

chronicles David's growth as he learned how a different set of life experiences can deeply impact science teachers' approaches to evolution in the classroom. David, an agnostic, had never worked with science teachers who also held to a deep faith until he moved to Georgia in the USA. David was surprised to find some science teachers who were staunchly opposed to teaching evolution in their classes. At first, David tried to correct their beliefs about evolution, but then he began to realize that he had skipped the essential first step of listening to them before trying to influence them. He began to find that, rather than being uninformed, many of these teachers were thinking through their religious beliefs, their scientific beliefs, and the interplay between the two. He began to see that science teachers had to consider the hearts, as well as the minds, of their students. Many of the teachers in the study, and by extension religious students like them in science classes, are actively choosing not to learn about evolution ... Evolutionary science pales in importance to the eternal issues of God, Heaven, and salvation.

I know well this tension between the heart and the mind because I've lived it. I was raised in a Christian fundamentalist home and church, and I'm now a science teacher and educator. Working through this tension was a perspective I brought to the Hearts and Minds study. My own faith journey has led me away from fundamentalism, but I do still hold to the view that the Christian scriptures are the inspired words of God. I find truth in both worldviews. Science provides truth from the basis of evidence, but my faith also provides an intellectual, durable system of knowing the world.[10]

[10] Lee Meadows, "Approaching the Conflict Between Religion and Evolution", in

Recent research has shown that good-quality teaching can help students from a fundamentalist position to learn about evolution and come to accept some of evolution's central tenets. David Long has reported on his anthropological research into the ways that university students interact with the concept of evolution during their introductory biology classes.[11] He concluded that a few lessons on the topic are most unlikely to change the views of students of a fundamentalist religious persuasion.

However, other research suggests that careful and respectful teaching about evolution can make students who initially reject the theory of evolution considerably more likely to accept at least some aspects of it. Winslow *et al.* (2011) studied fifteen biology-related majors or recent biology-related graduates at a mid-western Christian liberal arts university in the USA. The data were interviews, course documents, and observations of classes (in a course called "Origins").[12] The study found that most participants were raised by their families to believe in creationism, but came to accept evolution through evaluating the evidence for it, negotiating the meanings of Genesis, recognizing evolution as a non-salvation issue, and observing the teachers as Christian role models who accept evolution. For example, one student reported:

They can say they're Christian and be an evolutionist, but it would really help for Dr. [Origins professor] because she

---

Jones & Reiss, *Teaching about Scientific Origins*, p. 149.

[11] David Long, *Evolution and Religion in American Education: An Ethnography*, New York: Springer, 2011.

[12] M. W. Winslow, J. R. Staver, and L. C. Scharmann, "Evolution and Personal Religious Belief: Christian University Biology-related Majors' Search for Reconciliation", *Journal of Research in Science Teaching*, 48 (2011), pp. 1026–1049.

actually showed you. She'd talk about God and ... then
she also talked about evolution and so you kinda had to
reconcile the two ... My whole life it was just two things
that were separate and they must stay separate, but with her
they kinda came together and you had to reconcile them.[13]

This story indicates the importance of teachers who do not separate out evolution and religion or see them in conflict: Indeed "Six participants valued the influence of professors who authenticated a positive relationship between science and religious faith instead of isolating the two domains from each other". This is clear from another project carried out by Lee Meadows involving twelve teachers in US Christian schools who explicitly attempted to teach evolutionary biology and also to nurture their students' religious faith. He found:

Participating teachers refused to require their students
to accept a single view of origins, just as adult Christians
across America don't have a single view. Instead, they asked
their students to understand scientific evidence, consider
Biblical interpretation, and think for themselves. So often,
evolution education seems to drive to a single point, whether
in faith-based schools teaching a single creationist view or
in a public college classroom where a professor advocates
scientific materialism. Participating teachers refused to tie
themselves to such agendas, and their trust in their students
to think and make good decisions serves as a model for
evolution educators in all school types, not just faith-based.
Participating teachers appeared to have found a powerful
key for diminishing controversy during the teaching of

---

[13] Winslow *et al.*, *op. cit.*, p. 1036.

evolution by simply acknowledging what almost any teacher of teenagers already knows: teenagers make their own decisions. Students consider what their teachers say, but they come to their own conclusions, despite pressure from teachers or other adults with an agenda. These teachers lifted the reality of their students' decision making into the overt learning climate of their classrooms.

Participating teachers were passionate about teaching evolution well to their students. Their passion makes clear the profound importance of caring, skilled teachers when students from faith backgrounds are learning evolution. These teachers' words remind us how learning evolution is a matter of the heart for many students, with profound and often eternal implications in students' minds. These teachers' practices give us a good image of how teaching evolution and caring for children's souls can be intertwined successfully.[14]

Conclusion

Both the experiences of those who have contributed to this book and the published research noted here highlight the difficulties for people to change from a position in which the theory of evolution is rejected for religious reasons to one where it is accepted and the individual still retains their religious faith. This should not be unexpected. Individuals who reject the theory of evolution for religious reasons are likely to fear that accepting the theory of evolution will require them to reject their religious faith. Perhaps

---

[14] Lee Meadows, "Shepherding and Strength: Teaching Evolution in American Christian Schools", in J. Chapman, S. McNamara, M. J. Reiss, and Y. Waghid (eds), *International Handbook of Learning, Teaching and Leading in Faith-based Schools*, Dordrecht: Springer, 2014.

unsurprisingly but helpful in practice, the growing literature on the subject suggests that this transition can be facilitated by learning from trusted adults who combine in themselves an acceptance of the theory of evolution with a sincere religious faith.

Epilogue

David Fergusson, FBA, FRSE was a Church of Scotland parish minister before becoming Professor of Systematic Theology in the University of Aberdeen and then in 2000 Professor of Divinity and Principal of New College in the University of Edinburgh. He has given the Bampton Lectures (2001), the Gifford Lectures (2008) and the Warfield Lectures (2013). His publications include *The Cosmos and the Creator – an Introduction to the Theology of Creation* (SPCK, 1998) and *Creation* (Eerdmans, 2014).

The essays in this collection show the different ways in which a commitment to evolutionary science and Christian faith can coexist. They reflect different intellectual and spiritual journeys, and perhaps also register some competing claims about how science and religion should be combined. I should confess at the outset that my own conviction in the compatibility of evolutionary science and Christian faith has never involved a shift in perspective or the overcoming of antithetical claims that were held in tension. From an early age, I attended church in the west end of Glasgow. Many members of our congregation were students or teaching staff in the nearby university and it was widely assumed that the practices of science and faith were compatible. The world could be investigated and described by natural scientists but also characterized as the good creation of God. The order, beauty, and intelligibility of nature as displayed in scientific description could attest the wisdom of God. Darwinian evolution merely intensified a sense of the grandeur of nature. This confidence was also instilled in me by my father who was a doctor in Clydebank. His work had a pastoral involvement as well as a confidence in the practice of modern medicine. For the most part, he would not allow any conflict between his commitment to medical science and his Christian faith. These seemed to belong together, even though he could express scepticism about inflated claims for the efficacy of healing services. While these may have had a genuinely therapeutic quality, he was never persuaded that chronic or serious physical illness could be treated except by medication or surgery or the restorative power of nature. I well remember a woman in our congregation with serious heart disease who claimed that she had been cured, following a healing service in Greenock. My father was sceptical. Her chest pains and breathlessness seemed undiminished and she died some time later of cardiac failure.

Looking back, I have to recognize that none of this ever caused me seriously to question a deeply held assumption about the consistency of scientific and theological claims; it was an unexamined presupposition of my upbringing. Provided an over-literal reading of Scripture was avoided, theology could cheerfully coexist with natural science and preoccupy itself with other tasks. This harmonious premise was not much different from Stephen Jay Gould's NOMA (Non-Overlapping MAgisteria), with its differentiation of science and religion as belonging to distinct domains with different authorities and functions.[1] In retrospect, however, I may have underestimated the opportunities for a fruitful conversation between evolutionary science and Christian faith. A somewhat complacent understanding of the

---

[1] Stephen Jay Gould, *Rocks of Ages: Science and Religion in the Fullness of Life*, London: Jonathan Cape, 2001.

independence and consistency of different domains perhaps militated against this.

When I entered university, much greater challenges to Christian faith appeared to come from philosophy and history. My confidence in the design argument was shaken by the criticisms of Hume and Kant. The prevailing mood of analytic philosophy was sceptical, secular, and dismissive of faith-based convictions. My second-year ethics tutor, a son of the manse who had lost his faith, told me that philosophy departments were replete with those who had abandoned their earlier theological convictions. He expressed his own disillusionment with philosophy and religion, once remarking to his students that his preferred ambition was to run a scrapyard in Glasgow. I was never sure whether this was seriously intended, but his loss of faith and resultant angst seemed more the result of reading Hume than any encounter with Darwin. At the same time, the work of historical criticism on the Bible, and in particular the Gospels, seemed to threaten the standard account of the story of Jesus that existed in the churches. Could we really know very much about what Jesus actually said and did, if the Gospels were the product of early church traditions rather than first-hand reports of what had happened? And how should one speak of the resurrection of Christ? The work of Bultmann and other New Testament critics presented obstacles and anxieties that were closer to home and more threatening than any claims of neo-Darwinism.

In part, this intellectual preoccupation may have been determined by the way in which the culture of theology was much closer to the humanities than to the natural sciences. Most of the leading theologians of the day had been trained in philosophy, classics, or literature, and tended to engage, if at all, with colleagues in medicine and science only on pastoral and ethical issues. The exception, of course, was Tom Torrance whom

I encountered in Edinburgh where I went to study theology, after graduating in philosophy in Glasgow. TFT, as he was known, had obviously worked hard at familiarizing himself with the history of the natural sciences and had spent time talking to some of his colleagues in the university's science faculty at King's Buildings. His work on theological science was difficult to assess, and not only for undergraduate students. It seemed to take him beyond Barth, to whom he remained fiercely loyal, into the terrain of natural theology and cross-disciplinary dialogue. His interest in science was largely directed towards Einsteinian physics, both with respect to its methods and findings. However, his encounter with Michael Polanyi, whose literary executor he became, had an impact upon Torrance's writings from the 1970s onwards, and their interaction would merit further scholarly attention today. All this shaped his epistemology and resulted in fierce attacks upon philosophers, theologians, and biblical critics who held unscientific assumptions, usually of a dualist nature. Wherever they pointed to division, dichotomy, or uncertainty, Torrance insisted upon the integrity of science and faith, revelation and reason, divine being and action, and history and faith. That the mode of knowledge must be appropriate to the nature of the object became for him a methodological axiom. This resulted in a highly robust theological realism which he allied with Einsteinian physics, against all forms of positivism and instrumentalism.[2]

This was highly significant, and in retrospect I ought to have recognized more fully the importance of the kind of conversations that Torrance pioneered. Later this field of study became more familiar to me as a graduate student in Oxford through the work of Ian Barbour, Arthur Peacocke, and

---

[2] For a moving and perceptive reading of Torrance on science, see Peter Forster, "Theological Science in Retrospect", *Theology in Scotland*, 16 (2009), pp. 60–73.

especially John Polkinghorne.

Torrance's axis with the natural sciences was dominated by physics. His interest in biology was less evident and he seemed often to downplay the significance of evolutionary theory. I suspect that this was borne of his suspicion that much neo-Darwinism was materialist in its ideological overtones, or at least lacking the stronger teleological convictions and sense of quasi-religious wonder that seemed to characterize physics and cosmology at that time. He also judged that it suffered from some of the methodological problems which he associated with the social sciences. In one of my last conversations with him, he seemed dubious when I told him of my elder son's decision to study sociology.

In recent times, the significance of the biology-theology dialogue has grown considerably. Partly this has been on account of the need to engage with creationism and Intelligent Design theory, both of which seem mistaken enterprises to me and effectively rebutted by recent writers such as Kenneth Miller and Francis Collins.[3] Yet the cultural salience of these movements has necessitated some serious interaction. In my first year as a teacher in Aberdeen, I recall being challenged by a theology student who had a strong background in science. If Romans 5 is to be taken seriously, he asked, must we not reject Darwinism? My upbringing had not prepared me well for such questioning. Rather taken aback, I suggested that we might need to reconsider some traditional readings of Romans 5, as well as Genesis 1–3, in view of the modern scientific worldview. Yet perhaps more has to be said.

The dialogue with biology has a long way to go and it would be foolish to speculate where it might eventually lead. Simon Conway Morris has made the sensible point that given our knowledge

---

[3] Kenneth Miller, *Finding Darwin's God,* New York: Harper, 1999 and Francis Collins, *The Language of God,* New York: Free Press, 2006.

of developments in the natural sciences, it is unlikely that neo-Darwinism will look exactly the same in fifty or a hundred years from now. Some intellectual humility is needed here, and this must caution against making too absolutist claims for the status of current scientific thinking or of tying our theology too closely to any of the dominant scientific narratives of the day. The recent collaboration of the theologian Sarah Coakley with her Harvard mathematician colleague Martin Nowack on the role of altruism in evolution suggests one fruitful way in which this dialogue may progress.[4]

Yet many of the standard assumptions of Darwinian science seem inescapable. The long argument of *Origin of Species* was broadly correct when judged against the rival accounts of the day. Species had evolved over long periods from common origins under the pressures of natural selection. This may not be an exhaustive, final, or mono-causal account, but the direction of travel will surely not take us back to a young earth or prelapsarian humanity or indeed to a simple anthropocentrism in which the human species was ontologically distinguished, privileged, and set apart at the dawn of creation. Here the evolutionary story does create some points of tension with which I had not earlier reckoned. Despite his espousal of NOMA, Gould himself recognized that there could be friction between the discourses of science and religion.

The most significant of these stresses might be described as recognizing the decentring of human existence. The age of the cosmos coupled with the long history of life prior to the emergence of human beings suggests that God must have intended more than the creation of humankind. This necessitates a revision of earlier theological and ethical attitudes to non-human creatures. Similarly, the size of the universe with its

---

[4] Martin A. Nowak and Sarah Coakley (eds), *Evolution, Games and God*, Cambridge, MA: Harvard University Press, 2013.

multiplicity of galaxies and planets generates the possibility of other intelligent life forms in distant cosmic regions. The likely impact of this on our theology remains a matter of speculation. I have attempted to register these shifts in the theology of creation in a textbook on the subject, while at the same time seeking to appropriate more traditional themes.[5] The birth of a child does not diminish the love of a parent for the child's older siblings; nor does the existence of brothers and sisters limit the love of the parent for the newborn. Or at least it shouldn't.

How much more, then, is God's love sufficiently capacious to embrace a multiplicity of creatures, affirming each in a manner appropriate to its mode of living. Human beings do not need to be the only objects of God's love or indeed to have some uniquely privileged status in the history of the universe. Such claims can draw upon vital insights of Scripture, even if these have been overlaid by earlier traditions. In the book of Job, the mysterious power and wisdom of God are celebrated in the creation of the hippopotamus and crocodile, creatures that have little obvious relation to human beings. The hubris lies in assuming that we alone are of concern to God. Although the Bible does not teach this, it has often been assumed by the theological traditions of the church. Yet once divested of an excessive anthropocentrism we can return to understand more humbly the infinite love of God offered to us. In the act of naming, describing, and respecting other creatures and vast reaches of the cosmos, we enrich our relationship to the creation and its Maker. This seems to be our particular gift and responsibility, at least in the history of planet Earth, through which the wisdom of science can reflect the infinitely greater wisdom of God.

---

[5] David Fergusson, *Creation*, Grand Rapids, MI: Eerdmans, 2014.

Going Further

There is a huge amount of literature on the debate between evolution and creation. Many of the contributors to this volume refer to books which have helped them understand the issues better. The following is a very select list of the more worthwhile books; it should not be regarded as definitive, but as a supplement to other literature referred to in the text. Entries marked with † indicate an author who is also a contributor to this book.

Scientific Account of Evolution

Jerry Coyne, *Why Evolution is True*, Oxford: Oxford University Press, 2009.

Richard Dawkins, *The Ancestor's Tale*, London: Weidenfeld and Nicolson, 2005.

Richard Dawkins, *The Greatest Show on Earth*, London: Transworld, 2009.

Ernst Mayr, *One Long Argument: Charles Darwin and the Genesis of Modern Evolutionary Thought*, London: Allen Lane, 1991.

Reconciliation

Denis Alexander, *Creation or Evolution: Do We Have to Choose?*, Oxford: Lion, revised edition, 2014.

Francisco Ayala, *Darwin's Gift to Science and Religion*, Washington, DC: Joseph Henry Press, 2007.

† R. J. Berry, *God and Evolution*, Vancouver, BC: Regent College Press, 2001.

Francis Collins, *The Language of God: A Scientist Presents Evidence for Belief*, New York: Free Press, 2006.

† Darrel Falk, *Coming to Peace with Science: Bridging the Worlds Between Faith and Biology*, Downers Grove, IL: IVP, 2004.

† Karl Giberson, *Saving Darwin: How to be a Christian and Believe in Evolution*, New York: HarperOne, 2008.

† Stephen Godfrey and Christopher Smith, *Paradigms on Pilgrimage: Creationism, Paleontology and Biblical Interpretation*, Toronto: Clements Publishing, 2005.

† Denis O. Lamoureux, *Evolutionary Creation: A Christian Approach*, Eugene, OR: Wipf and Stock, 2008.

Donald MacKay, *The Clockwork Image*, Leicester: IVP, 1974, reprinted 1997.

Kenneth R. Miller, *Finding Darwin's God: A Scientist's Search for Common Ground Between God and Evolution*, New York: HarperCollins, 1999.

Michael Ruse, *Can a Darwinian Be a Christian?*, Cambridge: Cambridge University Press, 2001.

† Davis A. Young and Ralph F. Stearley, *The Bible, Rocks and Time*, Downers Grove, IL: IVP Academic, 2008.

Debates between creationists and Christian evolutionists

Derek Burke (ed), *When Christians Disagree: Evolution*, Nottingham: IVP-UK, 1985.

Richard Carlson (ed), *Science & Christianity: Four Views*, Downers Grove, IL: IVP-US, 2000.

Graeme Finlay, Stephen Lloyd, Stephen Pattemore & David Swift, *Debating Darwin*, Milton Keynes: Paternoster, 2009.

History

Peter Bowler, *Evolution: The History of an Idea*, 4th edn, Oakland, CA: University of California Press, 2009.

Peter Bowler, *Reconciling Science and Religion: The Debate in Early Twentieth-Century Britain*, Chicago, IL: University of Chicago Press, 2001.

Peter Bowler, *Monkey Trials and Gorilla Sermons*, Cambridge, MA: Harvard University Press, 2007.

Janet Browne, *Books That Changed the World: Darwin's Origin of Species*, New York: Atlantic Monthly Press, 2006.

Edward Larson, *Summer for the Gods: The Scopes Trial and America's Continuing Debate Over Science and Religion*, Cambridge, MA: Harvard University Press, 1997.

David Livingstone, *Darwin's Forgotten Defenders: The Encounter Between Evangelical Theology and Evolutionary Thought*, Grand Rapids, MI: Eerdmans, 1987.

David Montgomery, *The Rocks Don't Lie: A Geologist Investigates Noah's Flood*, London: W. W. Norton, 2012.

James Moore, *The Post-Darwinian Controversies: A Study of the Protestant Struggles to Come to Terms with Darwin in Great Britain*, Cambridge: Cambridge University Press, 1981.

James Moore, *The Darwin Legend*, Grand Rapids, MI: Baker Book House, 1994.

Ron Numbers, *The Creationists: From Scientific Creationism to Intelligent Design*, Cambridge, MA: Harvard University Press, 2006.

Chris Rios, *After the Monkey Trial*, New York: Fordham University Press, 2014.

Michael Ruse, *The Evolution-Creation Struggle*, Cambridge, MA: Harvard University Press, 2005.

Exposition

† R. J. Berry and Tom Noble (eds), *Darwin, Creation and the Fall*, Leicester, Apollos, 2009.

Henri Blocher, *In the Beginning*, Leicester, IVP, 1984.

† David Fergusson, *The Cosmos and the Creator*, London: SPCK, 1998.

† David Fergusson, *Creation*, Grand Rapids, MI: Eerdmans, 2014.

Ernest Lucas, *Can We Believe Genesis Today?*, Nottingham: IVP, 2005.

Keith B. Miller (ed), *Perspectives on an Evolving Creation*, Grand Rapids, MI: Eerdmans, 2003.

† Michael Northcott and R. J. Berry (eds), *Theology After Darwin*, Milton Keynes: Paternoster, 2009.

Robert Russell, William R. Stoeger and Francisco Ayala (eds), *Evolutionary and Molecular Biology*, Vatican Observatory Publications, 1998.

Melvin Tinker, *Reclaiming Genesis*, Oxford: Monarch, 2010.

John Walton, *The Lost World of Genesis One: Ancient Cosmology and the Origins Debate*, Downers Grove, IL: IVP Academic, 2009.

David Wilkinson, *The Bible Speaks Today: The Message of Creation*, Downers Grove, IL: IVP Academic, 2002.

Useful organizations

American Scientific Affiliation
A fellowship of Christians in science and related disciplines, who share a common fidelity to the Word of God and a commitment to integrity in the practice of science:

http://network.asa3.org/ (accessed 11 July 2014).

BioLogos
Seeks to convince church and world of the harmony between science and biblical faith as it presents an evolutionary understanding of God's creation:

http://biologos.org/ (accessed 11 July 2014).

Christians in Science
An international network of those concerned with the relationship between science and Christian faith:

http://www.cis.org.uk/ (accessed 11 July 2014).

Faraday Institute for Science and Religion
An interdisciplinary research exercise which is involved in academic research and promoting the public understanding of science and religion:

http://www.faraday.st-edmunds.cam.ac.uk/ (accessed 11 July 2014).

Index of Bible References

Index of Bible References

Index

Index

Index

Index

Index